The Purple Color of Kurdish Politics

"This compelling collection highlights a range of personal experiences of imprisoned Kurdish women politicians and their dedication to the collective feminist struggle against gender inequality, patriarchal social structures, and anti-Kurdish repression in Turkey. Through their prison writings, twenty-two deeply committed Kurdish women define their personal forms of resistance within a securitized society and its unremitting prison system. Relying on radical feminist principles, Kurdish women identify daily practices of implementing notions of gender equality and provide critical insights into their successes and failures to transform Turkey's political structures."

—Vera Eccarius-Kelly, Professor of Political Science and International Relations at Siena College in Albany, New York

"Twenty-two stories are woven together by Gültan Kışanak to reassert the enduring value of Kurdish women's collective resistance. The stories, translated by twenty-two scholars and activists, take the reader beyond mere political struggle to the vibrant interconnected memories and inner lives of Kurdish women political prisoners."

—Shahrzad Mojab, Professor at the University of Toronto and co-author of *Women of Kurdistan*

The Purple Color of Kurdish Politics

Women Politicians Write from Prison

Edited by Gültan Kışanak

Translation coordinated by Ruken Isik, Emek Ergun, and Janet Biehl

With contributions by Nurhayat Altun, Sadiye Süer Baran, Zeynep Han Bingöl, Yıldız Çetin, Çağlar Demirel, Fatma Doğan, Leyla Güven, Dilek Hatipoğlu, Selma Irmak, Servin Karakoç, Sara Kaya, Diba Keskin, Evin Keve, Mukaddes Kubilay, Burcu Çelik Özkan, Edibe Şahin, Zeynep Sipçik, Aysel Tuğluk, Sebahat Tuncel, Gülser Yıldırım, and Figen Yüksekdağ

PLUTO PRESS

First published 2018 as *Kürt Siyasetinin Mor Rengi* by Dipnot Yayınları

First English language edition published 2022 by Pluto Press
New Wing, Somerset House, Strand, London WC2R 1LA
and Pluto Press Inc.
1930 Village Center Circle, Ste. 3-384, Las Vegas, NV 89134

www.plutobooks.com

British Library Cataloguing in Publication Data
A catalogue record for this book is available from the British Library

ISBN 978 0 7453 4709 7 Hardback
ISBN 978 0 7453 4708 0 Paperback
ISBN 978 0 7453 4711 0 PDF
ISBN 978 0 7453 4710 3 EPUB

Typeset by Stanford DTP Services, Northampton, England
Printed and bound by CPI Group (UK) Ltd, Croydon, CR0 4YY

Contents

List of Abbreviations

PARTIES AND GROUPS IN THE KURDISH POLITICAL TRADITION

BDP	Peace and Democracy Party
DBP	Democratic Regions Party
DEHAP	Democratic People's Party
DEP	Democracy Party
DTH	Democratic Society Movement
DTK	Democratic Society Congress
DTP	Democratic Society Party
HADEP	People's Democracy Party
HDK	People's Democratic Congress
HDP	Peoples' Democratic Party
HEP	People's Labor Party
KCK	Kurdistan Communities Union
PKK	Kurdistan Workers' Party

OTHER ORGANIZATIONS

AKP	Justice and Development Party
CHP	Republican People's Party
DİSK	Confederation of Revolutionary Trade Unions of Turkey
DYP	True Path Party
ESP	Socialist Party of the Oppressed
İHD	Turkish Human Rights Association
KA.DER	Association for the Support and Training of Women Candidates
MHP	Nationalist Movement Party
SHP	Social Democratic People's Party

Translation Coordinators' Preface

Ruken Isik, Emek Ergun, and Janet Biehl

Turkey's political environment is notoriously difficult for activists seeking to affirm the human rights of Kurds, the country's largest ethnic minority. Official government policy is to reject the validity, if not the existence, of Kurdish identity itself. But that has not prevented Kurdish people from entering the political arena and being elected to office, whether as mayors of municipalities or members of the parliament in Ankara, the capital city. In recent years, however, as repression has tightened in Turkey, pro-Kurdish activism has almost guaranteed imprisonment.

In this book, 22 Kurdish women politicians, imprisoned since 2016, recount their revolutionary achievements and struggles in that difficult political environment. Indeed, Kurdish women have been fighting against multiple forces of oppression both within and beyond the boundaries of the official apparatuses of the state. The violent intersections of Turkish nationalism, colonialism, militarism, and capitalism with local patriarchal arrangements have created particularly difficult and dangerous conditions of resistance for Kurdish women. Yet they continue not only to survive but also to thrive as political subjects whose radically creative amalgamation of anticolonial, anticapitalist, ecological, and feminist philosophies and practices of democracy are inspiring for those who dream of a world of plurality, equality, justice, and peace for all. The color of that dream is purple, which internationally symbolizes feminism. And this book describes the ways in which a group of Kurdish women politicians have fought for that dream at the daring intersections of feminist politics with Kurdish party politics in Turkey.

Although the 22 contributors are victimized by multiple systems of oppression, they are not victims. As Gültan Kışanak, who edited the original Turkish edition from within prison, explains, "We managed to participate in politics by overcoming many barriers. We had to confront the various faces of male domination that exclude women from public life."* But confront them they did: "We carried women's words and demands to political platforms by defeating the prejudices of men, the family, and the society. It's been a challenging struggle."

We chose to translate the book because the stories of the political experiences of the 22 women are not only inspiring and uplifting, but also challenging, instructive, and insightful for women of the world who want to claim their place on the political arena that is too often ruled by the discriminatory, exclusionary, and assimilative forces of misogyny.

Just as the original Turkish edition was produced collectively, our translation too is the result of a collective process of feminist solidarity. It began in 2020 when Ruken reached out to Emek and Janet. As translation coordinators, we have complementary areas of expertise and skill sets. We then brought together 22 remarkable translators from a variety of academic and activist backgrounds and geographic locations. For all of us, translating this book has meant standing in solidarity with its authors as well as those committed to Kurdish women's liberation. That makes the translation a risky project for those who live under more precarious conditions: for instance, one of the translators who works as an academic at a state university in Turkey must remain anonymous for now because of the risk of potential government retaliation.

During the translation process, we used an email group, engaged in several phases of peer reviews and revisions, and conducted two workshops especially to decide how to translate certain words consistently, such as Kurdish *heval* and Turkish *arkadaş*. Both these words could be translated as "friend" or "comrade," and both claim gender-egalitarian camaraderie among political subjects dedicated to Kurdish resistance. For simplicity's sake, we went with "friend" for *arkadaş* and kept all Kurdish words as they were, but readers

---

* All Kışanak quotations in the preface are from her Turkish article "Sınır Tanımayan Hayaller" (Dreams Without Borders), written for the March 8, 2021 issue of the Swiss magazine *Femina*. You can see the full Turkish original as well as Kışanak's handwritten drafts at https://tinyurl.com/299u8cwz.

should keep in mind that in the Kurdish context *heval* and *arkadaş* refer to a highly politicized form of friendship. During the various phases of our collaboration, despite some differences and disagreements, we stuck with our shared vision of feminist solidarity and found common ground on most matters.

The collaboration process that made this translation possible also depended on the support of other individuals to whom we're deeply grateful: Beyhan Demir, Ayşe Düzkan, Evin Kışanak, Burcu Çelik Özkan, and Emirali Türkmen. We also thank the Freedom for Aysel Tuğluk and Ill Prisoners Platform for permission to reproduce their call for action. Finally, we're grateful to Neda Tehrani of Pluto Press for helping to bring this project to fruition. Ruken and Emek are also thankful to Janet for contributing her original drawings to the book. In editing, we've slightly reduced the length of the essays for space considerations.

The Purple Color of Kurdish Politics is a product of women's solidarity, so is its translation, and we hope that you, its readers—whoever you are, wherever you are located, and whatever languages you speak—will stand in solidarity with Kurdish women and become part of the anticolonial and anticapitalist feminist resistance that the book hopes to expand against fascist regimes of male domination. By bringing differently situated feminist activists and movements together across languages, translation enables cross-border flows and exchanges of feminist lessons on how to transform societies, states, institutions, and individuals to make the world a place of peaceful and democratic plurality. For instance, the revolutionary principles of co-chairing and co-mayoring as practiced by Kurdish politicians are not only interesting to explore and study, but also quite seductive to adapt and adopt under different political regimes. We intend for this translation to be an opportunity for English-speaking readers to learn from the political experiments of 22 Kurdish women writers on how to transform patriarchal political systems and revolutionize male-dominated cultures and mechanisms of rule even under the most repressive conditions. We invite you to engage with these narratives as testimonials to Kurdish women politicians' resilience, determination, and agency, even though they've been systematically subjected to colonial state violence and gender discrimination in Turkey.

Kışanak understands that you may be unfamiliar with Kurdish women's particular struggles: "When there is so much social and political development happening in the world, what the Kurdish women politicians are experiencing in Turkey might seem like a distant agenda to you." But, she explains, "the road that will take us to our dreams of freedom passes through following each other's footsteps." Her strong sense of feminist solidarity with her English-speaking readers stems from her awareness that in our intensely and violently globalized (and "manned") world, we cannot accomplish an equal, democratic, and sustainable future without cross-border cooperation and resistance. And translation is necessary to that process of working together across (and against) the borders that turn us into each other's enemies. Therefore, we also invite translators to make this book travel into other languages so that even more peoples and communities around the world get a chance to engage with its stories of resistance.

Since the original book was published in Turkey in 2018, some of the 22 women have been freed, but the majority are still in prison. (We've updated their status in the captions opening the chapters.) For those who are still incarcerated, prison authorities have been exploiting pandemic conditions to further isolate and torture them. In her 2021 *Femina* article, Kışanak reported that due to the pandemic, "all our socializing and communication rights have been banned." No conversations are allowed, and "we haven't seen each other for a year now." As a result, "Everyone is trying to cope with loneliness in their own cells." Since Turkey only recently (and partially) eased the distancing procedures of the pandemic, these isolation practices most likely lasted much longer. Yet despite the women's psychologically arduous conditions, Kışanak continues, "We overcome the material loneliness we're forced into by thinking of the women making a struggle outside. We augment ourselves with our dreams." The achievements of women elsewhere give them hope, because "every win achieved against male domination reaches us by surpassing the concrete walls and iron bars and warms our hearts."

Like Kışanak, we too hope that upon reading the Kurdish women politicians' stories, you'll share their commitment to feminist solidarity and anticolonial resistance: "I believe after you read these lines," she says, "you'll think that, as women, we aren't distant and different from each other at all even though we live under different social and political settings. As women, it isn't just the paths we walk but also the dream of a future of freedom, justice, and equality that bring us all together. As women, we learn from one another, and we gain strength and morale from women's solidarity. By crossing borders, we share experiences and increase our gains."

To which we can only add the cry of the Kurdish women's movement, *Jin, Jiyan, Azadi!* Women, Life, Freedom!

Preface to the English Translation

Gültan Kışanak

Translated by Umut Erel

In the global struggle for women to participate in politics, the fight for suffrage was the crucial first step. Gaining the right to vote and to be elected to office was a milestone in women's struggle for equality and freedom. By participating in political processes, women could ask questions like "How should we live?" and "What should we do?" and then put their responses into practice. The system of male domination, however, has tried to ensure that this political right remains on paper only. Therefore, women have had to continue fighting to expand their legal rights and achieve de facto equality. Today equal representation for women in politics remains a crucial goal for the global feminist movement.

The patriarchal order is structured like a pyramid. Predicated on race, class, and gender, it encompasses a complex matrix of systems of domination. Women occupy the lowest ranks, and the women of marginalized nations have had to struggle additionally to carve out a place for themselves in politics. Kurdish women's political experiences, as well as their perseverance and determination, expose the patriarchal system's complex relations.

In every country where Kurds live (Iran, Iraq, Syria, and Turkey), Kurdish women have fought for equality. Globally, the women's movement has come to know us through our distinctive experiments in Turkey's political arena. This book tells the story of those experiments, especially in the window of opportunity between 2014 and 2016.

Approximately 20 million Kurds live in Turkey, a country founded on the ruins of the Ottoman Empire. Since the 1920s, Kurds have demanded state recognition of their identity and cultural rights, including rights to use their mother tongue and participate as Kurds in politics and government. Unfortunately, those demands remain unmet even in the twenty-first century. The result, since the 1980 military coup, has been incessant conflict between the Kurdish people and the Turkish state. And like other conflicts, this one afflicts women the most. Yet even in this context, Kurdish women have managed to make important advances in their struggle for gender equality.

Kurdish women's political struggle arguably began in Diyarbakır Prison in 1980. After the coup, Turkey's military junta repressed all domestic opponents, including Kurds. It arrested thousands and imprisoned the great majority in Military Prison No. 5, located in the largest Kurdish city, Diyarbakır. For three years, authorities tortured prisoners with bone-chilling brutality. Kurdish women prisoners at Diyarbakır had their first experiences with political struggle when they resisted those atrocities. Their acts of resistance were the first skirmishes in a women's struggle that continues unrelentingly to this day.

During that coup period, I myself was detained in Diyarbakır Prison for two years. Almost 40 years later, I'm in prison again. In the fall of 2016, the Turkish state arrested Kurdish democratic politicians en masse and imprisoned dozens of women politicians, including myself. Nine of us who had been MPs and co-mayors found ourselves in Kocaeli No. 1 F-type High-Security Prison. Within those walls, as we spent long stretches of time together, friends* implored me, "Why don't you write something about your experiences with women in Diyarbakır Prison all those years ago?"

It was a good idea, but as I thought about it, I got an even better one. In 1980 only two women councilors had been imprisoned, but now in 2017 Turkish prisons were full of women MPs, co-mayors, and city councilors. Yes, it was important for me to write about the 1980 coup, the brutality at Diyarbakır Prison, and women's resistance there, but the journey of Kurdish women has continued nonstop since then. Connecting the past with the present seemed a better response to the situation we're currently facing. Hence this book.

---

* The term *arkadaş* literally translates as "friend" but denotes the politicized friendship and solidarity among Kurdish movement members.

The last thing I wanted was to draw solely on my own experiences and opinions. Every woman's story is a precious treasure, and considered together, they reveal amazing energy and power. Gathering, compiling, and publishing them all, I thought, would contribute to women's struggle for freedom. And making these women's struggles and victories visible would place them within the historical record.

I have a background in journalism,* so I decided to send interview questions to my friends via letters. *What made you dare to enter the male-dominated arena of politics?* I asked. *What challenges did you face? How did you overcome them? What changes has our struggle generated? What have we accomplished?* In my cover letter, I explained my plan to compile the interviews and publish them. "The more women contribute to the book," I wrote, "the better it'll be, and the more accurately and thoroughly it'll reveal our struggles . . . Without your contribution, the book will be incomplete. I want it to tell our story, the story of all of us."

My friends were scattered in different prisons across Turkey, so to send the letters, I had to track down their prison addresses. That wasn't easy. Some friends got transferred to a different prison before my letter arrived. Others couldn't respond because the prison authorities would punish them if they did. Still others wrote responses, but the prison authorities deemed the contents "objectionable" and refused to let them be sent to me. Realizing it would take a long time to overcome these problems, I set a cutoff date: I'd include only the interviews that reached me by February 2018.

As my friends received my questions, they told me later, a wave of excitement came over them, and in writing out their responses, they threw themselves into it. When my daughter Evin visited, I explained the idea to her—she was thrilled too, saying, "Mom, hurry up and write the book in case you get released!" (In fact, as I write this in late 2021, over five years have passed since we were arrested and three years since the book was published in Turkish. Thirteen of the women whose stories are in the book are still in prison.)

---

* Kışanak worked as a journalist, editor, and news director for various Kurdish newspapers in 1990–2004.

Soon the interview responses began to arrive, from those whose conditions permitted them to send letters to me. As I read them, I realized that we'd all walked similar paths and had similar experiences—the interviews repeated each other. But their written responses lacked the feel of face-to-face interviews. So, with my friends' consent, I turned their responses into narratives, under their own names.

I'd like to express my deepest gratitude to my friends who answered my questions under difficult prison conditions. I hope they'll forgive any shortcomings that have resulted from my editing. Once we are all free, we'll be able to delve more deeply into our memories to produce an even more comprehensive and multifaceted work.

Every narrative in this book recounts the experience of an individual within the Kurdish women's movement. The stories are not biographies; rather, each woman articulates where she started out, her progress, the obstacles she faced, and how she found the strength to stand up to the patriarchal system. By sharing these stories of our experiences in the women's liberation struggle—the tough setbacks as well as the sweet victories—we seek to leave our mark on history.

To enable non-Kurdish readers to understand their stories better, I've written an introduction recounting the history of the Kurdish women's movement. It provides the background for the women's stories, explaining the main events they refer to.

All our accomplishments in the political arena are grounded in the hard work of thousands of women who often paid a heavy price for it. As significant as all their efforts are, it would be impossible to include all their stories in this book, so I've limited its scope to the stories of women who held office in local or national politics and who were in prison between August 2017 and February 2018. The one exception is Leyla Güven, who was elected an MP from Hakkâri on June 24, 2018. At that time, we were in the final stages of editing the book, and we expected Leyla to be released, but she wasn't. So I sent her my interview questions quickly, then rushed her story into the book. I think her story highlights well the ongoing unlawfulness.

A further limitation: while this book uses the broad category "Kurdish women," it includes the stories only of women who have been involved in legal political party activities—specifically, women who worked in parties that follow in the political tradition initiated by HEP in 1990. Other Kurdish women work in different political parties or outside party politics altogether. The Kurdish women's movement, after all, works through a wide array of channels and mobilizes people in all arenas of life. Each arena gives rise to unique and precious experiences, which contribute to making the women's movement a complex structure that continually develops and renews itself.

This book doesn't focus on the charges for which the particular women were arrested; nor does it trace the course of their trials or emphasize the unlawfulness of those proceedings. I've included only short descriptions about the processes of detention, arrest, and imprisonment. We already know very well that the patriarchal system wants us to pay a high price for our struggle for a democratic future in which women have equal rights.

In their letters responding to me, the imprisoned women all thanked me for working on this book. But it's I who thank them, and I emphasize that this book is a product of a collective effort. On behalf of us all, I thank Hülya Osmanağaoğlu, who edited the book and made important contributions.

Translating and publishing this book in English is crucial to sharing Kurdish women's political experiences with a larger readership. Many women contributed to the translation. On behalf of all the contributors, I'd like to thank them for their hard work and solidarity.

I also thank the prison officers who had the privilege of reading the book before any other readers did, including me. I hope it became an occasion for them to start questioning gender inequalities in society.

Our biggest debt of gratitude is undoubtedly owed to all women who carry the torch of women's liberation struggle.

Gültan Kışanak
October 27, 2021

Women's Organizing in the Kurdish Party Tradition

Gültan Kışanak

Translated by Necla Açık and Paula Darwish

Throughout history, social inequalities have ignited social struggles. Although humans are considered the most intelligent creatures on earth, they've created inequalities, hegemonies, and hierarchies, dealing blow after blow to human values and rights, while decimating the natural world to the point of jeopardizing their future survival. History is littered with conflicts sparked by these inequalities and by nature's rebellions against the pillage of its assets, commonly referred to as "natural" disasters.

Gender inequality is the oldest inequality in history, and for a long time, women's struggle against male supremacy was purposefully obscured by ruling classes. Women's struggle for freedom continues today as a universal force, and the Kurdish women's movement is part of this universal struggle. Its accomplishments are remarkable, as Kurdish women have asserted their existence, power, and will in every area of life. All their experiences deserve to be thoroughly examined, but the stories in this book are about their experiences in a specific political party tradition in Turkey. That tradition began with HEP, the first legal party with a specifically Kurdish identity, and has continued with other parties to the present. The book also focuses on Kurdish women's experiences in local government, where over those years we've achieved co-mayoring and equal representation.

Working within a political party tests women's self-confidence repeatedly, every day and every minute. Even as they struggle against prescribed social roles, the traditional family structure, and state oppression, they must also face the party's own patriarchal mindset and gender roles internalized by women themselves.

And just when a woman seems to receive acknowledgment for her achievements, she realizes that it has been given to her as a special privilege; if she indulges in savoring it, she becomes a masculinized woman type, infected by the patriarchal mindset. In short, women's political party experience is endlessly challenging.

HEP AND DEP (1990–94)

HEP, established on June 7, 1990, was the first political party in Turkey to overtly identify as Kurdish. During the 1980s, the Kurdish struggle had gained ground, becoming a mass movement that provided the social foundation for HEP's establishment.

Turkey has a 10 percent electoral threshold, a high bar that any party must surpass to gain seats in parliament. So for the 1991 parliamentary elections, HEP made an alliance with SHP, merging their candidates on the same slate. HEP's only woman candidate, Leyla Zana, was a newcomer to politics and could easily have become invisible among the veteran men politicians. But the opposite happened—she became the center of attention, the most sought-after speaker at election rallies, partly because her husband, Mehdi Zana, the mayor of the city of Diyarbakır, had been detained in the 1980 coup.

During the 1991 campaign, a spirit of determination arose among the people to correct that injustice, but Leyla Zana's popularity had another basis as well. With her red, yellow, and green headband and her enthralling Kurdish-language oratory, she became the symbol of politicized Kurdish women. Her nickname "Xûşka Leyla" (Sister Leyla) reflected the era's outlook that women in politics were seen as men's "sisters." A ranked-choice voting system was then in effect: the voters could cast their ballots both for the party and for whomever they liked on the party slate. Leyla received enough preferential votes to put her in top place as the MP for Diyarbakır. Of the 450 seats in the 1991 Turkish parliament, only eight were held by women. One was Leyla Zana. On the new parliament's opening day, at the swearing-in ceremony, she said, "I take this oath for the fellowship of the Kurdish and Turkish peoples." For daring to utter these words, the Turkish media all but lynched her, and its hysteria persisted long afterward, reflecting the society's intolerance of women politicians, especially Kurdish ones.

In 1993 the Turkish state banned HEP, whereupon its activists proceeded to form a new party, DEP. In those years the Turkish state was forcibly evacuating and razing Kurdish villages, allowing extrajudicial murders of prominent Kurds to go unsolved, and maintaining an ongoing state of emergency. Kurdish democratic politics fell victim to those policies. On March 4, 1994, the state stripped the DEP MPs of their parliamentary immunity, frog-marched them out of the parliament, and arrested them. One of those MPs was Leyla Zana.

Women were not yet an organized force in HEP and DEP. They were present in local party chapters, but at the central party level, only two or three women held appointed positions. In those years, women could participate in Turkish politics only if they were "strong and deserving" or else held menial positions. Parties didn't nominate women as candidates for office and made no special effort to attract women's votes. Candidates made no outreach to women and addressed no speeches to them. Not only were women excluded as agents of politics, they couldn't even be the subject of politics. With a few rare exceptions, politics was a men's business.

Kurds began their struggle for democratic politics with the 1991 election rallies and continued thereafter with marches, protests, and press releases. Women joined demonstrations and rallies. The politicization of the streets swelled the Kurdish political movement, but women could mostly only knock on its doors.

HADEP (1994–2002)

After DEP was shut down in 1994, Kurdish activists regrouped as HADEP, and buoyed by the groundswell in the streets, more women got involved in local party work. In the larger provinces, the party established women's commissions to address the trauma of forcible evacuation from villages. These commissions held women-only meetings in neighborhoods, where women decried the impact of Turkey's war on themselves and their children. Out of these meetings, a specific women's agenda emerged, alongside the general political agenda. Many women said they wanted to get involved in grassroots party activism but were prevented by their fathers, husbands, and brothers, even those who themselves were party activists. Why couldn't women join men in fighting state oppression? they asked. Wasn't the ability to leave the house and become active a matter of freedom? Solving this problem became a priority for women in local party administration, who visited families to persuade men to let women participate.

Even as women performed more local party work, their efforts weren't replicated at the central party level. There women remained few in number, even to the point that a man on the Central Executive Committee was briefly put in charge of women's issues. But gradually local women's mobilization gained strength, and in 1997 party women created a Central Women's Commission to coordinate local work with the central party structure, and general political work with women's autonomous activities.

In 1999 HADEP participated in local elections, but most women didn't yet feel powerful enough to run as candidates. The political atmosphere was extremely tense, yet in a timid but courageous debut, women candidates did run in three districts: Mukaddes Kubilay in Bazîd (Turkish Doğubayazıt) in Ağrı province, Cihan Sincar in the Kızıltepe in Mardin province, and Ayşe Karadağ in Derik, also in Mardin province. Women participated enthusiastically in the campaigns. Overall, HADEP won control of 37 municipalities, including one metropolitan district (Diyarbakır) and six provinces (Ağrı, Batman, Bingöl, Hakkâri, Siirt, and Van). The three women candidates were elected and now had to figure out how to govern. With the support of the party's newly formed women's branches, they did exceptional work and gained the public's trust.

In 2000, Turkey's Law on Political Parties was amended to allow parties to establish women's branches. So that year at the HADEP congress, members proposed a resolution to amend the party's bylaws to institute women's branches. The congress approved the resolution, which also instituted a 25 percent women's quota:

> Positive discrimination will be applied for women in candidacies and delegates at all levels and to the ratio of speakers at all meetings. In elections for management roles at every level of the

> HADEP constitution, at least one in four of those chosen must be women. This rule applies to municipal council members, MP candidacies, and delegates for provincial or area congresses and conventions: at least one in four members, delegates, and MP candidates must be women. No upper limit can be set.

For the first time, a Kurdish political party adopted a women's quota both in elections and in all official party bodies at every level, down to the number of speakers at meetings. Over the next years, our effort to fulfill the women's quota reflected our determination to speak and our rejection of the silencing of women. The right to speak, after all, is the cornerstone of people's power to assert their will. Including women's right to speak in the resolution was a direct challenge to the existing patriarchal attitude of "It's not your prerogative to speak."

Soon after the HADEP congress, the party held its first women's congress. Thousands of women from across the country arrived in Ankara to participate, demonstrating women's determination and strength. They formed women's branches in accordance with the new bylaw, and for the first time, the party created a central office—head of the women's branches—whose main function was to support and promote women's activism.

Women now occupied a substantial position in HADEP. Ever more women were entering the party, the women's quota ensured that women held positions in the Party Council and Central Executive Committee, the women's branches were in place, women were mobilized in every province and district.

But all this was still not enough for women to achieve equality within the party, where the patriarchal mindset was firmly entrenched. Political parties are hierarchically structured bodies, with a powerful leader—generally a man—at the top. The weight of the party hierarchy tended to crush women's organizing. Mixed-gender meetings made decisions about which women would sit on the Party Council and Central Executive Committee, who would be candidates for elections, and what women's activities would be undertaken, but at these meetings, men were in the majority. That situation obstructed the development of gender awareness and prevented party women from recognizing their power and believing in themselves and each other.

The women's branches discussed the problem at women's conferences, then in 2000 they proposed that the party adopt four principles:

1. *Women's organizing must be based on autonomous self-organizing, and all decisions concerning women must be made by women.* In accordance with the new party bylaw, women set up their own structure within the party but outside the party hierarchy. The Central Women's Branch would coordinate women's operations and make all decisions concerning women. The head of the women's branches would present women's branch decisions to the Central Executive Committee; if those decisions were challenged, the women members of the CEC would defend them, ensuring their acceptance. The same process was applied in the districts and provinces; here too women in the local party administration were automatically members of the women's branches. Women throughout the party structure would mobilize to ensure that their decisions were implemented and to check attempts to undermine them. The formation of a collective women's voice would have a major impact on the party.

2. *In advance of election periods, party women must establish a Women's Election Commission, separate from the General Election Commission.* The Women's Election Commission would ensure that the women's quota was filled and take nominations for women candidates. Furthermore, it would support women candidates throughout their campaigns by giving interviews, conducting opinion polls, and producing election publicity and materials. It'd strive to increase women politicians' visibility and introduce women's agendas into the society at large. Such work would prove crucial in swaying politics toward a women-centered axis.

3. *The party budget must allocate funds to women's organizing.* That "politics is for those who have money" is fundamental to sustaining the hierarchical structure of parties. Women who lacked the resources to travel to party meetings could not be active in politics.

But they had trouble getting funding from the party because it didn't regard their activities as necessary. The fact that women were obliged to ask for money from their men at home or the party treasurer replicated traditional gender roles.

This problem was resolved at the central party level when a woman took on the role of general treasurer. But at the district and provincial levels, women were told, "The party has just enough money for general activities. You women need to find your own budget." That attitude, too, perpetuated traditional family roles. Women were reduced to organizing charity sales and selling handmade goods to fund the party's March 8 events. So it was crucial for the party to budget a set amount for women's activities. After a while, this principle was incorporated into the party bylaws.

4. *Men who were bigamous or violent toward women were barred from holding party executive positions.* At every congress and in every election, women made great efforts to enforce compliance with this principle. The party accepted it in theory, but implementation proved difficult. Some argued for flexibility, insisting that men who had pre-existing bigamous marriages prior should be exempt from the principle. Men pushed for "exceptions" during congress and election periods. But thanks to women's sheer persistence, the principle was ultimately incorporated into the party bylaws.

Thereafter when men were vetted as prospective electoral candidates, they were asked about their relations with women. Men who gave unsatisfactory responses were eliminated from candidacy. At least one woman sat on each interview panel. So before the interview, men nominees would frantically bone up on the subject by asking their women friends about women's perspectives.

Since 2000, women in Kurdish political parties have operated on the basis of these four principles. In tandem with the women's quota, the women's principles enabled women to move into active positions. But a long struggle remained before the general party entirely dropped the attitude that "politics is for men, women are auxiliaries," and empowered women's mobilization. In fact, the operations of male domination, together with the privileges handed to men by the patriarchal system, continued to affect the party's gender balance. Ultimately women couldn't easily become an "equal power" without unraveling all hierarchical relations.

THE 2002 GENERAL ELECTIONS

In the 2002 general elections, women's mobilization in the women's branches and implementation of the women's principles bore their first fruit. Women were nominated in places where they stood a chance of getting elected. And the first time, the party presented its women's policies to the people. In several provinces, the party's top-ranked women candidates got more than enough votes to be elected MPs.

But the party as a whole didn't get enough votes to surpass the 10 percent electoral threshold, so the vote-winning individuals couldn't take their seats in parliament. If not for the high threshold, there would have been many women representatives in the parliament in 2002. Clearly the 10 percent threshold constitutes a barrier to democratic politics in general and to women in particular.

In the wake of that failure to surpass the threshold, a hostile patriarchal backlash erupted. Some blamed the shortfall on the choice of women as preferential candidates, and some even blamed those candidates' religious identities. Male chauvinism kept this discourse on the agenda for some time, as sexist men in the party believed they'd finally found a legitimate reason to oppose women candidates.

Women and men turned out to have strikingly different styles of doing politics. Overall, Turkish political culture values a strong leader and a managed society, but political women tend to aim for a democratic politics grounded in cooperation, collective will, rights, and responsibilities. Kurdish politics also claims to pursue a democracy-oriented political practice, but it's nonetheless influenced by the patriarchal style. Men in the Kurdish parties conformed to the classical mode by seeking to accrue power as individuals, while women saw political work as a responsibility to the collectivity.

After 2007, the gender struggle within the party was transformed. In the past, party men took blatantly exclusionary approaches to ensure their continued domination, but now they found subtler, more deceptive ways to exploit the privileges that the patriarchal system so readily handed them. For example, in program planning, they'd recommend women to handle insignificant, small programs and men to lead major, large ones. When women objected, they invoked public opinion in that ever-ready excuse: "It's what the people want!"

Another subtle form of misogyny within the party was that it approached gender inequality as a women's issue. Although it specifically incorporated gender equality as a goal in its programs and bylaws, it made few concrete efforts to fulfill that goal in reality. One resolution required that in every internal party training and meeting, "women's liberation" was to be a main agenda item, but men violated this principle easily: in meetings where no women were present or where women's organizing was weak, women's issues weren't discussed.

The party bylaw on the quota had affirmed the principle of "positive discrimination," or affirmative action to include more women. But this principle proved even harder to implement than women's quota. Men consented to allocating some seats to women when more than one seat was available, but when there was only one seat, they roared against allowing a woman to have it. They howled about the woman's supposed lack of "qualifications" and threw at her every sexist prejudice known to the patriarchal system.

The question of whether women were "qualified" to hold political office was never-ending. Everything about women candidates was interrogated, and qualities that no one would think of looking for in men were demanded of women. Women were expected to work harder, be more decent, be more effective speakers, have more knowledge and experience, take more risks, and be more self-sacrificing. To some extent, women defused the "qualification" issue by choosing women candidates themselves, but the issue still surfaced far too often.

Whenever a man made a mistake or misjudgment, everyone quickly forgot about it. But let even one erroneous word slip from a woman's mouth, and she'd be castigated endlessly. The patriarchal mentality within the party would then join hands with the media, state, and society. But when the subject was a man, an unnamed male solidarity would come into play.

At press briefings, protests, events, and visits, some men would rush to elbow women aside and shove their way forward—yet another sign of their inability to accept women as equals. In fact, once the party implemented equal representation, some men interpreted standing even one step behind a woman as a blow to their pride.

During elections, men would try to undermine the women's quota by grousing, "Why do women always want *guaranteed* places?" And when a man candidate lost an election, men would conjure up so many excuses on his behalf that the candidate's actual shortcomings would become virtually invisible. But if a woman candidate lost an election, they'd pin the blame on her alone and ignore all other possible factors. No wonder women hesitated to run for election in places where the outcome was uncertain.

In the face of this double standard and other sexist attitudes, women learned to reject all relations of dominance and power and look instead for ways to root their collective force in democratic principles. Our experience showed over and over again that the only sure path here was the one that passed through women's autonomous self-organizing. During times when women's organizing was strong, the patriarchal mentality regressed, and when women's organizing weakened, the patriarchal mentality became prominent, pushing back against women's will. Women understood that relinquishing the fight against the patriarchal mentality would put all their gains at risk, so they continued their struggle within the framework of democratic political principles.

On March 13, 2003, Turkey's Constitutional Court shut HADEP down. Thereafter the mantle passed to DEHAP, a new party in the same Kurdish tradition. DEHAP carried over women's accomplishments and principles, and women continued their work there.

Organized women's work was by now well established within the Kurdish political tradition, but the party realized that it needed to raise and deepen gender consciousness, so it instituted gender awareness trainings. These trainings taught women to question every institution and perception formed by a male-dominant mentality, to challenge existing codes of femininity and masculinity, and to strive for a future that embraced women's emancipation and democracy. Over time they even learned to challenge the hierarchical relationship that human beings formed with nature. Asking Kurdish women "What kind of a future?" introduced them to the ideology of women's liberation. This work gave the Kurdish women's movement momentum and depth.

Women in DEHAP sought to extend women's struggle into every area of life, by creating independent women's institutions. After 2000, DEHAP set up women's structures one after another. During the period 2000–5 autonomous women's organizations examined the historical origins of the woman question, analyzed issues of violence and discrimination against women, and discussed the preconditions for women to achieve economic, social, political, and cultural power and agency. The most intensely discussed topics were the social contract and the ideology of women's liberation.

The Dicle Women's Cultural Center, in Istanbul, became a focal point for women's education. The Amargi Women's Cooperative, also in Istanbul, offered consciousness raising. And in 2002 the Selis Women's Counseling Center, in Diyarbakır, worked to prevent violence against women. In 2001 the Diyarbakır Metropolitan Municipality established the Center for Research and Application on Women's Issues to conduct fieldwork on issues affecting women, search for solutions, and offer counseling services. Over time other municipal administrations opened women's centers, strengthening the links between women and local governments.

The autonomous women's organizations and DEHAP's women's branches needed to collaborate and coordinate their work. Together they held women's conferences, bringing together women from different fields to share experiences, discuss ways of furthering the women's liberation struggle, and organize campaigns around common themes. They established the Democratic Free Women's Movement (DÖKH) not as a centralized organization but as a dynamic, flexible, and inclusive "movement" that allowed principles and agendas to be determined, planned, and executed collectively.

LOCAL EXPERIMENTS

Building on the rise in gender awareness and the spread of women's organizing, women prepared for the 2004 local elections with more confidence. A year out from the elections, women met to draft feasibility reports, make situational assessments, and discuss questions such as "How can we increase the number of women mayors and councilors? Where can we nominate women candidates?" Following the recommendation of their feasibility reports, the party chose about 15 places where women candidates could be nominated, including one province, Dersim.

In places that were designated for women, the party didn't accept nominations of men. They raised howls of fury and unleashed all the familiar sexist arguments, starting with "We're gonna lose with women candidates." Then sexist party men decided that the party's candidates should be chosen in primaries. "Let both men and women run in the primary," they said. "Whoever wins will be the candidate." It was yet another way to evade the women's quota. When women objected, they argued, "What kind of democracy is it if it won't even accept our candidacy for nomination?" But in all those years when not a single woman was elected mayor, no one had questioned democracy. No man had thought to ask, "What kind of democracy is it if no woman ever becomes a mayor?" But when they heard, "Let's make room for women," they suddenly remembered: "Democracy!"

The women's movement fought such attitudes tooth and nail. In the 2004 local elections, for the first time, a party election manifesto dedicated a special section to women, spelling out the kind of work that the party would carry out for women in the municipalities. In addition, women ran as candidates, and they distributed flyers, leaflets, and brochures specifically addressed to women.

When the time came for people to cast their ballots, they elected a total of 56 DEHAP mayors. Nine were women. Women were elected as district mayors in Bağlar and Bismil in Diyarbakır province, in Bazîd in Ağrı province, and in Kızıltepe and Mazıdağı and Sürgücü in Mardin province; in Bostaniçi in Van province; in Küçükdikili in Adana province; and in Dersim province. The proportion of women mayors in DEHAP didn't reach the targeted women's quota but reached 16 percent—a success unprecedented in any Turkish party. The success highlighted the positive impact of our collective struggle.

The women elected to these positions found themselves shouldering a huge weight, but the women's movement didn't leave them to fend for themselves. After all, it had persuaded them to run in the first place by promising to support them. So immediately after the elections, women experienced in local activism took up positions in support for the new women mayors. The party held women's local governance conferences to share experiences. The new municipal administrations went on to develop women's projects and allocate funding for them. They launched women's centers, and women began to visit local government offices. Town halls finally opened their doors to women.

Up to that point, municipalities employed hardly any women staff, and women at the managerial level were all but nonexistent. Still, the women mayors, and a few women councilors and advisers, did their best to get the job done.

SEXIST ATTITUDES IN LOCAL POLITICS

Kurdish women had difficult experiences in national politics, but their experiences in local politics were even harder, due to gender discrimination. I can say that the most significant prejudices are the following:

- *Women can't be executives:* The patriarchal mindset seeks to limit the government roles available to women. That is, a woman can be an MP, but not a prime minister or a cabinet minister—and in local government, a woman cannot be a mayor. After all, the mayor is the person who runs the city, and women cannot handle executive authority. The constitutional provision that everyone has the right to vote and run for office has no reality in the actual world. The fundamental objective of the struggle for women's liberation is to change this reality and to achieve real equality.
- *Municipal services are men's business:* One of the jobs of a mayor is to coordinate local services and manage local affairs. The

patriarchal mindset perceives almost all municipal services as men's business and holds that women know nothing about infrastructure, road construction, town planning, urban development, or firefighting. Therefore, women are unfit to be mayor.

- *Women don't have a head for economics:* Municipalities have budgets. According to the patriarchal mindset, women don't understand financial matters; economics and budget management are men's jobs. So a woman mayor is incapable of managing a budget.
- *Women can't be "chiefs":* The mayor represents the entire city. Women can be MPs representing women, but they can't represent an entire city where both men and women live. Just as the father is the "chief" of the family, the mayor is the city's "Sir Chief." We still hear women mayors being referred to as "Lady Chief" or "Sir Chiefwoman."
- *Other leaders are men, so the mayor should be a man too:* Municipal mayors have to deal with elected neighborhood officials, businesspeople, professionals, opinion leaders, notables, and employers, as well as regional and local officials such as governors. In short, they must be in touch with all the major actors in the city. Since those actors are almost exclusively men, naturally the mayor must also be a man. But given that half the residents of a city are women, one might well ask why all the city's top economic, social, and political positions are in the hands of men. Instead the patriarchal mentality asserts, "The mayor must be a man," and seeks to reinforce male power by using the local government's resources.

The way to challenge such conservative attitudes was to build a strong women's organization. Political women organized, worked hard, and took strong stands, while those who served their electorates successfully gained the people's confidence. Nothing else really mattered. Gradually the patriarchal mentality, which saw politics as the achievement and exercise of "power" and couldn't bear yielding to women, was losing ground.

In fact, in some places men candidates competed so abrasively that the party stood to potentially lose the election, so the public begged, "Assign the women's quota here too, or we'll lose the election. We stand a chance of winning only with a woman candidate." Other suggestions were along the lines of "Let's nominate women candidates even in places where there's no possibility of winning." Women welcomed this latter proposal too, because electoral campaigns were good opportunities for women to engage with the public and become politicized. So the party applied the gender quota even to constituencies where it had no chance of winning.

DTP (2005–9) AND CO-CHAIRING

After 2004, DEHAP began to discuss ways to restructure mainstream politics. It held a series of local and regional meetings to gather suggestions from the public. This process culminated in the establishment of DTP in 2005, whereupon DEHAP ceased its political activities.

As DTP was formed, party women decided to strengthen their organizing. First, they replaced the women's branches with women's assemblies. The assembly is a horizontal model that strengthens local initiatives. The assemblies would make women part of the struggle, rather than leaving them to wait for a solution from elsewhere, a crucial step in fostering women's agency.

Second, party women decided that the party should implement a system of co-chairing, or dual leadership. That is, instead of one individual holding a party position, one man and one woman would hold the position jointly. As expected, men in the party resisted this proposal, asking "What's the point?" and "It's against the law." Others weighed in with "Okay, when a deserving woman comes forward, we'll make her the chair."

But by then, DTP had already expressed its recognition that gender equality is the most fundamental criterion of democracy. Co-chairing would represent the institutionalization of equality between men and women. In the end, the party incorporated co-chairing into its bylaws.

The party then submitted an official application to the Turkish state to legally establish co-chairing. But the Supreme Court of Appeals rejected the clause on the grounds that it was "not part of the Law on Political Parties" and demanded that the party remove co-chairing from its bylaws. This reignited the debate.

The women responded by saying to the party, "If the Supreme Court insists that we remove the clause from the bylaws, we will, but let's not give up co-chairing itself. Let's implement it de facto." That led to some difficult discussions in the Central Executive Committee, where some claimed that women were trying to get the party shut down, while others suggested that the party remove co-chairing from the bylaws and go back to the old leadership system. But the women refused to back down. Thanks to their determination, co-chairing was implemented on principle, an important gain not just for DTP but for democracy itself. At its first congress, DTP elected Aysel Tuğluk and Ahmet Türk as co-chairs.

It would take almost a decade of hard work to spread co-chairing to all levels of the party. But backed by the women's quota, women's principles, women's assemblies, and ever more women elected officials, co-chairing became widespread. Kurdish women were becoming political agents.

As the 2007 general elections approached, party women wanted to see more women's candidacies. DTP, meanwhile, was determined that this time the party must surpass the 10 percent threshold and get into parliament. Rather than risk another failure, it decided to advance its candidates as independents.* And rather than run candidates in all provinces, it would run them only in places where they had a chance of winning. The party's target was to have 30 to 35 MPs elected. Based on this target, women did the math and put forward the number of candidates required for the women's quota.

Our effort bore fruit: 22 party candidates won parliamentary seats. Eight were women: Aysel Tuğluk, Sebahat Tuncel, Fatma Kurtulan, Ayla Akat Ata, Gültan Kışanak, Emine Ayna, Sevahir Bayındır, and Pervin Buldan. The victory of women's assembly spokesperson Sebahat Tuncel was notable because she was impris-

---

* The 10 percent electoral threshold effectively shut Kurdish parties out of parliament. But that threshold applies only to parties; in a curious loophole, it doesn't apply to independents. So Kurdish candidates had a better chance of getting elected if they ran as independents than as party members.

oned during the elections. Undoubtedly, if the women's movement had not insisted on fulfilling the women's quota, fewer women MPs would have been elected. These women would turn in impressive performances.

Meanwhile at the local level, in the nine districts that had elected women mayors in 2004, the public was satisfied. The women mayors had undertaken many exemplary projects and performed well. Their successful administrations debunked the patriarchal argument: "Women can't do it." For the 2007 local elections, the patriarchal mindset came up with a different objection: "Women might succeed as candidates in other places, but they won't in our area, because it has its own particularities." But they turned out to be wrong. In fact, in the 2007 local elections, 14 more municipalities elected women as mayors and deputies, wherever they were nominated, by large majorities.

LOCAL GOVERNMENT

In local government, the new mayors had not only to carry out the work but also to entrench it by making structural changes that could be implemented in all municipalities. They had at least one woman vice mayor, hired more women personnel and administrators, formed a women's caucus in municipal councils, and established gender equality commissions. Almost all the women-led municipalities replicated these practices. They established women's directorates, whose members were elected by the women employees, to act as a bridge between the administration and working women, ensuring that women's hard work made an impact on upper-level decisions. They conducted gender awareness trainings for municipal employees and offered workshops on gender-based budget planning, allocating funding for women's programs. In collective agreements between municipalities and labor unions, they added the following provision: "If a man employee inflicts violence on his wife, she'll receive half of his salary."

All these activities contributed to a structural transformation in the municipalities, where male domination had been formerly deeply rooted. It wasn't easy to transform municipalities to incorporate women into them, to ensure that they delivered services to women, and to develop women-oriented practices in urban planning and municipal services. But by the 2009 local elections, women's successes as elected officials rendered most sexist opposition meaningless. The "we'll lose with women" fearmongering was discredited. The public's confidence in women grew by leaps and bounds.

The strengthening of democratic politics, however, and women's participation in both local and national government must have unsettled the patriarchal system, because in April 2009 the Turkish state initiated an arrest operation against Kurdish activists.* In this political genocide operation, which continued for several years, more than 10,000 people were arrested, and 70,000 to 80,000 people had to deal with detention and make court appearances. Almost everyone who was engaged in democratic politics was detained.

One of the operation's main objectives was to disperse the women's movement, force women to withdraw from the political sphere, and eliminate the gains women had made. The women's assemblies were a major target. The state arrested approximately 500 members of women's assemblies, party administrators, and municipal councilors, including Viranşehir mayor Leyla Güven and Derik mayor Çağlar Demirel. Although women had taken care to protect their achievements, these arrests did substantial harm to their work.

BDP (2010–14)

On December 11, the Constitutional Court shut down DTP. Once again, a new party, BDP, took over the tradition and inherited the accumulated achievements of the women's struggle. In BDP, as in DTP, co-chairing, women's assemblies, and women's principles formed the basis for the goal of achieving equal representation in the party.

---

* From 2009 to 2012, the Turkish state's so-called anti-KCK operation detained thousands of Kurdish activists, intellectuals, academics, publishers, trade unionists, and human rights defenders, as well as duly elected local officials, on the grounds of their alleged links to KCK, an umbrella organization that includes the PKK, which the Turkish state considers "terrorist."

For the general 2011 elections, the pro-Kurdish parties once again joined with other democratic, left-socialist forces to form an electoral alliance, to strengthen the struggle for democracy and surpass the 10 percent threshold. This new bloc did gain seats in parliament, and the number of women MPs rose to eleven. That success generated a positive atmosphere, and BDP agreed that henceforth Kurdish parties would participate in such blocs. Their allies agreed on the need for a structure but not on what kind or how. So BDP facilitated an initiative to bring together all these groups, as well as other individuals and organizations supporting a democratic and egalitarian future. It organized a series of meetings. At the epicenter of this work were two Kurdish women, Sebahat Tuncel, and myself, who met with numerous women's organizations, activists, and academics.

In 2012 this process gave rise to HDK, in which the women's perspective had substantial influence: women were the main constituent of its platform for social change. Although the participating groups failed to achieve the desired level of collaboration, the experience paved the way for Kurdish women to consider partnering with the Turkish women's movement.

Meanwhile, discussions had begun about a new constitution for Turkey. The country was still governed by the constitution that had been introduced with the 1980 military coup. In the intervening years it had been amended, but a new constitution was clearly necessary. After the 2011 elections, parliament established a Constitutional Reconciliation Commission, to which BDP was entitled to appoint a member. It chose Ayla Akat Ata, who became the only woman on the commission. BDP drew up a draft constitution that was based on freedoms and gender equality and that proposed democratic solutions to all issues of identity and cultural rights, including the Kurdish question. Women's demands were front and center as a result of constitutional meetings convened by the women's movement. The work of the Constitutional Commission was aborted due to disagreements, but during the process, the Kurdish women's movement and the Turkish feminist movement found common ground, developing relationships that remained strong.

Also, in the years 2010–14, the Turkish-Kurdish conflict seemed on track to move toward a peaceful, democratic resolution. In 2013 the AKP government initiated talks at İmralı. Very different assessments have been made about this peace and resolution process, but I'll touch here only on the aspects related to women. To ensure that any prospective resolution would be democratic, the Kurdish women's movement insisted that women have representation in BDP's delegation to İmralı: hence Ayla Akat Ata, Pervin Buldan, and Ceylan Bağrıyanık participated in the delegation. Because the Kurdish side included women in the process, women's demands were on the table. Hence too the remarkable emphasis on women's freedom in the 2015 program announced at Dolmabahçe Palace.*

THE 2014 ELECTIONS

After the Turkish state cracked down on women's assemblies, BDP decided to rebuild and strengthen them, especially in districts and provinces identified by women's conferences. Its belief was that if the party could set up women's assemblies in every province, district, neighborhood, and village, then women would become stronger as individuals, and women collectively could become an organized force. The women's assemblies in fact became the driving force in fulfilling the principle of equal representation.

For the 2014 local elections, women in HDP and BDP insisted on fully implementing the women's quota. They organized women's conferences to discuss and assess women's local governance experiences. They conducted feasibility studies to gain a better understanding of local particularities. They decided where to apply the women's quota by factoring in the numbers and safety of seats.

Co-chairing had been implemented de facto for nine years in DTP and later in BDP. In 2014, as a result of women's struggle and determination, Turkey amended its Law on Political Parties to add a clause making co-chairing legal in all political parties. Now in

---

* After two years, the talks produced a ten-point agreement, presented to the public on February 28, 2015, at the Dolmabahçe Palace. This agreement consisted of ten principles for peace and democracy in Turkey, including a new constitution that guaranteed women's rights. The AKP government subsequently reneged on the agreement and initiated a war of annihilation against Kurdish cities, towns, and villages.

BDP, women discussed extending co-chairing to local government. Instead of running one candidate for an office, like a mayor, the party could run two, one man and one woman, and if they won, they'd become "co-mayors." It wasn't easy to broach this subject in the party, I recall. It carried considerable challenges and risks. Given how difficult it had been, in some places, to persuade men to accept women as single leaders, pushing for co-mayoring would shake the very foundations of male domination and power. It could also tear the party apart.

Our discussions were interminable, but finally we decided to set aside our fears. Women had come a long way in politics, and now we wanted to take this further step toward gender equality. We decided to go for co-mayoring in local government. The party agreed.

Time was pressing, as the elections were drawing near. Women mobilized all their resources and chose their co-mayor candidates, who then entered the fray alongside men, except in a few small places. The party ran co-mayor candidates in almost every province, district, and town where it entered the elections. Women held rallies and campaigned as co-mayor candidates. Although we heard occasional remarks such as "It'll create divided leadership," overall the public greeted our candidates with enthusiasm. It was a revolutionary step for women. We were everywhere now.

In the local elections of March 30, 2014, BDP's co-mayor candidates won in a total of 102 municipalities, three of which (Diyarbakır, Van, and Mardin) were metropolitan districts, and eight were provinces. It was a tremendous victory, a momentous turning point in women's journey toward equality and freedom. We'd started in 1999 with only three women mayors, and now the door was opened to a new era, when women could participate in leadership in all municipalities. That success paved the way for HDP to enter the 2015 local elections on the principle of equal representation.

CO-MAYORING

Co-mayoring had never been done before, and at first it presented a lot of challenges. Although co-chairing was legal within political parties, it was not legal in local government. So we had to bring about co-mayoring de facto. It doesn't mean literally sharing the mayoral position—dividing the power to rule—between a man and woman. Rather, it means implementing principles of equal representation and collective governance in order to shape local governments from women's perspective and manage cities and living spaces according to the goal of gender equality. Accomplishing this required not simply tweaking a technical regulation or even making a political decision but rather undertaking a radical and concerted shift in mentality.

We had presented our co-mayor candidates to the people as such, and the people approved them as such. We then wrote a regulation defining the purpose, function, and operation of the co-mayorship and proposed it to the municipal councils. The councils accepted it, but the central government bodies that oversaw local administration opposed it and obtained a court order to revoke it. Co-mayoring never got legal approval. But the important point was that we implemented it as a *mode of governance*. It didn't matter whether co-mayors could legally exercise certain authority, because co-mayoring isn't a practice of sharing power. Rather, it's a principle of collective governance and decision making that includes women's will.

Co-mayoring was easy to define in theory, but in reality, since it lacked a legal basis, women co-mayors had difficulty asserting their will, particularly in local government, which in Turkey is subordinate to the central administration. Only a radical shift in mentality would make that possible, one that went beyond traditional political templates—such as centralism, autocracy, and populism—and that internalized instead an egalitarian and collective mode of governance. Such a radical change could be achieved only in practice, by a struggle to break, one by one, the habits dictated by domination. Curbing men's hegemonic and hierarchical attitudes, while strengthening women's self-confidence and willingness to assert themselves, required a process of concentrated work and creativity.

The existing scarcity of women in decision-making bodies and leadership positions in municipalities was also a problem. As I mentioned, local governments had made some structural changes—such as having women vice chairs and creating women's directorates—but these remained insufficient. In addition, in newly won municipalities, everything had to be built from scratch. If the women's group in a municipal council was strong, the co-mayor experienced fewer problems; if not, she was on her own. Some places also failed to understand co-mayoring as a system of governance, reducing it instead to a simplistic notion of two simultaneously elected representatives dividing power.

Local governance requires around-the-clock collaboration with the public and local organizations. So local social structures, dynamics, and attitudes of civil society groups toward women's political work were also important in shaping co-mayoring experiences. Such local conditions could either empower or obstruct women.

Despite all the challenges, we successfully implemented co-mayoring, giving women a voice and a platform to articulate their interests and make decisions in local governments. However, they were able to do so only for about two years. In 2016, as part of its political operation against the municipalities, the AKP government removed the co-mayors from their positions and appointed *kayyums*—so-called "trustees"—to replace democratically elected mayors and run local government their place.

Nevertheless, the short-lived experiment exceeded our expectations, proving that co-mayoring could mitigate the chauvinistic mentality, empower women, and generate social change. Co-mayoring had, so to speak, a multiplier effect. A success in one area made an impact in many others, and not only in municipal services. Women became more visible in cities, they could navigate public spaces more easily, and they made known their political views and will more clearly.

HDP (2014–PRESENT)

In 2014 HDP entered Turkey's political arena as the common opposition platform of diverse democratic forces. It carries on the Kurdish party traditions of co-chairing and women's assemblies. The Kurdish women's movement is a constituent of HDP, where they came together with the Turkish feminist movement. I won't go into detail here about women's activities in HDP but will simply outline their political successes.

The first elections in which HDP participated were those of June 7, 2015. For women, the goal was to achieve equal representation, so in drawing up the candidate lists, HDP women sought to apply the zipper system—that is, alternating the names of the men and women candidates, to ensure equality. But achieving equal representation for women and at the same time fair representation of the various HDP factions was a challenge. Some factions created candidate lists using the zipper system, but other factions circumvented equal representation and nominated candidates who were men, invoking local sensibilities or the particular sensibilities of the factions themselves.

That June the electoral outcome was a great success for HDP—80 deputies were elected, 32 of whom were women. The proportion of elected women MPs within the party was now 40 percent. HDP's relatively high ratio raised the overall ratio of women's representation in the Turkish parliament to a historic 17 percent. Unfortunately, the people's and women's will wasn't upheld, as AKP rejected this outcome and repeated the national elections. In these "re-elections" of November 1, 2015, HDP won only 59 seats in parliament, 23 of them women.

Even in November, however, HDP had won enough seats to establish a Women's Group in parliament—honoring the principle of women's autonomous self-organizing, which is anchored in the party program. At its first press conference, the HDP Women's Group called on the women MPs of the other parties to collaborate with them on women's issues and carry out parliamentary activities from women's perspective.

The HDP Women's Group held meetings where women's issues—rather than general politics—were the focus of discussion. Women from many groups did attend, from the Peace Mothers to families of mineworkers who had lost their lives in a recent mine disaster, and from union representatives to women's organization activists. Members of the women's and feminist movements took the floor to express their opinions and offer suggestions. The meeting agendas included the violence experienced by all women, including Dilek Doğan, who was killed at her home during a police raid in Istanbul; Özgecan Aslan, who was raped and killed on a bus she boarded; Taybet Ana, who was killed by a sniper in front of her house and whose body couldn't be recovered from the street for a week; and women workers who died in workplace accidents or were murdered.

HDP women also played a significant role in parliamentary commissions, as the party assigned members to the commissions based on the principle of equal representation.

On November 4, 2016, the AKP government arrested 15 MPs, including HDP national co-chairs, in its political genocide operation against democratic politics. It continued the operation by arresting more MPs and stripping them of their parliamentary status. It targeted democratic politics in general and the women's struggle in particular. The government was attempting to smash women's will.

It was at this time that the AKP government replaced elected co-mayors with appointed *kayyums* to run municipalities. At the same time, it shut down municipalities' women's centers and terminated their women's directorates and women's departments. It demolished women's work and achievements, showing that the patriarchal system couldn't stomach the emerging women's regime. But this isn't the end of the story; rivers, after all, don't flow backward.

RELATIONS WITH THE FEMINIST MOVEMENT IN TURKEY

Turkey's feminist movement is broad and diverse in political thinking, attitudes, and practices. Relations between Turkey's feminist movement and the Kurdish women's movement can be divided into three periods: 1991–2000, 2000–14, and 2014 to the present. They started out by taking joint stands against human rights violations in the 1990s and later moved toward sharing experiences and collaborative interactions after 2000.

In the 1990s Kurdish women focused on problems faced by the Kurdish people as a whole, but step by step they raised their consciousness of oppression, violence, and discrimination based on their gender identity. In those years, they freed themselves from being the "auxiliary force" to the national struggle and considered women's historical journey in its own right. They examined, for example, why real socialism, like that in the Soviet Union, had failed to realize women's liberation. The feminist movement had also been asking those same questions and charting its own course by particularly drawing on the ideological legacy of western European feminism.

In the 1990s, Turkey's feminist movement and politically active Kurdish women were aware of each other, but their relations were far from close. Kurdish women tended to regard the feminist struggle as a bourgeois enterprise, while feminists saw the Kurdish women's struggle as an extension of the Kurdish national struggle. Another reason for the distance was that while Turkish feminists worked in autonomous women's structures, Kurdish women worked within an organized political party. Turkish feminists had experienced firsthand that women couldn't go beyond secondary positions in political parties where male dominance was solidly organized. So they'd given up on political parties and turned instead to independent women's organizing.

In the 1990s, Kurdish women and Turkish feminists found common ground mainly in the struggle against human rights violations. In those years, unsolved murders of individual Kurds and the burning of thousands of Kurdish villages caused a mass Kurdish migration to the western provinces, especially Istanbul. This commingling of people increased social interactions and also laid the groundwork for the development of a common opposition to gross human rights violations. In 1994 a group of feminist women launched the "Don't touch my friend" campaign, an important breakthrough. The campaign, "to reject racism and nationalism, be it overt or covert," helped Kurdish women feel they weren't alone. In 1995, during the sit-ins initiated by women in Istanbul to protest the disappearances of people in custody, women of different identities got to know each other and witnessed each other's suffering.

March 8 events, for International Women's Day, were also important contact zones. Working side by side in the planning meetings and at marches, women had a chance to learn from each other's experiences. A joint women's march on March 8, 1997, boosted everyone's morale. For Kurdish women, being free to speak in Kurdish, shout Kurdish slogans, and carry Kurdish banners meant that their identity was fully accepted.

But every March 8, the discussions about slogans and demands would become heated. Some feminists questioned whether the Kurdish women who participated in the protests had any gender consciousness at all. In essence, these discussions wrestled with the problem of how gender identity intersects with other identities. How does oppression on the basis of ethnic and cultural identity affect women? How should women approach domination and hierarchies within their various ethnicities and cultures? Should women set aside their national identities? Or does identity override sisterhood? To say the least, when women with different identities came together in the 1990s, they lacked satisfactory answers to these questions.

In the 2000s, relations between Turkish feminists and Kurdish women improved. Kurdish women established autonomous women's organizations, and they also started working to oppose domestic violence and gender discrimination, in addition to state-induced violence, which played a major role in that change of relations. As women sharing experiences in the fight against violence against women, efforts to collaborate took center stage. The struggle to prevent women's murders took on particular importance. When a Kurdish man murdered a Kurdish woman, Kurdish women arranged for her funeral and so challenged social conservatism. The mainstream media framed such killings as "murders of tradition," dismissing the violence as a matter of "backward, feudal Kurds." Kurdish women needed feminists in Turkey to help them reject these insults and point out that calling such killings "murders of tradition" or "honor killings" served only to justify them. The Kurdish women's movement highlighted that these murders were instances of the systemic violence that exists under male domination in all societies. They called them femicides and launched the "No to femicide!" campaign.

Another important basis for coming together was the Women's Shelters Conventions, where discussions between Turkish feminists and Kurdish women revealed difficulties in understanding that state violence against women and domestic violence were nourished by the same source. Although theoretically everyone accepted that nationalism, militarism, and sexism fed on each other, diverging perspectives emerged when it came to understanding actually existing conditions. Nevertheless, Kurdish women and Turkish feminists needed to come together on the same platform and be open to mutual exchanges of views and mutual transformation. When Kurdish women mayors opened women's centers and shelters in the municipalities they governed, they were able to draw on Turkish feminists' political experiences in combating violence against women.

After 2000, Turkish feminists and Kurdish women jointly called for peace between the PKK and the Turkish state. Their peace rallies, vigils, and meetings highlighted the shared suffering of women. In 2013 the peace process opened between the Turkish state and the PKK, raising hopes that the Kurdish question would be resolved through dialogue. Women held important meetings about women's participation in political solution processes. The Women's Freedom Assembly (KÖM) became a ground for unity, solidarity, and common struggle. However, after the elections of June 7, 2015, the AKP government terminated the peace process and initiated a new wave of repression against democratic politics. Nevertheless, shared participation in the peace process gave women important knowledge about one another's experiences.

Party politics was arguably the area where Kurdish women had the least in common with Turkish feminists. During every recent election season, Kurdish parties made electoral alliances with Turkey's other pro-democracy political parties and organizations. Starting with the 2007 elections, such alliances had allowed Kurds to gain some representation in the parliament. For our part, we Kurdish women found it striking that the left-socialist parties failed to propose women candidates and always nominated men. Perhaps the Turkish feminist movement's self-imposed distance from political parties, seeing them as a male domain, was a factor, but more crucial was the question of why the Kurdish women's movement and the Turkish feminist movement couldn't establish electoral alliances. Yes, in general, feminist groups supported women candidates and made important contributions to Sebahat Tuncel's campaign in 2007. Kurdish women, for their part, voiced feminist demands in parliament. But no electoral women's alliance for parliamentary representation was ever formed.

With the emergence of HDP, we can now certainly speak of new relations on that ground. But that joint experiment, as I've said, is outside the scope of this book.

In general, the Kurdish women's movement's experience in political parties has been a process of successive, overlapping developments in four phases.

In the 1990s, women organized within the political party. Some joined the party primarily in pursuit of political-national interests and developed an awareness of women's issues only later, though their party activities. The shared struggle to take part in the party's decision-making mechanisms strengthened women's solidarity. After 2000, with the establishment of self-organized women's institutions outside the party, women held in-depth discussions to raise gender awareness. These independent women's institutions and the women's organization within the party were in mutual dialogue. Three women mayors were elected in 1999, but only after 2004 did a particular women's policy in municipal governance begin to emerge. The following years saw the founding of numerous women's organizations affiliated with municipalities. After 2007, women entered the parliament, and ratios of representation gradually increased in each national and local election. During this period marked by "political representation," people's expectations from MPs and mayors substantially rose.

Women's organizing within the political party, self-organized independent women's institutions, municipal women's initiatives, and women's representation in the parliament and local governance are pillars of an integrated whole. All are major building blocks of the women's liberation struggle, and each is important in its own way. Their constant interaction with each other helps drive the women's liberation struggle forward. Neither area can replace the other. They're all the driving forces of the women's movement, each with an equally important role.

Independent women's institutions are important for raising gender consciousness and showing women how imposed roles hold them back. Here groups can accelerate the process of questioning the patriarchal mentality, rejecting gender roles, breaking away from relationships in which women are secondary to men, and externalizing women's political will. That allows for a radicalization in gender consciousness. Political parties, on the other hand, expand the reach of gender awareness and promote social transformation. Centralism, power struggles, and hierarchies are the biggest obstacles to parties becoming fully democratic. In parties that claim to fight for democracy, women must constantly challenge those obstacles and remain actively engaged against male domination.

Bringing about equal representation has been an immense success of the women's movement, and it arose from the foundational work of women's organizing, without which women wouldn't have become "political subjects" but have remained in the passive position of being "those who demand" something of "those who promise." This type of relation isn't conducive to aspirations for freedom. The women's approach involves "doing together" and "being powerful together." Women's will can be expressed only through women's organizing, and political representation is a reflection of that will. Horizontal and assembly-style organizing, claiming political subjectivity, and questioning relations of domination have been important political principles. Such organizing will further strengthen women's will and representation.

Autonomous women's institutions experienced a similar interactive relationship with local governments. Since 2004, women's representation in local government has grown in tandem with the rapid proliferation of women's institutions affiliated with municipalities. Breaking sexist power in municipal administrations has been a tremendous achievement, enabling local governments to provide services to meet women's needs. As municipality-based women's centers, women's cooperatives, women's shelters, and the overall struggle against violence against women proliferated, however, the self-organized women's institutions seemed to fade into the background. So, although the approach of "Municipalities have lots of resources, let them do it" was justified in a sense, it brought its own problems. The bureaucratic and "cadreist" procedures of municipalities are still formidable handicaps to local governance, which also affects women's mobilization. Plus, local governments operate under the tutelage of the central government. We see the heavy consequences of that reality today more than ever.

The women's movement, having created a great synergy with its model of equal representation and co-mayoring, will continue to walk on its path to freedom, learning from its own experiences and from those of global women's movements. And what determines its progress on this path will be women's dreams of building a free and democratic future in peace.

Those small arms
were wrapped around my waist,
"are you leaving?" the voice asked,
while the eyes said "stay"
Should I respond to the question,
or to your eyes?
Or,
to your heart
that trembles like a dove?
The weight of hope
how can it be so heavy?
In my country where death is rampant
words are useless
I just gave you a snug hug
we made a ladder from our hopes
we hid peace away in the rainbow.
For the children playing hide and seek
to find . . .*

* These are the lines I wrote on the way back from our journey against the Silvan blockade (Kışanak).

1

"How Will You Find That Many Women?"

Aysel Tuğluk

Translated by Hazal Hürman

Aysel Tuğluk (b. 1965) was vice co-chair of HDP. She served two terms as MP for Diyarbakır. She was arrested on December 26, 2016 and was sentenced to ten years in prison. Currently in Kocaeli No. 1 F-type Prison, she is struggling with dementia; please refer to the "Freedom for Aysel Tuğluk" appeal on pp. 275–6.

I was born in Elâzığ. My family is originally from Dersim, but they moved to Elâzığ for my dad's job. I grew up there. My brother was involved in the revolutionary movement, and I spent the 1970s observing him and his friends with keen interest. Then in 1979 state security forces arrested him and took him to a torture center. He was tortured brutally, then taken to prison. A few months later a group of fascists were dispatched to the same prison with weapons. One day they opened fire on prisoners in the yard and injured several of them, including my brother. His condition was critical, so he was taken to Diyarbakır. But they couldn't save him. We were told that he was taken off the respirator and left to die.

Losing my brother was devastating for my family. Our sorrow and suffering made me wonder why he'd died. What were he and his friends trying to accomplish? His death was a turning point: I had no choice but to become a dissident, a leftist, and a rebel.

I attended law school at Istanbul University. After graduation I went to Bayrampaşa Prison, where political prisoners were incarcerated, and I visited the revolutionaries I'd observed as a child. In the 1990s, I chose to serve as a lawyer in political trials, considering it my duty. I joined a group of patriotic* Kurdish lawyers who were monitoring rights abuses, investigating torture allegations, and providing legal support. In 1994 we established the Foundation for Research on Society and Law (TOHAV) to provide medical and mental health treatment for torture survivors and support their lawsuits. I served on TOHAV's administrative board for two terms. I also joined İHD. Supporting the human rights struggle was my profession's raison d'être.

Around the same time, a group of women friends and I established the Patriotic Women's Association. For the first time, Kurdish women would pursue their struggle institutionally. My friends and I were proud of founding the association and considered it a great achievement, but the government soon shut it down.

In 1999, dear Abdullah Öcalan was imprisoned on İmralı, and as a human rights lawyer, I joined his defense team. To organize our

* Used commonly by the Kurdish movement, the term *yurtsever* refers to someone in support of Kurdish liberation and advocating for Kurds' cultural, linguistic, and political rights.

work, we established the Asrın Law Office. I followed his lawsuit and met him many times before 2005. We talked about the legal process and political issues, but at every meeting, Öcalan would make an assessment of women's situation. He viewed women's freedom as a necessary precondition for the freedom of the whole society. He insisted that women must create their own democratic structures and organize themselves autonomously. Every meeting with him had a great impact on me.

I wasn't much interested in politics, but around 2005 some party activists launched an initiative to lay the groundwork for a new political party by creating a broad alliance of Kurds and Turks, leftists, socialists, and democrats. I was recommended to sit on the board, along with Leyla Zana. For several months, we held open meetings in provinces, towns, and villages, where we presented the principles of the proposed new party and took suggestions from the public. We established a democratic process to elect delegates, setting up ballot boxes in local areas. Approximately 350,000 people cast votes for delegates, who founded the alliance, DTH, which then decided to become a political party, DTP.

Women friends, including Leyla Zana, worked hard on the founding process. At meetings about the party's principles and program, we added a proposal for co-chairing on the agenda, as a new model of party administration. The party's women were thrilled, but the men couldn't make sense of it. At every turn, they objected, claiming it would cause problems in administration and decision making. Besides, they argued, co-chairing "wouldn't be legally approved" by the Turkish state. They hid behind that rationale: "Well, maybe it could be done, but it's legally impossible." They even tried to block a vote on the proposal. But women stood up for it and insisted, "Let's make our own decision about co-chairing and put it into practice regardless. If the state rejects it, so be it."

A second issue that stirred great controversy was bigamy. Women asked for the party to adopt a rule barring men with more than one wife from taking administrative positions. But almost all the men balked, arguing that the rule would exclude many men who were involved in founding the party. Besides, they said, bigamy was widespread in the society, so if the party adopted the rule, people would complain, and the party would lose support. And without polygamous men, the party wouldn't be able to find enough administrators. They proposed applying the rule, if at all, only to men who took a second wife after the party was established.

Finally, the issue of the women's quota stirred controversy. Men's biggest argument was, "How will you find that many women?" We reminded them that half of the population was women, so then they raised the issue of women's supposed lack of qualifications.

We women felt that we had powerful political support on all three issues and didn't back down. Digging in our heels, we made sure that co-chairing and the women's quota were included in the party's program and bylaws, and we took a principled decision against bigamy. These victories infused us party women with a sense of triumph.

Meanwhile, the founding delegates made the decision to establish DTP. Since it was going to enact co-chairing, women formed a committee to determine who would be the woman co-chair. We asked several women to take on the task, but all turned it down for one reason or another. At a loss, my friends turned to me and said I should be co-chair. My first thought was: *Here comes trouble.* It was, of course, an honor to become the first woman co-chair. In a way, I knew I had to do it, but I was afraid I wasn't up to the job.

When DTP's founding became official, Ahmet Türk and I were elected co-chairs. We had adjacent offices in the party headquarters. What happened in these two adjoining rooms was quite interesting. When men—be they members or administrators—came to visit, they'd directly go to the man co-chair's office, where they held all kinds of weighty discussions of politics. But they'd visit my office only in passing, out of courtesy. The kinder ones would tap on my door and say goodbye before leaving. Even more interesting, a sign that read "Mr. Ahmet Türk/Co-chair" appeared on the door to his room, but nobody bothered to put up a sign on mine. The woman co-chair was being disregarded. My women friends were outraged—they had a sign reading "Aysel Tuğluk/Co-chair" made up and installed it on my office door themselves.

Thanks to the determination and solidarity of the party women's organization, co-chairing survived, and gradually men's attitudes improved. But then Turkey's Supreme Court of Appeals notified us that co-chairing violated the Law on Political Parties and thus wasn't approved. The men on the Central Executive Committee came to my office to express their "sadness." They explained that if we were to continue with co-chairing, the state would shut the party down, and we couldn't afford to take that risk. Sorrowful as they were, they proposed an alternative: they'd make me "the general vice chair in charge of organizing."

I told them that that decision wasn't for me to make, and that our women's assembly would discuss it and decide. The women's assembly convened and refused to accept a vice chairpersonship. We would continue to implement co-chairing de facto and fight for passing it into law. We launched a signature campaign, demanding legislation to legalize co-chairing. In no time at all, we collected 98,000 signatures and presented them to parliament.

We continued with co-chairing on a de facto basis until 2014, when Turkey finally amended its Law on Political Parties to allow it. Meanwhile, the presence of a woman co-chair moved the women's agenda to the center of mainstream politics. We know from experience that wherever no women are present, nothing is done for women. Conventional politics is practiced in accordance with the male-dominant ideology. The men in the party's decision-making bodies dictate politics. But women's determined struggle for co-chairing and the women's quota elevated us to the status of political actors. The mentality that perceived women not as decision makers but as auxiliaries was crumbling.

Here's a tragicomic incident that took place before co-chairing gained institutional recognition. One day my co-chair Ahmet Türk and I attended a party event in the Şemdinli district of Hakkâri. After the event, we went to a restaurant along with other party executives. The waiter asked Ahmet Türk, "My chair, what would you like to have?" Then he turned to me and asked, "Auntie chair, what would you like?" Everyone at the table tittered. "You've misunderstood co-chairing," I explained, smiling too. "Co-chairs are a man and a woman who have equal rights and responsibilities." Later we laughed when we remembered this dialogue, but it shows the kinds of challenges that women's struggle for equality has had to overcome.

Today co-chairing is a baseline criterion of any democratic organization. Once it was legally allowed, many political parties and nongovernmental organizations adopted it and practice it now. Today an organization that doesn't use co-chairing is regarded as deficient. But we didn't achieve this success easily. It took grit and determination. Some of the challenges we encountered stemmed from us, from women ourselves. Women too often hesitated to take on positions of responsibility. Men were immediately ready to become co-chairs and made special efforts for it, but women persistently avoided it. Yes, all the women advocated co-chairing and fought fiercely for it, but in practice, when it came to taking charge, they preferred to remain behind the scenes. That only contributes to the reproduction of male domination in the political arena.

As the 2007 elections neared, DTP faced the problem of overcoming the 10 percent electoral threshold for sending MPs to the parliament, which we knew had been set high as a barrier to exclude us. Fortunately, we could build on existing forces and we ran independent candidates to improve our chances of being elected MPs. DTP was committed to filling its women's quota, so the party formed a Women's Election Commission to determine which women would be candidates. The commission prepared feasibility reports, took proposals from locals, then announced the women candidates.

The result was an uproar, as members objected to particular women for things that they'd never objected to in men. "Women can't handle it!" some wailed. "Who are these women, anyway? No one knows them!" others moaned. "They have no political experience!" and "The public doesn't want them!" and "They're gonna lose us votes!" they cried, giving fervent voice to the patriarchal mentality that politics was a man's job. But we women ignored them and threw ourselves into the election campaigns. In the end, DTP won 22 seats in the parliament, eight of them held by women and 14 by men. The public showed that the patriarchal forebodings had been groundless. I was elected MP for Diyarbakır. For the first time since 1994, the Kurdish people's will would once again be represented in parliament.

The Kurdish women's political struggle was now twofold: the struggle for the freedom of Kurds, whose existence was denied, and the equally urgent struggle for women's liberation. Those of us elected as MPs carried out our work along both axes in the rather short time we had. In 2009, Turkey's Constitutional Court shut down DTP. Thirty-seven people, including myself and Ahmet Türk, were banned from politics.

In 2010, at the urging of our friends in the party and nongovernmental organizations, Ahmet Türk and I took on the task of co-chairing DTK. Established in 2005, DTK was an umbrella platform encompassing women, youth, nongovernmental organizations, notables, professional associations, and business groups. Implementing co-chairing in such a diverse amalgamation was of utmost importance to achieving gender equality and a critical experience for me personally.

When I look back, I see that despite our inexperience, we women did manage to overcome male-dominant politics. The political style that we put into practice gradually gained acceptance both in parliament and in the eyes of public. We didn't hold back from addressing all social problems openly and courageously in parliament, including the Kurdish question and women's issues. Furthermore, the parliament wasn't our sole political arena: we also carried out work at the local level, both with the public and with women, in unique projects. We did politics in tandem with the public, and we marched alongside them in protests. All these activities enabled the public to support us. We invalidated the perception that "women can't handle it" simply by building our political practice one step at a time. So successful were we that in advance of the 2011 elections, the party's committee to nominate candidates received suggestions for women candidates from all over the country. Our commitment to do politics with the people; our presence in neighborhoods, on the streets, and in every area of life; and our rejection of the conventional political style created a positive public reception. I consider it a huge accomplishment that we pushed back against the dominant male style in politics.

Despite all our efforts, we were unable to achieve a democratic and peaceful resolution to the Kurdish question in Turkey. Nor did we bring an end to Kurdish suffering. This, as a woman, is my greatest self-criticism. We could have played a leading role in achieving peace.

In late 2016 I was serving as the vice co-chair for law and human rights in HDP. On December 26, I was detained in Ankara, then transported to Diyarbakır. My detention was an extension of the November 4 operation against HDP. I was held in custody for a day at the Diyarbakır police department, then arrested and taken to Kocaeli No. 1 F-type Prison. For two months, I was held in solitary confinement. Then I shared a cell with HDP co-chair Figen Yüksekdağ. A couple of months later, DBP co-chair Sebahat Tuncel joined us. The three of us are currently in the same cell.

All my legitimate activities on behalf of democratic politics were listed in the indictment against me. They pretended to conduct a fair trial, but after only three hearings, I was sentenced to ten years of imprisonment for "founding and leading an armed terrorist organization." Several other indictments, filed concerning my activities for freedom of thought and expression and democratic politics, are ongoing.

Since the 1990s, the state has been trying to exclude Kurds from democratic politics by using the judicial system. For Kurds who engage in politics, the price has been death, prison, or exile. Now women, who have become a major force in democratic politics, are in prison, too. Nonetheless we'll continue our struggle for democratic politics, not only for our own sakes but on behalf of all the peoples we live among and for all women. We'll continue to fight for our work, our identity, and our freedom. As women, we have no option but to endure despite the sexist mindset that would reduce our identities to those of "mother, sister, and wife" and imprison us at home. We women must fight back. There is nothing that a woman's emotional and analytical intelligence cannot achieve.

Taking as a precept the words of Samuel Beckett, "Fail again, fail better," after every lost battle we should continue to take the risk of failing again with the pleasure of playing a game. We may lose a little more, but so what? Failing time and again but losing now to do better later is part of the struggle. What matters is taking responsibility for life.

2

Mother, Child, Prison

Burcu Çelik Özkan

Translated by Berivan Kutlay Sarıkaya

Burcu Çelik Özkan (b. 1986) was elected an MP from Muş in both June and November 2015. She was arrested on April 19, 2017 and released in October 2019. In a new trial, she was sentenced to prison. Her case is pending in the Supreme Court of Appeals.

In the general elections of June 7, 2015, I was elected to serve as one of the MPs from Muş. I got 72 percent of the vote, but the government didn't accept the people's will: it annulled the election results and called a new one. In the re-election of November 1, 2015, I was elected an MP from Muş for the second time. And this time I went to parliament to serve. There, as a member of the Parliamentary Human Rights Investigation Commission, I worked on activities related to the rights of women, children, and workers, and as a spokesperson for HDP's Prison Commission, I worked on violations of prisoners' human rights.

On April 19, 2017, I met with local tradespeople in Varto, a district in Muş province. Afterward I got in my car and headed back to Muş city. Along the way, the police stopped my car. The district manager of the Office of Counter-terrorism told me there was an arrest warrant out for me and detained me. I was taken to the police station. Everything happened very quickly. After a so-called "health check," I was taken to the Muş courthouse and brought before a judge. The police were inexperienced and acted with dizzying haste, stressed about detaining an MP. I'd witnessed the detention process many times as a lawyer, but this time I was the accused. I gave my statement at the courthouse and that same day was arrested.

On October 6, 2017, at the last hearing of my expedited trial, I was acquitted of all the charges that were included in the police investigation report as well as those that had been added to the indictment later. Nevertheless, I was sentenced to six years imprisonment for a crime that I hadn't had a chance to "defend myself" against because it hadn't appeared anywhere in the indictment. My conviction violated all the basic judicial procedures and principles.

Later, in a retrial, a court of appeals quashed my conviction, but then, as a result of the retrial itself, the court increased my sentence to seven years and three months on account of, again, allegations that hadn't been included in the indictment. As of this writing in 2018, the case is pending before the Supreme Court of Appeals.

According to Turkey's constitution, MPs are immune to legal prosecution. But now for the first time, MPs were being stripped of parliamentary immunity. It was the ruling alliance between AKP and MHP that had so clearly violated the constitution. CHP, the opposition, supported the ruling, saying, "It goes against the constitution—but yes." Thus, the government united to remove the constitutional barrier to politically motivated police investigations.

Fake police investigation reports had already been prepared against us; they were quickly turned into investigative files. The authorities completed the investigation with lightning speed, and the prosecutions started. By ignoring not only domestic law but also the European Court of Human Rights and international law, the AKP-MHP government violated the rule of law in unprecedented ways.

The government went on to coordinate an operation that arrested DBP mayors, thousands of executives and employees of HDP and DBP, and numerous academics and journalists. Simultaneously, on November 4, 2016, it began detaining MPs. As just one episode in this sequence of terrible experiences, my turn had come on that fateful day, April 19, 2017.

Upon my arrest, I was taken to Muş Prison. After processing me, they put me in . . . a room. Actually, it was neither a room nor a cell. It was a storage closet that had been hastily emptied of kitchen supplies and supposedly made suitable for lodging—probably because of a ministry order that said, "Don't put her in a cell." They opened the door of the storage closet and said, "You'll be our guest here tonight." I knew that the MP friends who had been arrested before me were being kept in solitary confinement, but I'd never have believed it if anyone had said I'd be put in a food supply storage closet.

I entered the closet with great curiosity. In one corner of the long, empty space was a bed with sheets. I thanked the staff and settled in. There was a wire-covered ventilation window, which I'm calling a window out of courtesy; you understand what I mean. After collapsing early from exhaustion, I awoke and listened to the trees outside rustle like a lullaby. The minutes ticked by slowly. The next day they were going to transport me, but to where? To Kandıra? Silivri? The uncertainty was irritating. Finally, I dozed off fitfully.

In the morning, I opened my eyes to see rays of sunshine trying to enter through the wired window. That gave me hope. Even in prison, you have to start the day with hope. Officers came and took me out of storage. They did whatever processing had to be done. As I waited, I joked, "Generous people of Muş, don't you have a cup of tea for me?" The answer was short and unmistakable, and a bit helpless: "Forbidden."

We left Muş Prison, and I hoped they were going to transfer me to the prison where other imprisoned MPs were held. But instead they put me on a plane to Ankara. On the plane, I saw some people I knew. It was strange. They were silent, and I didn't know whether to be afraid or sad. A few people dared to come over and sit by me for the duration of the trip. When we touched down, they said, "*Geçmiş olsun*"—an act of great courage, which was required now when speaking to an MP they'd elected.

We disembarked in Ankara, and I was taken to Sincan Prison under extraordinary security, accompanied by more vehicles than I could count. After I waited for a few hours, they took me into a ward. As I walked down the corridor, I passed women friends in cells. Their familiar eyes smiled at me—I knew most of them. But the authorities had decided to isolate me. They put me in solitary confinement and kept me there for 35 days. During that time, I was physically alone, but I felt deeply that the hearts of millions were with me and with the other women friends in prison, judging from the hundreds of solidarity messages and letters arriving from home and abroad.

Everyone who has spent time in prison has a story about birds. I shared my loneliness with birds, then watched them fly off—it was like experiencing freedom myself. Superficially birds may seem all the same, but they're not at all. Angry, smiling, lazy, excited, sullen—every one is different. Maybe it was because of my loneliness, but I got to know them individually.

Thirty-five days later, my friend Süheyla joined me in isolation. I shared my pain, sadness, and happiness with her, and she became my closest and only friend. I have no doubt that my friendship with Süheyla will last forever.

At first, I tried to make sense of prison, to find meaning in the experience of being here. I got the opportunity to read and write here, and as I had more time to think, my values, priorities, and goals became clearer. In this sense, I came to feel good about myself.

Every day in prison is different. Little by little I started to write. Based on the pages I've written so far—I've been here seven months now—I want to write a novel.

On April 30, 2018, my three-year-old daughter Asmîn was brought to this prison to share my detention with me. That small child's eyes, turned toward the future with hope, have filled my cell with light. But the days I've spent with her here have also been sad and hurtful. Asmîn's dreams have been stolen from her, and she isn't alone. Hundreds of Kurdish children are growing up with the same feelings. Some like Asmîn are in prison, some must visit their mothers' and fathers' graves, some live in burned-down homes, some in the ruins of their homeland. That Asmîn is in prison has put me and Süheyla through hell.

The day she arrived, she knew nothing about prison, only that something was restricting her. Doors opened in the morning and closed in the evening. She noticed the fences and the iron bars. Yet she was happy, because she didn't know how much those conditions were harming her. That first day, Asmîn ran out into the prison courtyard. She tried to talk to the birds and asked me about everything she saw. In the evening, the guards came to close the courtyard gate, and she ran over to me. "Mom, let's go home," she said. I didn't know what to do or say. How could I tell her that we couldn't go home? Just then she took my hand, and we went back to the cell. "Mom," she said, "we're home." Thanks to her, a great burden fell off my shoulders. In that moment, I realized that you can steal a small child's life, but not their hope. The prison cell had become her home.

Later that evening she jumped onto my lap and said, "Mom, I found you." "Were you looking for me, darling?" I asked. "Yes, Mom." Again, I didn't know what to say. We just hugged each other and went to sleep.

I was born in Muş province in 1986 and grew up there. Muş experienced the darkness and cruelty of the 1990s more than most. Every day brought unsolved political murders, armed clashes, police searches, and house raids. Whenever a White Toros entered a neighborhood, children playing on the street would rush off to raise the alarm.* Our neighborhood, Muratpaşa, was frequented by White Toroses. But those of us who lived there had great solidarity. When a White Toros came to our neighborhood, everyone would turn their eyes to our house. At the time, I didn't understand why, but I remember the anxiety that would suffuse my mother's eyes.

One morning in 1993 we were forced to migrate. My mother, my two siblings, and I climbed into the back of a truck with chickens and left behind our memories, home, and neighbors. It was my first time away from Muş.

We drove for a long time, as if we were traveling around the world. Finally, we arrived in Çiftlikköy, in Yalova province. There we'd begin a new life, which I soon realized was nothing like our old life in Muş. In my seven-year-old's mind, I noticed every difference. For example, we had a satellite antenna in our house. It affected our social relations in the neighborhood. What was this antenna for? Later, I kept looking for houses with satellite antennas.

We lived in Çiftlikköy from 1993 until the 1999 Izmit earthquake. After that we moved to Bursa, a large city. Now, Bursa's population was mostly immigrants, but many of its residents didn't welcome people different from themselves and felt a strong desire for a homogenous society. We lived in a neighborhood with people who were immigrants like us and had experienced similar things. Compared to the rest of Bursa, our neighborhood comprised a wealth of differences. The poorer part of the neighborhood was Kurdish.

I attended school in downtown Bursa, so my school life was distant from my neighborhood life. Over time, I realized that my neighborhood life was more real. I started meeting with my school friends outside class. Together we listened to Kurdish songs, read books, and talked about ourselves and our neighbors. Gradually our sense of Kurdish identity matured.

I attended law school at Marmara University in Istanbul, where I started to think about democratic politics and the women's

* Renault's white Toros-model cars were the symbols of kidnappings and unsolved murders in 1990s Turkey.

struggle. During my college years, I couldn't fully express myself because I was shy. But after I graduated, I felt freer.

As a lawyer, I volunteered especially for political cases of women and children; I wanted to take responsibility for what our people had gone through. But it turned out that being a lawyer wasn't enough for me. I wanted to do more active political work, so I got involved with HDP. Although I was new to political parties, I got elected as the party's co-chair for Istanbul's Beylikdüzü district. Fortunately, my friends gave me indispensable assistance.

Meanwhile, women friends and the party suggested I run for parliament in the 2015 elections, and they nominated me as an MP candidate from my old hometown Muş. I was so excited. If I won, I could renew my connection to Kurdistan, which I'd left in 1993. Campaigning for parliament in Muş would be an honor but also, I knew, difficult as a woman, because extremely patriarchal attitudes prevailed there, and social relations were grounded largely in religion.

First, I studied the people's social values and expectations. I realized that if the party were to win the election there, we'd have to appeal to women and mobilize their solidarity. But how? At that time, not many women in Muş were active in HDP. We ran a vigorous election campaign, together with our women friends in the party administration and precious elderly mothers. I met many dedicated women in the neighborhoods—in fact, once I got to know them, I saw that their enormous power was just waiting to be mobilized, which made it impossible for me not to be hopeful.

But we constantly ran into problems. "Can women really be MPs?" I was asked. "How can women speak in public? Are you saying a woman can enter any men's space?" Some people flat-out refused to accept that women could do politics. It wasn't easy, but as we continued to explain ourselves and model strong behavior, we made significant inroads into that segment of society.

Once when I was scheduled to visit a certain house, a crowd was waiting outside to welcome the MP candidate. My colleagues and I got out of our vehicles and I heard people ask each other, "Who is the candidate?" Their eyes were searching for a man, but the person in front of them was a woman. As I stepped into the house, my hosts looked at me with a bit of embarrassment for not seeing what they were expecting, and a little hesitancy, as if they were asking, *Is she really the candidate?*

They led me into a large room, crowded with some 60 people, including the village notables, the *rûspîs*, wise elders. I was the only woman present. All eyes were fastened on me, although sometimes they averted their gaze. Truthfully, I wasn't all that comfortable. And as I talked to them, I was wondering how I could get to meet the women. Finally, I just asked, "Where are the women?"

As if they'd been waiting for that moment, a young man took me into another room. I opened the door and found about 35 women waiting curiously for the MP candidate. The young man introduced me. Interestingly, if he hadn't, the women wouldn't have realized that I was the candidate. But when they did, the moment was indescribable—they hugged me tightly and beamed at me with pride. With each woman I talked to, I truly felt myself getting stronger, and my faith and hope swelled. Later, gradually, they accepted that women could be MPs, and that made everything feel a little more normal.

Something else I had to overcome was that as the MP candidate, I was the only woman who was allowed to go to certain men's spaces—other women friends were barred. In some districts—Varto, Malazgirt, Bulanık, and Korkut—women's actions had overturned such taboos. But in Muş city and the surrounding villages, we did have the problem. But eventually we made progress.

When you're a woman candidate, people feel they can question everything about you—your private life, your friendships and social life, even your outfit. And this is deemed perfectly normal! One way to avoid this scrutiny is to express yourself clearly and to be open and sincere. Over time you'll realize that people actually don't expect all that much from you and that even small touches will make them smile. People you meet may have certain sensitivities, but if you pay attention to those—sincerely and without putting on an act—while also maintaining your position, you'll see that they'll accept you, and as a result, the bond between you and them will become stronger.

Of course, it's impossible to achieve gender equality and women's participation in all areas of life overnight. But as we raised women's political awareness, materialized our political will, and worked to unsettle established norms, we unleashed an optimistic sentiment that portended that all those things could change. It was important just to begin this social transformation. I must underline that I shared many beautiful and precious moments with these women. We all drew strength from the solidarity that emerged at our meetings.

In August 10, 2015, in the Varto district of Muş, police shot and killed a woman called Kevser Eltürk, and afterward her naked body was publicly displayed. That outraged people. The local women's assembly called a meeting, and hundreds of women came, in a fury. Never before in Muş had a women's event drawn so much participation. The day started with nerves and questions, but during the day we all felt the power of women's solidarity, and by the day's end I felt stronger and more hopeful.

The simple wisdom of elderly mothers had an incredible impact on social change. One day Mother Sîsê, age 80, was arrested and imprisoned. Muş women were incensed and organized to free her, with solidarity that was precious. As police were taking her to prison, they asked her, "What organization are you from?" Mother Sîsê couldn't answer since she didn't understand Turkish well. Then the officers asked, "To whom would you like to go?" She immediately answered, "Take me to the *friends*!" Mother Sîsê told me this story herself after she was released. Unfortunately, she's now in prison again and seriously ill.

Once I became an MP, I joined the parliament's Human Rights Commission and its subcommittee on the rights of prisoners. I made many prison visits, where I met political prisoners who had been in solitary confinement for 20 years, and women who were imprisoned with their children. But the most wrenching meetings were with prisoners who were seriously ill.

During one visit, I noticed a man lying on a bed near the door to the prison yard. He never spoke, but his eyes told me he wanted to say something. His friends explained to me that the man, Abdulkadir Fırat, couldn't speak and was paralyzed. A report from the Institute of Forensic Medicine said he had a 97 percent disability and couldn't remain in prison—he should have been released long before. But after 2015, Turkey's political atmosphere changed, and such reports were altered, and his had been revised to read: "He can stay in prison."

During another prison visit, I saw a woman standing in the hallway with a baby in her arms. When I approached her, she burst into tears. I decided to accompany her back to her ward. Leaving the other members of the delegation—all men—downstairs, we went upstairs. Her friends there were surprised to see me. They welcomed me, but begged, "Sorry, but please let our friend get to bed. She just gave birth." I was shocked. How could this be? A woman who had given birth just a few hours earlier was standing with her baby in her arms?!

Her friends had prepared a bed for her. The mother lay down, but I held the baby awhile. She was so tiny and cute. I sat with them until visiting hours ended. When it was time to leave, I wondered, *What can I do?* But I could give them only words of hope and strength. *Mother, child, prison*—it's hard even to use these three words in the same sentence. But now I'm going through the same thing, living in prison with my child.

In June 2016, during Ramadan, I visited some provinces and districts that had been under curfew and attacked. We Kurdish people went through a lot during that time. In one place, the curfew had been lifted, and people were returning. I organized a committee to begin healing, and people told me about their terrifying experiences. I sat with one mother in what had been her yard—her four-story house had been reduced to rubble, and some parts of it burned. I took her hand, and a few moments passed in silence. I wondered what she was feeling. Angry? Offended? Heartbroken? Finally, she said to me in Kurdish, "My dear, raise your head and keep it held high. May the Kurdish people live long. May you all live long." Then she embraced me with faith and hope. It seemed unreal. All I could do was bow and kiss her hand.

Not only do women belong in political struggle, they excel at it—that's more obvious today than ever. I'm convinced that women's solidarity and struggle will prevail over male domination. We'll continue to work for an egalitarian and liberatory society in the parliament, in prisons, on the streets, and at home. Nothing can stop us. We'll find solutions to ever-worsening political, economic, and social problems. We'll give our children back their stolen lives—no one should doubt it. But until that day comes, the fates of our children will lie in our hands.

3

"We Never Thought of It That Way"

Çağlar Demirel

Translated by Elif Sarıcan

Çağlar Demirel (b. 1969) was elected an MP from Diyarbakır in both June and November 2015. She served as the HDP group vice chair. She was arrested on December 13, 2016. On September 21, 2021, she was released because she had served more time in prison than her prison sentence.

That day—December 12, 2016—in Turkey's parliament, we were discussing the budget. The session ended, we left, and on our way home, at around 12:30 a.m., police stopped our official car. We were three women: Besime Konca, an MP for Siirt; Aysel Tuğluk, HDP vice co-chair; and me. The officers told Besime and me, "We have a warrant for your detention." We demanded to see it; they showed us a piece of paper with our information on it, but no signature or seal. We argued with them, then, pointing guns at us, they said, "We don't have time for this. You're gonna come with us."

They put Besime in one car and me in another and sped off, more or less kidnapping us. I kept insisting on seeing my warrant, but all they said was "They told us to bring you in, so that's what we're doing." They wouldn't tell me where they were taking me, but then, they didn't seem to know. They shuttled between the hospital and the police station, then got a new order and took me to the police station.

After holding us there for a while, they drove us to the airport and put us on a noncommercial flight to Diyarbakır. After we landed, they shoved Besime into a car and sped off with her, and they took me to the police headquarters in Bağlar, a district of Diyarbakır. The next morning someone said I was to be transported to a prison far away, and my family could pack my bags.

I said, "I still don't know why I'm detained." My lawyers arrived, but they didn't know either. At the courthouse, just before they saw me, they'd been told, "The detention warrant hasn't been signed off yet." The police had detained me, an MP, with no legal authorization! The operation was patently unlawful and was being carried out under a political order.

At the courthouse, I learned that an arrest warrant had been issued for me. This was utterly lawless. As an MP, I had parliamentary immunity, which could be lifted only if an investigation report were submitted to parliament. Without that report, neither the police nor the court could legally take action against me. But who cared about the law? My lawyers' efforts were fruitless. The paperwork was filed out in the courthouse, and the pre-cooked arrest decision was framed to make it look lawful.

They took me back to police headquarters and kept me waiting awhile. Besime had been released and gone to the Diyarbakır courthouse looking for me. But the court had issued an arrest warrant for her too, so when she turned up at the courthouse, they arrested her. They took us both to Diyarbakır E-type Prison, where we were kept in the observation ward overnight.

Early the next morning, they flew us both to Istanbul on a commercial plane. We exchanged greetings with the passengers, holding our heads high. As we disembarked, people shouted, "We're proud of you!" We were taken to Kocaeli No. 1 F-type Prison. After processing us, they took us to separate cells, where our solitary confinement began.

Some friends, all elected officeholders, were already in this prison and also being kept in isolation. It was very cold. The vent was frozen. I could hear distant voices but couldn't make out any words. Once when I was taken outside my cell for a lawyer's visit, I spotted Gültan. She called out to me, "Why are you here!?"

"I couldn't leave you alone!" I said.

They kept me in solitary for 53 days.

The unlawfulness continued during my trial process. I demanded to go to the hearings, but they refused. I demanded an end to the unlawful actions—refused. I asked for an expert to transcribe my Kurdish speeches, the subject of the indictment against me, but even that was rejected. All the many speeches I'd given at women's events as a representative of the people's will were now framed as crimes.

On July 14, 2017, after a cursory trial, the court sentenced me to seven years and six months. The Antep district court approved the sentence without even examining my case and sent it to the Supreme Court of Appeals. They were railroading me to terrify other women. They were also, inadvertently, revealing the patriarchal order's fear of women's liberation.

I was born in 1969 in the Pasûr (Turkish Kulp) district of Diyarbakır province. My family moved to Diyarbakır for schools, and we made our home in the city's Sur district. I graduated from Dicle University with a degree in nursing. The Family Planning Association of Turkey had recently opened a women's health center in the

Huzurevleri neighborhood of Diyarbakır, where a lot of migrants lived, and I started working there.

A team of friends stationed in the streets would direct women to the center, where they could get free healthcare. But I soon realized that these women needed much more than that. For one thing, they knew very little about sexual health and had no idea even how to talk about it. It embarrassed them. It was a taboo subject. Sexual violence was even harder to talk about.

I found it impossible to separate health from all the other issues that affected them, so in effect the health center became a counseling center. Some women, pregnant as a result of rape or incest, were traumatized and felt helpless. They'd try to induce a miscarriage by lifting heavy sacks, jumping off a roof, or taking wrong drugs—and seriously harm themselves. They couldn't tell their family members, because they said they'd be blamed for it and even be killed. They needed shelter and safe transportation, not to mention support after they left the shelter. Sometimes in emergency cases, we sheltered women in the homes of trusted acquaintances until we could find a place for them.

We gave workshops on these subjects and got requests for one-on-one consultations. My speaking Kurdish to them was important in building trust. Once they trusted us, they talked more freely about their experiences. We told them they had the right to make their own decisions about their bodies, and we taught them contraception methods. We explained that the decision to bear children was theirs alone, to be made under the influence of no one else. We held trainings to raise awareness of violence against women.

Our health center was funded by a three-year grant from the European Union. When that term came to an end, the center was to be closed. I said I wanted to continue the work voluntarily, but everyone said, "You can't do it alone." I said, "I can, if we borrow personnel from other institutions." With assistance from Dicle University's school of public health, we continued the project for four more years.

Other kinds of women's institutions had been opened in the city. With the participation of them all, we developed a joint women's platform and collectively helped prevent femicides. One woman who became pregnant as a result of rape was murdered by her brother. The women's institutions took charge. We persuaded her mother to claim her body. Then we attended her burial, where we denounced femicide. Working one-to-one with women in neighborhoods was invaluable to me—it taught me about the connections between women's health and gender consciousness, political awareness, and solidarity.

For the 2004 municipal elections, our party decided that a woman would run in Bağlar district, in fulfillment of the women's quota. Men objected because they saw local government as a male domain, but the women were determined and nominated Yurdusev Özsökmenler as the party's candidate for mayor of Bağlar. All the women's institutions mobilized and campaigned vigorously for her. Among Diyarbakır's districts, our party received the most votes in Bağlar, and Yurdusev was elected. Under her leadership, the municipality initiated women's projects.

Gültan Kışanak served as the projects' general coordinator. She persuaded me to take charge of opening and running the Kardelen Women's House, to provide counseling and legal services to women experiencing violence, poverty, and health problems. I put together a team. Our first problem was finding a space—the municipality had no building to house the center.

We found a place to rent, on the ground floor of an apartment building, but the residents objected, saying, "It'll disturb our peace." To help overcome their doubts, we called a meeting for the residents. Mostly men showed up. Mayor Yurdusev explained the project and its importance. But after she spoke, everyone who took the floor said something like: "Mayor, we love you and our party very much. We voted for you. But we don't want a women's shelter here. It'll bring divorced women here. Men will come and harass the young women. It'll disturb our peace."

We explained that we were planning a women's counseling center, not a shelter, but we couldn't sway them. Then Mayor Yurdusev said, "Let's talk to the women. Their views are more important." We did, and the women said they liked the idea, but frankly, they were somewhat under the men's influence. "Who do we turn to if we have a problem?" they asked. "You'll go to Çağlar," said the mayor, meaning me.

Some of the women were from my old district, Pasûr, and they knew me. We brought them around and opened Kardelen soon afterward. Some of the women who lived in the apartment building got involved with it, and we developed friendships and solidarity with them.

Our work at Kardelen was multifaceted. We held gender awareness trainings that attracted a lot of interest. Our priority was preventing violence against women. We provided education and counseling services and wanted to refer women in crisis to shelters, but there were no municipal women's shelters in the area. There was a "women's guest house," but its staff didn't care about confidentiality, and that jeopardized the safety of women who were already victims of violence. So, we formed a team and learned how to run a women's shelter and went on to open one in Diyarbakır Metropolitan Municipality, then another in Bağlar district.

At Kardelen, at the women's request, we offered art and craft classes, vocational training, and university preparation courses, and they were well attended. We got requests for music lessons and for cultural education and events, so we offered classes in *bağlama* and *arbane.** We formed the Kardelen Women's Choir, which took the stage at a March 8 rally, to great acclaim. The musical performances bolstered the women's morale.

On the eve of November 25, the International Day for the Elimination of Violence Against Women, we decided to visit coffeehouses and talk to men about violence against women. The women's institutions and the municipalities teamed up for this work. Mayor Yurdusev joined us at the coffeehouses. She asked the men, "Can any of you honestly say you've never been violent with your wife or sister?" Usually their response was silence. Then she talked to them about the importance of preventing violence against women and encouraged them to reject it. It was superb.

The fact that our mayor was a gender-conscious woman had an incredibly positive impact on Kardelen's work. We needed to be able to discuss and plan together without getting stuck in the municipal

---

* A *bağlama* is a long-necked lute, commonly used in folk music in Turkey. *Arbane*, or *erbane*, is a traditional Kurdish tambourine (frame drum) that accompanies folk dances.

bureaucracy. Moreover, having the city's support cleared the way for many of our projects. Our activities at Kardelen strengthened my own gender awareness and taught me how to deliver municipal services from a women-centered perspective.

In advance of the 2009 local elections, our party finalized its list of candidates and began planning campaigns. Selma Irmak was to run for mayor in Derik, in Mardin province. But then Turkey's Supreme Election Council decided, unlawfully, to cancel her candidacy leaving our party without a candidate. The people of Derik came into the streets and stayed there for days and nights. The Election Council backed down and gave the party one day to nominate a new candidate. Our party's Women's Election Commission proposed me, and I accepted.

When I arrived in Derik, a crowd welcomed me joyously. I worked hard to prove myself worthy of their confidence. Women especially mobilized for the campaign. When election day came, we won with a record number of votes.

The day my election was certified, I walked through the streets to the town hall, accompanied by the people of Derik, with women at the forefront. At the town hall, women threw out the executive chair, replaced it with a regular chair and had me sit on it. I got up and let an elderly mother sit on it.

The town hall had more than 100 employees, but only one was a woman, who had worked there for years. The building didn't even have a women's restroom. First thing, we had one built. For this, as for many other changes we made, men would say, "Huh, we never thought of it that way." How hard would it have been for them to stretch their minds and realize women needed a restroom, too?!

Just outside the town hall entrance was a men's coffeehouse. Men sat there all day playing Rummikub, at tables lining the path to the town hall door. To get to the door, you had to walk past them, which could be disturbing, and it prevented women from coming to the town hall altogether. It wasn't easy, but eventually we got the coffeehouse closed.

The women of Derik had never set foot in the town hall before. Now it belonged to them as well as to men. It turned out, they had strong opinions. We made decisions with them and implemented them together. Most notably, we opened the Peljin Women's Center to carry out women's projects. We hired women staff, including the sociologist Zeynep Sipçik to coordinate its activities. We got a lot done with the support of our women councilors. In 2014 Zeynep was herself elected co-mayor of the Dargeçit district, although now she's in prison too.

Derik's most important source of income was olives, cultivated in its historic orchards. In recent years, part of the town had been zoned for development. Women wanted us, instead, to create new olive orchards there and open a facility to process olives into oil. But we didn't get a chance in the two and a half years I served as mayor. The political genocide operation that had started in 2009 finally reached me, as it reached many elected officeholders. In 2011, police raided my house—they broke down the door and stormed in, their faces covered with masks, pointing guns at me and my father.

The townspeople converged in front of the town hall and protested. As I was driven away from the town, they followed us in their cars to the border of Mardin province. The municipality that they'd won with their resistance and votes was being taken away from them again.

I was detained in Diyarbakır. After four days I was arrested and taken to Diyarbakır E-type Prison. The charge against me: participation in women's activities. So many people were detained in this case that before I had a chance to make my defense in course I got released in July 2014. By then, local elections had taken place, and our party was implementing co-mayoring. The state had tried to stop us, but now women held office in more than 100 municipalities.

In the elections of June 7, 2015, Kurdish women carried their claim to equal representation into national politics. Their strong turnout made it clear that HDP was a women's party. I ran as a candidate for MP from Diyarbakır. On June 5, two days before the election, two bombs exploded at an HDP rally in Diyarbakır, killing five people. More than 400 were injured. The hospitals were filled with the wounded. Those who were conscious kept repeating that they wanted to cast their votes on election day. And so they did; the ones who were allowed by their doctors voted, then staggered back to the hospital. Some women who had worked on my election campaign had lost arms, legs, or eyes. When I visited them, they asked only about the election. Despite that brutality, the people of Diyarbakır made history, awarding HDP ten out of its eleven MP seats. Across Turkey, HDP received 13.2 percent of the vote and won a total of 80 MP seats, of which 32 were women. We broke a record, and the women's struggle achieved a victory.

But the AKP government didn't accept the people's will that was expressed on June 7 and called for a re-election to take place on November 1. On October 10, ISIS bombs exploded at a rally in Ankara, resulting in a massacre. This crime against humanity was another effort to undercut democratic politics, carried out by those who couldn't stomach women's liberation.

Despite this and other massacres, on November 1 people in Turkey elected enough HDP women to the parliament that we could establish a Women's Group there. The Kurdish women's movement joined forces with Turkey's feminist movement, creating a powerful synergy. Our Women's Group started holding autonomous meetings. Then on November 4, 2016, the next political genocide operation began, attacking democratic politics in general and women's electoral success in particular.

Nevertheless, women's liberation cannot be stopped.

4
"Hurry Up and Fix Things"

Diba Keskin

Translated by Kumru Toktamış

Diba Keskin (b. 1973) was elected co-mayor of Erciş, in Van province, on March 30, 2014, with 49.5 percent of the vote. She was arrested on October 13, 2015. She was sentenced to ten years in prison but was released on September 23, 2019.

I come from a conservative family in Van province. My father was an imam. In the 1990s, due to his political work, he was detained and tortured in prison. Most of my family then emigrated to Europe, but I continued living in Van. Once my children were old enough, I started working at the local branch of BDP. I joined its neighborhood and village committees. Later, still in Van, I participated in HDP activities. With my conservative identity, I was involved in the party's faith commission and also at the Democratic Islam Congress.

At the urging of friends, I applied to HDP to run for co-mayor of Erciş, in Van province, in the 2014 local elections. My husband supported me wholeheartedly, although he too is conservative. That he supported me indicates how years of political struggle have advanced our society. In previous local elections in Erciş, HEP and its successor parties had never been successful. But this time HDP prevailed, and I became the first woman elected to Erciş municipality in its 90 years of existence.

During the election campaign, some AKP men tried to smear me, saying, "How can a woman govern this town? Our religion doesn't allow that." Then, one day while speaking to a crowd, I said calmly into the microphone, "Okay then, let's talk about this. Look at the Quran and show me which verses say women can't be leaders. You won't find any—they're not there." From then on, I made this point every time I spoke.

Women's struggle is essential not just for women but for the entire society. Unfortunately, the system of male domination manipulates religious faith to condemn women to live in darkness. Before 2014, as I said, no woman had been elected mayor in Erciş, and out of the 400 municipal workers, only two had been women. And the municipality had never undertaken any programs to address women's needs. But once I was elected co-mayor, the town hall's administrative culture changed. Co-mayoring was so new to the people of Erciş, and a woman co-mayor meant a new political mentality.

Fortunately I wasn't alone—eight women had been elected as councilors. Yes, we all had previous experience in civil society organizations and political parties, but local governance was another story. In municipalities, power was institutionalized in deep-rooted ways. It wasn't easy, but together we worked hard to institute the co-mayoring. It'd take even more time for us to institute democratic politics, a democratic culture, and democratic governance principles.

We prioritized hiring women in every division, from technical to social services, from accounting to municipal security to bus drivers. Before we finalized our projects for 2015, we called a meeting of the district's women. They took their seats, and then engineers and architects presented their project proposals in Kurdish and Turkish. Next, we solicited women's comments and suggestions. Some burst into tears—they later explained that it was the first time anyone had ever asked their opinions. Such meetings were absolutely normal, yet no previous mayor had ever considered asking for women's views about the services in a town where they also lived.

Then we went into the neighborhoods and called women's meetings there. At first, they hesitated to speak up, but then they cautiously took the floor to raise issues and propose solutions. Some men found it bizarre that women were offering solutions. But over time women gained confidence, saying, "I live in this neighborhood, I live in this town, so of course I'm going to make suggestions."

Here's another incident. Early one morning a group of women came to the town hall and said to me, "We're from the Salihiye district in Erciş. For years, whenever we had a problem, our husbands would go to the mayor to seek a solution. When they came home, they'd brag about how they'd met with the mayor. Well, this time we women are coming to you. We want to tell you about our issues, Mayor, and have tea with you." We sat down to tea, and they detailed the problems in Salihiye. As they were leaving, they said, "Hurry up and fix things—don't embarrass us to our husbands!"

Meanwhile, certain power-hungry individuals and groups wanted to return to patriarchal governance. They tried to smear us by suggesting that we were exclusionary toward men. Disconcertingly, some of them had voted for our party in the election. They shared our party but not our principles. According to them, the power to speak and make decisions belonged to men. Women belonged at home.

One smear campaign claimed we were opposed to tribal structures. Now, tribes are an integral part of our social fabric, providing bases for solidarity and cooperation, maintaining our cultural values, and upholding our heritage. But *tribalism* is something else. It's an obstacle to democratic development because it hinders the expression of the people's will and promotes hierarchical relations. Our position was, "Yes to tribes, no to tribalism," and once we made that clear, it put an end to that smear campaign.

Another challenging issue was condolence visits. When a family is bereaved, co-mayors have the responsibility to visit family members, sit with them, and pay respects. Men and women family members sit in separate tents. I'm a religious, conservative woman, but as co-mayor, I had the responsibility to enter the men's section and sit with them too.

My first condolence visit came right after my election. Accompanied by councilors, party executives, and 80-year-old Mele Kemal, I went to the condolence tent to pay my respects. A young man standing nearby warned, "This is the men's tent—that other one is for women." Mele Kemal smiled. "Do you know who she is?" she said. The young man recognized me but looked bewildered. "But Mayor, this is the men's tent—" he began. "Young man," I said, "do women and men recite the El-Fatiha prayer differently?" And with that, I stepped into the men's tent along with several friends, both men and women.

Inside, all the men rose and surveyed us, some with smiles, others agape. We said our prayers and conveyed condolences. My accompanying men friends expected me to promptly move to the women's tent, but I said, "Let's have tea here and then go to the other tent." Meanwhile I got to conversing with some of the men. After a while, the confusion in their faces disappeared. More men gathered around to join the conversation.

That was a breakthrough, and we continued that way with later condolence visits. Sometimes during these visits, I explained the significance of women in our religion by mentioning revered historical figures such as Hatice, Ayşe, and Fatima.* I quoted from the

* Hatice is the Turkish name for Khadija, Prophet Muhammad's first wife. Ayşe was his third wife and Fatima was his daughter.

Hadith to clarify that women's exclusion from society had nothing to do with Islam. During my first month in office, these condolence visits were the talk of the town.

I believe our administration was the most transparent and participatory ever to govern in Erciş. When we took office, we inherited a municipal debt of 184 million liras. The creditors demanded that we pay them immediately. They even resorted to withholding further funding. Within three months, we prepared a report on the municipality's financial status.

And we shared it with the public. We modeled transparency by showing the citizens how much money was coming in each month and what was being spent on what. We shared all the so-called confidential information, or "information only to be known by important individuals." Secrets of those formerly in power became publicly known. The people were stunned but appreciative that we were exposing the dirt underlying their charmed circle. They were tired of lies and corruption and were ready for a clean page.

Three years had passed since a large earthquake shook our region, but our district's previous administrations had done nothing to rebuild. The 173,000 people of Erciş were still living in rubble. We filed an application with the Ministry of Internal Affairs to investigate the previous administrations, but as you can imagine, we got no proper response.

Even as we paid down the debt and rebuilt, we initiated new projects. Erciş's small businesses, such as butchers and cheesemakers, didn't have their own spaces to sell their products. They were scattered around the town and did their selling in unhygienic conditions. We met with butchers and cheesemakers, took their comments, and worked with them to design a project that met their needs. And we built two large parks in the town center. Viticulture had existed here since the time of the ancient Urartians, so we cultivated three acres of vineyards and surrounded them with walnut trees. We called them the Peace Vineyards.

On October 12, 2015, the municipal council was holding its monthly meeting. At around 4 p.m., the meeting was adjourned. As the councilors filed out of the room, one of them approached me, saying, "Mayor, the police have surrounded the building, and they're outside that door." I strode over and opened it. The officers said they were there to detain me. I told them that if an investigation was underway, I'd go to the prosecutor's office to give my statement. The district chief of police told me that the order to detain me had come from the prosecutor's office. They had the right to use force, so I'd have to follow them. None of the officers were women, and I told them I wouldn't leave without a woman officer. We argued for a while, and finally, on my insistence, councilor Güler Avcı accompanied me to the precinct.

The pretext they gave for detaining me was a press conference that I'd held earlier that morning about democratic self-governance. Now, this topic is part of DBP's official program. In fact, we'd run our election campaign on the slogan, "We'll govern ourselves; we'll govern our cities." For years, at every demonstration and press conference, we'd made speeches about democratic self-governance. Our MPs regularly brought it up in parliament. Why was the central government suddenly worked up over an issue that had caused no problems up until now? I think the government was disturbed that the public was embracing our party's municipal governance and services. So they invented nonexistent crimes to use as a wedge to separate us from the people.

I spent that night at the precinct. The next day, at 11:30 p.m., they took me to court and arrested me. I heard roars of protest, whistling, and jeering outside. The police wanted to rush me out of the courthouse. "I demand to see my children," I insisted. The judge consented, and my children came to see me. My younger daughter was crying. The older one's face was red with anger, and she was verging on tears. I hugged them both tightly and said, "Don't cry. I'm being arrested for defending the values of the people, not for committing a robbery." My children said, "Mom, we're so proud of you and everything you've accomplished." We said goodbye, and they left. And I spent that night at the precinct too.

On October 14 at 6 a.m., our HDP district co-chair, Seval Çadırcı, and myself were put in a civilian car and driven from the town, accompanied by an armored police vehicle. No one told us where we were going. Judging from the road signs, we guessed our destination was Bitlis Prison.

After we were processed at Bitlis, I was in a sorry state, angry, stressed, and sleep deprived. I hadn't taken off my coat or headscarf for days. Finally, I had a moment to wash my hands and face. For both Seval and me, it was our first time behind bars. There were no other political prisoners in our ward. After we spent a week at Bitlis Prison, we were transferred to Sincan Prison in Ankara.

In Sincan, we were held in solitary confinement for 20 days. When we were finally allowed to see other prisoners, we realized some friends were there: Sur co-mayor Fatma Şık Barut, Silvan co-mayor Yüksel Boğdakçı, Batman co-mayor Gülistan Aker, Edremit co-mayor Rojbin Çetin, and Hakkâri co-mayor Dilek Hatipoğlu. I treasured my time with them, sharing conversations, exercise, and experiences.

Then came the coup attempt of July 15, 2016, and social activities in prison were forbidden. The prison authorities even surveilled our lawyer meetings and installed cameras in the meeting rooms to record them. In protest, we refused to see our lawyers for three months. After a while, they stopped recording and surveilling the meetings, but they imposed restrictions on other social activities—including library visits and exercise—and they're still in place. Our weekly phone conversations with the outside world, to which we have a right, have been reduced to once every other week. We aren't allowed to receive visitors except for immediate family members. And we can have closed (noncontact) visits with them only once every other week now. In short, our already limited rights have been even further restricted.

I was staying in a ward with Rojbin Çetin, Dilek Hatipoğlu, and Sabahat Çetinkaya. Rojbin's father was in the hospital and critically ill, but we were hiding this from her. When our day came to make phone calls, Rojbin went for hers first. We worried among ourselves, hoping that she wouldn't come back with bad news. When she came back, other friends gathered around her. But then as I stepped toward them, they all suddenly came to me. Something wasn't right. Rojbin told me gently that my mother had passed away that morning (August 10, 2016), after morning prayer. Of course, losing a loved one is always painful, but being in prison, away from your family, unable to perform your final duties to them heightens that pain many times over. Unfortunately, just 23 days later, I had to give the same bad news to Rojbin about her father.

I know this punishment wasn't really directed at me; its real target was the people of Erciş who elected me as co-mayor and the other women to the council. In 2016 the government appointed a *kayyum* to govern the district. The *kayyum* fired many workers, shut down the women's directorate, and halted all social programs, especially those for women. He canceled most of our incomplete projects and renamed the completed ones, claiming them as his own accomplishments. In effect, he resurrected the old power structure predicated on rule by one race and one gender. The will of the people of Erciş has been overturned, and their right to elect and determine their local government has been violated.

On March 16, 2017, Erciş Second High Criminal Court sentenced me to 13 years and nine months imprisonment. At this writing, my case is pending at Erzurum Appeals Court

5

Never Give Up

Dilek Hatipoğlu

Translated by Elif Genç

Dilek Hatipoğlu (b. 1975) was elected co-mayor of Hakkâri on March 30, 2014, with 60.83 percent of the vote. She was arrested on August 20, 2015, and is currently serving a sentence of 15 years in Sincan Prison.

If in 1975, the year I was born, a fortune teller had said, "This child will grow up to be co-mayor of Hakkâri," she'd have been believed about as much as Galileo was when he said the world was round. The distance women have come since then is truly extraordinary.

Originally my family is from Varto in Muş province. I graduated from the College of Open and Distance Education with a business management degree. My husband is from Çukurca in Hakkâri province. Because he's Sunni and I'm Alevi,* we had to elope to get married. We lived in Van province and had two children.

I regularly visited the local party headquarters and participated in its neighborhood activities. I helped out in election campaigns, but it never crossed my mind to become a candidate myself. Then in 2014 women friends urged me to run for co-mayor of Hakkâri. I declined, reminding them that I had no political experience. "We're implementing co-mayoring in all the municipalities now," they pressed me, "and we need women candidates. Come on, why not contribute to women's struggle by running for office?" "Let me think about it," I said.

I called my husband at work to ask for his opinion. "You won't be able to do it," he said. "City governance is tough anywhere, but in Hakkâri it's even tougher." That made me angry. If men could be mayors, why couldn't women? It had been precisely in response to this claim, "Women can't do it," that women had initiated co-mayoring. I told my husband, "You come home and take care of the kids. I'm going to Hakkâri to apply."

It was the last day for applications, so I rushed to Hakkâri and submitted mine. On December 20, 2013, I won the nominating election, which finalized my candidacy. In the next weeks, the party held a series of public meetings to introduce the candidates. I was supposed to give a speech in Gever (Turkish Yüksekova) in front of a large crowd, but I panicked. *How am I ever going to speak in front of these people?* I agonized. *I hope the other friends talk for a long time, then they won't ask me to.* But this meeting, it turned out, had only one speaker: me.

* Alevis are the largest religious/cultural minority in the Sunni-dominated Turkey.

I climbed atop a campaign truck and was handed a microphone. My heart was pounding in my ears. *How am I ever going to do this?* I had no choice but to dive right in. Clutching my prepared speech, I delivered it haltingly, brows knit, face pale. And you know, I never even looked down at the paper in my hand; it turned out that in my excitement, I'd memorized the entire speech. And I clambered down from that truck as fast as I could.

During the March 8 week, our campaign visited a number of villages to celebrate International Women's Day. We met with village women and explained that we were planning to implement co-mayoring. How overjoyed they were to hear about this brand-new idea—it made them so happy! Actually, those March 8 celebrations and women's meetings were a lot of fun.

But giving speeches at rallies—that still made me terribly uncomfortable. A March 8 rally was planned for Hakkâri city center, and I was to give another speech. Once again, I was agitated as the program began. I couldn't sit still and kept pacing back and forth. A friend, Saadet Becerikli, was there too. She was also going to give a speech. "I wasn't nervous at all before," she exclaimed, "but now thanks to you I am!" I wouldn't be exaggerating if I told you that just writing down this story is reviving my anxiety about that March 8 speech.

But what could I do? If you leave your house and set out to become a mayor with no experience, well then, of course you're going to have moments of stress. But breaking that barrier is the first step to coping with the difficult necessity of seeking public office. Even if you're skittish, or shy, or inexperienced, your life belongs to you. You can't become "experienced" in something unless you actually experience it. Luckily, I'd set out on this journey to combat the "Women can't do it" attitude, and I set out to prove that I could do it.

We won the election—and then the real challenges started. In general, if you're a woman, your whole life is a challenge, but if you take office in city government where the mentality of "Long hair, small mind"* is deeply rooted, your challenges are all the greater.

* This patriarchal idiom in Turkish implies that women aren't suitable for roles that require intellect.

And here we were trying to install co-mayoring, a collective governance model that had never been tried before. Implementing this system meant overturning the political routine. No wonder we ran into difficulties—old ways of doing things die hard, especially the single-power governance mode.

Yes, I lacked experience, but I had a moral code of truth, honesty, and conscientious responsibility. Keeping that in mind, I got to work. And when it came to co-mayoring, none of us had had any prior experience. There had been co-chairing within the party, but not co-mayoring in municipal government.

Social life can become meaningful only if it's built on the basis of equality, but the current system is discriminatory and exclusionary, both in mentality and in practice. Only democratic politics and women's liberation can change this situation. By instituting co-mayoring, we aimed to establish equality in social life. We ran all municipal activities based on that model and developed our projects in partnership with both men and women. We established a women's directorate in the municipal administration and connected it to the Binevş Counseling Center for Women, thereby strengthening women's work there. To help prevent violence against women, we conducted field studies and held awareness trainings in the neighborhoods.

In the past, women rarely visited the town hall—it was mostly men who came to voice their concerns and ask for things. But now 15 or 20 women from a neighborhood might show up at the town hall and say, "We're here because a woman co-mayor will understand us." One group told us, "Our roads are made of dirt, and our houses are full of dust, so we need you to pave the roads with asphalt." For the first time, women, instead of their husbands, were expressing their needs. We did pave their neighborhood roads, and they were very pleased. Women had raised a problem, and then other women had solved it.

Another time, some women told us they needed us to build paved roads to Biçer and Kiran. In those neighborhoods, whenever people fell ill or got injured, ambulances couldn't get to them, so people lost their lives. Also, in the absence of good roads, women had to carry their children on their backs to school or to the hospital. So, we built a paved road to Biçer.

But the road to Kiran was harder—it would have to run through an old cemetery. People wanted this road, but then they hesitated because of the cemetery. We consulted the mufti [Muslim scholar of the Quran], who gave permission for the road. That settled it. But the workers who would do the paving weren't persuaded—they kept delaying the work, coming up with new excuses every day. Then, the big day came and I said, "Okay, get everything ready. Tomorrow we're all going there to start the road." We arrived at 8 a.m. Just as the machines were about to break ground, the driver raised his hands into the air and prayed, "God forgive me. I swear, this wasn't my idea! It's the co-mayor's fault!" Finally, the road was built, and then I heard a more important prayer, from the neighborhood women. Every time they saw me, they'd say, "Bless you, Mayor—you saved us from so much anguish!"

In fact, Hakkâri lacked a lot of infrastructure. It needed a reliable water supply, a sewage system, a wastewater treatment plant, and a landfill, all of which required large expenditures. For years, the municipality had been prevented from taking out loans or getting grants to launch such projects. A drinking water supply project had been prepared seven years earlier but was never approved. We initiated a bidding process right away, so that work could begin. (It was supposed to be finished by March 2017—I'm not sure what stage it's at right now.)

We also implemented, or started to implement, sewage and wastewater treatment plant projects. I won't go into detail about these municipal services, but I mention these examples for a reason. People long ago had abandoned all hope of progress. When we moved forward on projects, however, the attitude of "A woman can't do it" gave way to confidence in us. Public opinion shifted to, "This woman co-mayor solves problems!" Needless to say, in the brief 16 months that we were in office, we couldn't complete all our projects. But we made a good start in democratic local governance and women's participation in it.

Co-mayoring was a great success and an important victory for women. But the patriarchal mentality didn't easily accept it. In my first few months, I had to deal with a conflict involving rancorous tribalism. Two young men had catcalled a young woman, fighting broke out, and it escalated to a full-blown intertribal clash. The two parties smashed each other's shop windows and damaged property. Shots were fired, wounding several on both sides. Co-mayors, MPs, and civil society organizations stepped in to try to make peace, but every time things simmered down, the parties would stoke up another brawl.

Clearly it was all being deliberately provoked to create chaos, and we kept saying so, but to no avail. To fuel the fight, certain people would stop vehicles that were entering the city from different districts and beat up men from the other tribe. Then the injured men's friends would visit them at the hospital—and they too would be attacked.

The city was in turmoil. The police just sat back and watched what was happening. I raced around talking on the phone to the governor, the police chief, and the tribal leaders, but I wasn't getting any results. The situation was out of control, houses were randomly being fired at, no one could go outside, and my telephone wouldn't stop ringing with people pleading "Mayor, please stop this, don't let it get worse."

I tried to meet with the governor, but I was told that he was attending an *iftar* dinner at the police guesthouse. Apparently, the governor, gendarmerie commander, AKP provincial chair, mufti, and tribal leaders were all going to discuss this issue over dinner. I showed up uninvited. "Right now," I told the men, "guns are being randomly fired in the neighborhoods. It's our job to put a stop to this. If anyone dies, you're responsible." Then I stalked out. I later learned that after I left, the governor sneered, "She's a woman, so emotional."

I went over to the town hall. A few minutes later I learned that an elderly man had been killed—he'd been going to the bakery to get bread for *iftar*. Upon hearing that someone had lost his life, I burst into tears, not knowing what to do. After that the governor declared a three-day curfew. We held talks with everyone involved, joined by a delegation from our party headquarters. After ten days of negotiations, everyone agreed to a truce. People had been provoked into a senseless, futile tribal fight that had left dozens wounded and one dead. Two young men had catcalled a girl—surely that was no reason to spill blood. I was the co-mayor, elected by the people. Yes, I was a woman, I was a mother, I was emotional, and I was new at politics. Yes, I struggled, but I didn't give up and resign although people expected me to.

On August 20, 2015, an arrest warrant was issued for me, and I went to the Hakkâri courthouse to give my statement to the prosecutor. He made me wait at his door for nearly two hours, then handed me over to the police without even seeing me. After four days of detention, they subjected me to a show trial, convicted me, and sentenced me to prison.

I was in shock but also angry. What crime had I committed? Was it a crime to work honestly as co-mayor and constantly search my conscience? Was it a crime to believe that 60,000 people had a right to drinking water? To provide services to the public instead of telling them a pack of lies? To stand by them in hard times and share their sorrows? Which of these had been my crime?

I entered Van M-type Prison with these feelings and thoughts. As I made my way down the ward, I wondered what life here would be like: the walls, the cold iron gates, the crowded maze. It wouldn't be easy to accept life there. I stayed there for a week. On August 30, I transferred to Sincan Prison in Ankara, along with Edremit co-mayor Rojbin Çetin. After we arrived there, Rojbin and I sat down on the stairs to the prison yard and smoked cigarettes. We talked about our cell—it was grimy, but we had no cleaning supplies. While we were talking, someone called out to us. That's how you communicate in prison—you call out to each other. We yelled back, letting them know what we needed. Shortly afterward friends sent us a television and a refrigerator. We were very touched.

I couldn't buy what I needed from the prison commissary because my funds weren't transferred to my new prison account. But then I discovered that the commissary didn't have what I needed. I didn't even have a kitchen sponge. When a delegation from the Human Rights Foundation of Turkey visited, we explained our problems, and the prison administration sent us a package of four sponges. In the third week, after some HDP ministers visited us, we got some plastic dinnerware. We still had no teakettle—we had to brew our tea and drink it from an empty tomato paste jar. Teakettles finally arrived at the commissary a month later.

We were in isolation for 40 days, deprived of all common-area activities, such as exercise, conversations, and library visits. The women friends in the prison demanded our release from isolation. In the end, for whatever reason, the prison administration let us out for activities.

The day came when I was allowed to have a conversation for the first time. I was so excited to meet with the women friends whom I knew only from their voices. The warmth and intimacy of that first encounter cannot be described. Some of the friends had been there for 20 or 25 years. They provided enormous support to every newcomer. Following the example of these friends, I also decided to try to make my own prison life meaningful.

It took the prosecutor three months to prepare for my case, and my first hearing was held on December 4, 2016. They didn't take me to court—they wanted to take my statement with SEGBİS,* which I refused. For my third hearing, I was transported back to Hakkâri, where I made my first defense. At my fourth hearing, the verdict was read. Although I was right there in Van Prison, I wasn't allowed to attend my fifth hearing, which sentenced me to 15 years imprisonment. Later the Supreme Court of Appeals approved five years of the sentence and sent the overturned ten-year sentence back to the Second High Criminal Court.

You'll remember that when I first entered the prison, I'd asked myself "What crime did I commit?" After considering all the large-scale lawlessness committed by the state, I now have a more meaningful answer. We women threw a monkey-wrench into the patriarchal order. They put us in prison to stop us, but they can't. Women have already emerged from their cages. We're already flapping our wings freely. No walls have the power to suppress that growing resistance.

* An audiovisual communication interface similar to Skype that the Turkish state uses to record testimonies, interrogations, and hearings, including over distances.

6

"We Have Your Keys. Come and Get Them."

Edibe Şahin

Translated by Seda Saluk

Edibe Şahin (b. 1960) was mayor of Dersim from 2009 to 2014. In June 2015, she was elected Dersim's first woman MP. She was arrested on November 17, 2016 and sentenced to prison. She is currently in Kocaeli F-type Prison. Her case is pending.

On November 6, 2016, police broke into my house in Dersim and raided it. They found no one at home. Ten days later, on November 16, they raided the house again, and once again no one was in. I was away in Istanbul, getting treatment for a digestive ailment. That day the gendarmerie in Dersim called me. "We searched your house," they said. "We have your keys. You may come and get them."

Now, I'd previously served as mayor of Dersim for five years, and on June 7, 2015, I'd been elected an MP. So, my phone number was a matter of public record. Instead of raiding my house, they could have just called me and told me they needed me to give a statement. Instead, they broke the door down, searched my home, then brought in a locksmith who installed a new lock. Only after they were finished with all that did they call me to let me know.

Despite my illness, I went to Dersim to retrieve the keys. Then I went to the prosecutor's office to give my statement. I had to wait a week before he'd see me because he was so busy. Finally, I gave statements for eleven separate investigations, all for press releases I'd previously given.

I returned to Istanbul to continue my treatment. As my ailment was severe, I was admitted to the hospital immediately. Two days after the hospital released me, the police detained me. They took me to police headquarters on Vatan Street in Istanbul and put me in a room with two young women in chadors. They'd been captured in an ISIS operation. I had to spend the night in the same room with them.

Early the next morning, I was flown to Elâzığ and from there driven to Dersim, accompanied by two plainclothes police officers, one of them a woman. As we arrived, police greeted us with armored vehicles. They'd closed off all roads into the city. The convoy blared their sirens, trying to create an extraordinary atmosphere and intimidate the public with a message of "The mayor and MP who you elected is now our hostage." It was as if they were gloating over my arrest. They took me to police headquarters.

When I entered the prosecutor's office, I saw that the prosecutor conducting the investigation was the one to whom I'd given my statement a week earlier. "Are you going to finish your business from last week?" I asked. I was arrested, based on the press release I'd issued when the HDP co-chairs, Selahattin Demirtaş and Figen Yüksekdağ, had been detained.

That night I was taken to Elâzığ E-type Prison. They processed and searched me, then took me into a cell. I looked around and saw Dersim's current co-mayor Nurhayat Altun, councilor Cemile Ataş, and DİSK's Dersim representative Şükran Yılmaz. These friends had been detained in Dersim the same day I was.

The cell had been prepared for us in a hurry. Its walls were only half tiled. There were only bunk beds, mattresses, and blankets. It was freezing cold. I was exhausted because I'd been on the road for 24 hours and was ill. Şükran and I shared a bed. The next day we were taken to the women's ward. Since I'd been imprisoned before, during the 1980 military coup, I knew what to expect.

How happy I was to be reunited with friends! Despite the frigid cold, their welcome was so very warm. There were 13 of us. They fixed me some hot tea and breakfast right away. In addition to the younger women, there was a mother around my age. She was one of Batman's *koçers* [nomads]. Her whole family was imprisoned, but each member was in a different prison.

One morning a week later, a guard announced that co-mayor Nurhayat and I would be transferred in half an hour. Friends rushed to prepare for our departure. Somehow, they simultaneously hugged us and packed up plates, spoons, glasses, napkins, and other stuff. They wanted to give me books, but they had so few, and I didn't have the heart to take them. Then we all went outside, and they saw us off with applause and ululations.

Nurhayat and I were handcuffed and put in a compartment inside the transport vehicle. There was a camera over our heads. We thought we were alone in the van, but when it stopped for a bathroom break, we saw someone emerge from another compartment in the vehicle. It was Dersim's co-mayor Mehmet Ali Bul, who was being transported with us.

That handcuffed journey lasted for hours. Finally, in the evening, we arrived at Sincan Women's Closed Prison in Ankara. They put Nurhayat and me in a room they called the guesthouse to spend the night and said we'd get back on the road in the morning. We were so weary that we slept using our coats as pillows.

Early the next morning, we set off again. At noon we arrived at Kocaeli No. 1 F-type Prison. Nurhayat and I were taken to a room with the sign "Men's Guesthouse" on the door. It was filthy—the remains of an unfinished meal were still on the table. We were held there for several hours during processing. We asked for the belongings we'd brought from the other prison, but they refused, saying, "This is a high-security place."

They took Nurhayat and me to separate cells. I entered mine, the door was slammed behind me, and then . . . utter silence. I'd been wondering who my roommates would be—it had never occurred to me that I'd be alone. The cell was furnished with a plastic table and chair and an old kitchen sink. A small beat-up cabinet, corroded with rust, stood by the door, and old newspapers lined the floor. There was a plastic water bottle in the toilet. I climbed to the upper level and saw three empty bunk beds and lockers. The walls were dripping with condensation. This was where I was to stay.

I was terribly thirsty but couldn't drink tap water due to my health problem. After a while someone opened the hatch in the door. I asked for water, and they said, "Drink from the tap. The commissary is closed till next week." Then they brought in a dirty mattress. I was exhausted, I wanted to take a bath, but there was no hot water. It was provided only for a few hours on certain days of the week. Most of all, I wanted tea. I'd been on the road for three days and hadn't had any tea. But whenever I asked the officers for anything, all they said was "Write a petition." There was nothing for me but to sleep. The cell had no TV, no newspapers, nothing to get news from outside. The room was utterly silent. I didn't have a watch. Other prisoners shouted slogans at certain times of day. I tried to guess what time it was from those shouts.

The first voice I heard was that of Mayor Gültan. It turned out our cells were adjacent. She called out to me and pounded on the wall, and I recognized her voice. We managed to greet each other, and on Friday when the internal mail arrived, I had a welcome letter from Gültan. I learned that Ayla Akat Ata was in the cell on my other side, but I couldn't make my voice reach her. The fact is, I was hoarse. I have a problem with my vocal cords, and when I go without speaking for a while, I lose my voice entirely. This condition made life in solitary even more onerous for me. On visiting days, my relatives came, and I would croak at them, then lose it altogether again.

This wasn't my first experience with an F-type prison. My older brother, who was arrested in 1980, had been transferred to Eskişehir F-type Prison in 1991.* We families of prisoners had protested their transfer in front of the prison for days. Inside, the prisoners were on hunger strike. The protests continued for days, both inside and outside. Finally, the prisoners were transferred back to their old prisons.

Now here I was in an F-type prison myself, in solitary confinement. The first thing I did was make my room more colorful. I hung postcards with nature scenes on the wall. I covered the rusty cabinet and sink with garbage bags. There was a surveillance camera inside the living space, so I bought a bedsheet from the commissary to make into a curtain. I had no scissors, so I cut it with a tiny knife and sewed the curtain. It brought some cheer to my cell and also helped against the cold by keeping the heat inside the covered area of the big cell. The cell was so damp that water pooled in one corner, and fungi grew every day on the floor. Trying to dry clothes was a torment. The only items available for us to purchase in the commissary were those for men's needs. Women were still new in this prison. The smallest slipper size was 40-41. They didn't even have a simple hairpin. I eventually cut my hair short because the commissary never got hairpins.

The new year arrived; for me, it was no different from any other day. I sat on the bunk bed and read a book. "Happy New Year!" shouted Mayor Gültan, banging on the wall. I answered of course, banging back. I could hear the voices of women friends from elsewhere, saying, "*Sersala we pîroz be,*" happy new year.

A month later Gültan, Ayla Akat Ata, Nurhayat Altun, Figen Yüksekdağ, Gülser Yıldırım, and I were allowed to meet for the first time in the common area. We huddled together for two and a

---

* F-type prisons are high-security prisons where prisoners stay in small cells either in solitary confinement or in groups of two or three. The first high-security prison was that of Eskişehir, built in 1991.

half hours and talked. Having been in solitary for so long, it was a bit tiring but so very wonderful. We'd so missed chatting.

In February 2017, our isolation was lifted, and we could now share cells with one or two people. They put me in a cell with Ayla. Our yard had three dovetail nests. Sparrows settled in one of them, and then our friends sent us a parakeet named Jîr, a marvelous creature. She had an aversion to her cage and preferred to perch on us. She loved to peck at our plates and hands and drink water from the tap. She also jogged with us around the yard. She got furious when we ignored her, and if we dared read a book, she'd fly over and peck at the pages. One day Jîr flew to freedom, along with the sparrows who had nested in the dovetail. We missed her terribly but were happy for her that she'd found freedom.

In April 2017 three of us started sharing a cell: Nurhayat, Gültan, and I. Once we became a threesome, our lives got far more colorful.

I was born in a village in Dersim's Nazimiye district as one of seven children, five of them girls. My mother wanted a boy but kept giving birth to girls, one after another. When I was little, and my mother got pregnant, I remember people whispering, "She'll have another girl."

When I was very young, we moved to Istanbul. I learned Turkish there. But my mother missed Dersim and yearned to go back. My father, a civil servant, asked for a position there, so we did go back. There I encountered another language problem—I'd forgotten my mother tongue, Kurdish. Whenever I tried to speak it, I made mistakes, and everyone laughed at me. One day I tried to say, "This dog will eat me," but instead I said, *Mi nû kutik werd*, which means, "I ate this dog." I kept making mistakes like that. But I stayed at it, and soon my mother tongue came back to me.

After middle school, I attended Ağrı Teachers' High School as a boarding student, along with a lot of other girls from Dersim. My mother objected, but I wanted to stand on my own two feet. At school, there were a lot of us girls from Dersim. On holidays, we'd rent a car to drive home. We had to pass through Erzurum, and that wasn't easy because in the 1970s it had lots of right-left clashes. As we drove through the city, police officers from POL-DER [Police Association] would accompany our car. It was in that school that I first heard the insult of "putting out the candle" against Alevis.* I was shocked when a classmate said, "Don't get me wrong, but that's what they say." Of course, that made me wonder.

I first got politicized in high school. Once on May Day, I was reading the May 1 declaration. Soldiers came into the school and ordered us all to wait outside in the snow. They blockaded the door. We'd done nothing wrong, but our school was directly across from the military base, and we'd been making a lot of noise. Then a rumor spread around the city that "the communists raided the school!" People were shocked to hear it, they'd never met any communists, so they rushed over to the school to see them. But when they got there, all they saw was us students. "What communists?" they said. "These are our girls!" Faced with this community reaction, the soldiers allowed us back into the classrooms.

After I graduated, I first worked as a substitute teacher in Dersim, then in the city's treasury office. I was there during the 1980 coup. That morning, September 12, I left the house to go to work and saw military vehicles everywhere. All the shops were closed. A soldier stopped me and told me to go home, saying, "There's been a coup." A curfew was imposed. Soldiers checked IDs and raided houses.

Life became very different. Police detained people every day. One day they detained me at work. I didn't know why. During torture, I learned that they actually wanted my brother—when they couldn't find him, they'd detained me instead. After ten days, they released me. I'd been wearing a skirt when they took me, and it caused problems, so after I was released, I wore pants all the time. A week later they detained me again, this time for wearing pants as a civil servant. They took me to the torture center known as "1800 Houses" in Elâzığ and tortured me severely for a month. After six months, they released me—on the day my brother was arrested. Clearly, they'd been holding me hostage.

For a while I fought legally to go back to my job, but my employment had been terminated with Martial Law No. 1402, so that was futile. I decided to go to Istanbul. When I told my parents, my

* The author is an Alevi. "Putting out the candle" refers to a derogatory myth claiming that Alevis engage in orgies after blowing off the twelve candles representing the twelve imams in their rituals.

mother was distraught, and my father was angry—I was engaged to be married, and society would look askance if I up and left. But I insisted on going my own way and went to Istanbul.

There I stayed with relatives, and I worked—and I participated in the protests in front of the prison gates on behalf of my imprisoned brother. At one point the authorities forced prisoners to wear uniforms, and to protest that, we and they went on hunger strikes and death fasts. Those days were tormented. The prisoners weren't in good health. As their families, we were constantly outside protesting and demanding to meet with the authorities. In the end, they revoked the requirement that prisoners wear uniforms. But for the rest of my life, I'd be a woman who got politicized at prison gates.

I started working at the Istanbul Mesopotamia Cultural Center (MKM), which had been founded to preserve and advance Kurdish culture. I ran the library and archives. We held a fundraiser, and soon 1,000 books arrived. We organized book signing events with Kurdish writers and poets that attracted great interest.

The MKM had only one woman on its board of directors, but we tried to hire and train women and ensure that women participated in all MKM activities. A children's choir would rehearse there. Mothers would bring their children, then wait for them until practice was over. While the mothers waited, we connected with them and discussed women's issues. Many of those women later became active in politics, including several who served as district chairs, provincial heads, and mayors.

While I was at the MKM, we published a Kurdish magazine called *Rewşen*, which included articles, stories, and interviews on Kurdish language, culture, and history. As the editor-in-chief, I handled the editing, printing, and distribution. I also helped found the Istanbul Kurdish Institute, serving two terms on its board of directors, the only woman to do so. The institute published a journal called *Zend*, which mainly included academic works and studies.

Undeniably, women played an important role in keeping the Kurdish language alive and transmitting it from generation to generation, but at the time, writing and research remained largely men's work. Men dominated the institute. Women were few and didn't write as much.

While I was working at MKM and the Institute, I had to make a long daily commute, since I lived way off in the Kadıköy district. Additionally, I had small children at home. I wanted to participate in women's organizing, and since the party had a women's commission in Kadıköy, I began attending their meetings. Our district chair was a woman, and I helped out in the district administration. Then I was elected district head for Kadıköy. At the party congress, we went to great lengths to ensure that half of the district administrations were headed by women, and we were successful. At that time, party women's mobilizing activities in Istanbul were generally strong. The heads of nine districts were women. Our neighborhood activities were multidimensional: at meetings we read aloud from the women's newspaper and discussed articles collectively. To create the budget for women's activities, we made a centralized decision to have women pay their membership dues directly to women's branches. We met with our women members more often, which improved women's organizing and relieved us financially. However, although women were involved in neighborhood activities, they were too often reluctant to participate in party leadership because their circumstances didn't allow it.

As the 1999 local elections approached, we nominated a woman candidate to run for Kadıköy mayor. Our neighborhood-based campaign was so effective that it became party culture to ensure that women took part in all neighborhood committees. No doubt the most critical factor in our strong relationship with women was Kurdish patriotism. In the 1990s, many Kurds had migrated to Istanbul as a result of village burnings, which caused many problems for women, such as poverty, unemployment, and housing.* We addressed those problems and also worked on ending blood feuds and preventing animosities from arising between families.

---

* For centuries, most Kurds in Turkey lived in small villages in southeastern Anatolia. Starting in 1985 and reaching a peak in 1992–4, the Turkish military forcibly annihilated some 3,000 Kurdish villages by evacuating the residents and razing the buildings. Some 30,000 people were killed, and hundreds of thousands of survivors fled to the large cities.

And when women suffered coercion or violence in the family, they learned that they could tell us. At that time, shelters for abused women were almost nonexistent. If an abused woman was in a crisis, we'd bring her into our own homes until the problem was resolved. We organized trainings to prevent violence against women.

We made home visits to meet women and tell them about our party and the women's struggle. When we started out, we needed more women to participate right away. We even recruited women who were new to the party and had no idea how to help abused women. One day two of our newer friends went on a home visit. The woman in the house told them about her husband's violence toward her, and of course, our friends listened sympathetically. The woman cried, and one of our friends cried with her. The other friend didn't know what to do. She picked up a copy of the party's bylaws and browsed through it, then turned to the other and said, "There's nothing about this in our bylaws." Afterward, back at party headquarters, they told us this tragicomic story, and we explained to them how to handle such situations. Clearly, we were all learning together as problems arose in practice.

In the 2000s, university students started a petition drive demanding "mother tongue" education. Our women members who had children in primary schools petitioned the District Directorate of National Education to support the campaign. One evening the homes of all these women were raided, and the women were detained. In a flash, we organized solidarity for them among other women in the neighborhood. Women volunteered to take care of the detainees' young children. The chair of our district women's branch was also arrested.

Their trial began, and the required language was Turkish, but most of the women didn't speak it so they asked for an interpreter. Just then a Kurdish man happened to be cleaning the hallways—and the judge summoned him to act as interpreter. But he couldn't translate properly into Turkish, so the women corrected him. At one point, the judge said, "It's all women in this court. Don't these kids have fathers? Why is it the mothers who petitioned?" Of course, they snapped back, "Judge, we're petitioning for use of our mother tongue, and you ask about fathers? What do fathers have to do with the mother tongue?" In the end, they were released.

I was under a lot of strain during this period. Every time I gave a press conference, I'd be detained afterward. Women, especially elderly mothers, would sit and wait in front of the police station, saying, "We won't leave without our chairwoman." Their solidarity was powerful. Whenever any of us were taken into custody, the police would snarl at us, "Go to the mountains or stay home."* This attitude summarizes well the role expected of women, particularly Kurdish women.

Sometimes people would say to us politically active women, "You have it easy." One day a newly married young woman friend decided she wanted to participate in party activities and went to consult her husband. "You can't—you have children," he told her. She told him about us, pointing out that we had children and yet were still in leadership positions. "They have nannies," he said. The next day she came to my home, saw that I didn't have a nanny for my children, and started working in party activities.

We had problems with party men. Our men friends would say, "Oh, we've overcome this problem of male domination," yet they maintained their sexist roles at home. Their wives, after putting in intense workdays at the party, came home to face cooking, cleaning, and tending to the children and the sick. And when our men friends visited us at home in the evenings, they'd sit and watch the news and discuss it, while we women did the chores, and then we got up earlier than them to do all the housework. Only after that did we catch up with meetings and party work.

We party women discussed these pressures among ourselves. Other women friends, who worked so hard to address women's issues every day, couldn't always see what we were going through. At a provincial women's meeting in Istanbul, we added a married women's agenda item, and our discussion enabled single women friends to see our problems. From then on, thanks to our strong organizational structure, they took our situation into consideration while planning events, especially in setting meeting times. The sol-

* "Go to the mountains" means join the Kurdish guerrilla forces fighting the Turkish state on the mountains.

idarity between older and younger women friends got stronger as we better understood each other.

After I served as Kadıköy district chair, I was elected to the Party Council, working mainly in the Marmara region. As the 2004 local elections drew near, we pored over Istanbul's membership lists, searching for women to become candidates for city councilor in places where they could be elected. After lengthy debates, we managed to get Çiçek Ariç into the candidates' list in Sultanbeyli. We came up with a final list but worried that the men would make last-minute changes. To prevent that from happening, we needed to safeguard the list until it was handed over to Turkey's Supreme Election Council. A friend named Dilber had recently had eye surgery and couldn't help with many activities. "I'll stay on guard," she said. She stayed overnight at party headquarters, keeping watch. Male friends teased her, saying, "She only has one eye, and she didn't let us see. What wouldn't she do with two eyes?" Çiçek won the election and became a councilor. That was important for Istanbul at the time.

In preparation for the 2009 local elections, the party's Women's Election Commission met to discuss recruiting women candidates to fill the women's quota, based on a feasibility report prepared by women friends. I was assigned to work on the commission and would participate in the organizing activities in the Marmara region.

After a while, the commission asked me to be a candidate for mayor of Dersim. At first I said no, but women friends encouraged me. Three women in all applied for the nomination, and we got together and agreed to compete in a comradely way. We went to public meetings together. I won the primary election, and the three of us congratulated one another. In the general election, I won by a small margin. My victory was certified, and I started my new job.

The previous Dersim mayor, Songül Erol Abdil, had served in 2004–9 as Turkey's only woman mayor. Now she was handing the position over to me. We got to work quickly. I attended a training meeting in Van for women mayors, where we discussed women's municipalism, our particular cities, and our priorities. Dersim would prioritize democratic participation, ecology, and women's activities.

In Dersim, two-thirds of the city councilors were women, the highest proportion in Turkey, and they represented almost every segment of society. We established a gender equality commission in the city council, which reported on the gender aspect of every issue on the council's agenda. Committed to transparency, we discussed the council agendas down to the last detail. Decisions now had to be taken unanimously, so that councilors could easily explain their decisions to the public. We opened ourselves to public scrutiny, and it was effective and robust, allowing our work to produce results.

We established a women's directorate to strengthen women's participation in the municipal administration. We encouraged women to become leaders. We opened a women's solidarity house. As we developed our projects, we discussed them with the democracy organizations, the unions, and the city residents; we met with women to solicit their suggestions.

We opened the town hall to the public twice a week. Eighty percent of those who came to meet with me were women, and most admitted they came because I was a woman. One day a middle-aged woman burst in crying, which startled us. She composed herself a bit, then threw her arms around my neck and exclaimed, "Now that I've seen this, I won't regret dying!" When I asked what she meant, she said that when she entered the building and heard us speaking in Kurdish, she was overwhelmed. Her feeling summed up our success.

The municipal services that women need can be different from the services that men require, and so we created projects to address women's needs. For example, women in particular would visit Gola Çeto to light candles. On certain holy days, people would visit the site in large numbers.

Gola Çeto lies on the Munzur River, which flows through Dersim. Starting in 1994, a dam was under construction on the river, about nine miles to the south of Gola Çeto. In 2009, the year I took office, the dam was completed, its gates were closed, and water accumulated to form a lake. But the dam threatened to inundate Gola Çeto—the site would soon be under water. As the waters rose, we could no longer hear the Munzur's current. An air of mourning hung over the city. Every day women went to Gola Çeto to witness and lament. They came to us and asked us to save this place.

We mobilized all our resources, built a barrier, and filled in part of the lake, intending to turn the reclaimed land into a park. But men opposed the construction of the park, arguing, "Dersim is a natural park area already. There's no need to build a park." Yes, Dersim was a natural park, but to go for a picnic, you needed a car, and cars belonged to men. Women needed green spaces that were accessible on foot. We built the park, and today it's one of Dersim's most popular places. It was women who asked us to save the site, and women who designed the project to save it.

Women asked us to create easily accessible green spaces in their neighborhoods, too. So, we initiated the Park in Every Neighborhood project, planting vegetation native to Dersim, much to the people's satisfaction.

One day of the nature and culture festival that we used to organize every year was reserved for women. All the speakers and artists of that day were women, and the exhibits and events were performed by women. Before the festival, we would take suggestions from the public on how to do it. The most popular suggestion was to clear a festival area and build a monument of Seyit Rıza there.* We picked a square and renamed it Seyit Rıza Square. We held the 2010 festival there, and inaugurated the Seyit Rıza monument, which was very emotional.

All Turkish municipalities are members of the Association of Municipalities of Turkey (TBB). Political parties are represented in the association council in proportion to the number of the municipalities they've won. Our party was to send a representative to the council. We decided our representative would be a woman, and the party recommended me. I was the only woman on the 15-person council. At the council, at my initiative, the council decided to hold trainings for women mayors and women council members, and

* Seyit Rıza (1863–1937), an Alevi Kurd, was a leader of the 1937 Dersim rebellion. The Turkish state suppressed the rebellion and executed him.

twice it organized two-day women's meetings where we discussed gender policies that municipalities could implement.

Our party also sent a woman member—Viranşehir mayor Leyla Güven—to represent us at the European Congress of Local and Regional Authorities. When Mayor Leyla was arrested in 2009, I took her place there. In conventional politics, it was unusual to send women members to such bodies. The fact that we did was an achievement of our party's women's organizing.

My term as mayor ended in 2014. On June 7, 2015, I was elected to parliament as an MP from Dersim. It was the first time Dersim had elected a woman MP. But the AKP government canceled the results of that election and held a re-election on November 1, overturning the people's will. I wasn't elected in the November 1 balloting. At the time of my arrest in 2016, I was an HDP council member.

Kurdish women, wherever we are, have never given up in our struggle against sexist attitudes and policies. Nor have we allowed our fight to be perceived as secondary or to be postponed. Under all circumstances, we'll continue to resist male domination. The stories told in this book cover only a tiny fraction of what we've experienced. It's impossible to describe them all. But with this book, we're opening a crucial door.

7
Women's Work Viewed as Frivolous

Evin Keve

Translated by Demet Arpacık

Evin Keve (b. 1987) was elected co-mayor of Çatak, in Van province, on March 30, 2014, with 68 percent of the vote. She was arrested on January 3, 2016, released on March 28, 2016, arrested again on February 3, 2017, and released on December 19, 2019. Her case is still pending.

The winter months were the hardest for our municipality in Çatak to provide services. On January 3, 2016, a snowstorm hit, with avalanches in some places. My phone rang off the hook, with neighborhood representatives and others demanding that the roads be plowed. Some needed the roads cleared to care for the sick, others were stranded and needed urgent help. I met with the councilors, and we got the plowing underway despite our limited means. It was an exhausting day.

At midnight I heard a knock at my door. I opened it to find a cluster of special operations police. They could have waited till morning, but no, they chose to come at midnight, although the district precinct wasn't even 200 feet from my house. Someone growled out the reason for this midnight raid: "You have to give a statement." They took me to the prosecutor's office, where I learned that I was being rushed into custody because of a statement I'd recently given to Jinha, the women's news agency. Then I was arrested, on the grounds of "having the potential to declare self-governance."

They transported me to Van M-type Prison. On my fourth day, I was to be transferred—to Sincan Prison in Ankara, they told my family and my lawyer. I was flown to Ankara under police escort. But then at the Ankara airport, they bought more tickets. "Where are they taking me?" I asked the woman soldier on duty. "Erzurum," she said. Without informing me properly, they more or less abducted me. I was outraged but also anxious—this would be my first prison experience. And I was worn out from traveling all day, after leaving Van that morning at 9 a.m.

We arrived at Erzurum Oltu Prison around midnight. There, to my horror, they told me Oltu had no ward for political prisoners, so I was to be put in the ward with ordinary prisoners. I refused, but the guards snapped back at me. We argued until 3 a.m., but nothing changed. Finally, they hauled me into a cell with two women who had been convicted of killing their rapists.

On Monday, the prison administration called my family to let them know where I was. It was unacceptable that I was in an ordinary prisoners' ward. I wrote to the prosecutor demanding to be moved to a political prisoners' ward. I wrote to my family, my lawyer, and my MP, Pervin Buldan. But nothing changed for two weeks. In the third week, two political prisoners arrived from Bingöl. Three days later the three of us were transferred to Bayburt M-type Prison.

On March 28, 2016, I was acquitted of all charges against me and released.

In January 2017, I traveled to Ankara for eye surgery. On January 3, while I was away, many people in our district were detained, including my fellow co-mayor, the vice chair, and some of the councilors. Five people got arrested, and the others were released. In February police detained me while I was still in Ankara for follow-up doctor's visits. They contacted the prosecutor's office in Çatak via SEGBİS, then arrested me, this time for "membership in a terrorist organization." They'd prepared an indictment against me—it consisted of the press releases I'd issued in 2013–14 and lists of the funerals I'd attended, and hydroelectric dam protests I'd supported. Frankly, they concocted the case to justify ousting me as co-mayor and replacing me with an appointed *kayyum*.

At the time of this writing (September 2017), I've been in Sincan Prison for eight months. Two months ago, the prosecutor filed another indictment, but the court didn't accept it due to insufficient evidence. Since then the prosecutor has been collecting evidence or, more accurately, inventing some new crime to say I committed.

Çatak officially became a district in 1923. From that year until the day I was elected—March 30, 2014—the municipality hadn't had employed a single woman as an administrator, not even as a staffer, let alone a co-mayor.

To be honest, back in 2014, when I was first nominated, I hesitated to run because I had no political party experience. Born in 1987, I was educated in Çatak and Van and graduated with a degree in child development and education. I taught kindergarten for a year. I lived with my parents and seven siblings. That's why I hesitated. Besides, it wasn't easy for a woman to run for co-mayor in a small conservative town. But our party was committed to establishing the co-mayor system and ensuring women's equal participation in local governments. Women friends encouraged me, and with their support, I agreed to run for co-mayor, and four other women became candidates for municipal councilors. Local women managed the campaign and made it forceful—they charged the atmosphere with their extraordinary energy.

We five women candidates also came up against problems in our own party. Too many party men still regarded women as menial workers. And while we women were going door to door to tell people one by one about our party program and about the importance of co-mayoring, the men candidates held neighborhood meetings. We decided to go with them.

Still, obstinate men threw clichés at us like "This is a feudal town—people here can't handle women in leadership." But I was born and raised in Çatak, and the people knew me and accepted me as I was. It wasn't the people who were feudal, it was the patriarchal mentality that wanted to obstruct women.

Our campaign was successful—I won with a whopping 68 percent of the vote. Ninety-one years after becoming a district, Çatak finally elected a woman co-mayor. And the four women friends were elected as councilors.

It really wasn't easy for us at first, as the patriarchal mentality constantly created the perception that women's work could only be frivolous. For example, the distinction between "mayor" and "co-mayor" tended to blur. Too often people perceived the man who was elected co-mayor along with me as the mayor, while I was seen as the vice mayor.

But we five elected women decided not to worry about such things—we rolled up our sleeves and got down to work. Knowing we represented the agency of all women in Çatak, we were determined to be strong. And in advance of every general meeting, we'd meet with women and create a women's agenda, then present it at the meeting.

No other women were working in the town hall, we had to recruit women personnel. Some families, when they heard we were hiring women, came to the town hall and asked, "Would you mind hiring my son instead of my daughter?" Naïvely, they thought that all a municipality did was collect garbage and take care of water and sewage issues. That was the common perception. But a municipality also had to address social problems.

At first, women wary of even setting foot in the town hall; just walking past it made them uncomfortable. But after we set up the women's directorate—it took almost a year—and got women's programs underway, women strode easily into the building to communicate their needs and articulate their wishes.

Initially the municipality's public relations office tended to sideline women. Sometimes men would go to the villages without informing us and hold meetings without inviting women. Over time this attitude changed—sort of. They started sending us women out to meet with people who they expected would be critical. Or if someone couldn't fulfill a need due to a budgetary shortfall, they'd forward the matter to me to handle.

As I write this essay, I'm realizing how hard I struggled in those days. Whenever I had a tough day, I remember, I'd go home, shut myself in my room, and have a good cry, then pull myself together and get back to work.

Here's a funny thing that happened. We announced that on March 8, International Women's Day, women would take the platform and run the town council. The men had a hard time accepting that, because in their view that platform belonged to them. When the day came, the women made their way to the platform anyway. The next day the photos in the newspapers were hilarious: they showed that as women were talking, some men were looking down at the ground, while others covered their faces with their hands. We laughed so hard!

8
"You're Going to Eat with the Men?"

Fatma Doğan

Translated by Ronay Bakan

Fatma Doğan (b. 1974) was elected co-mayor of Bozova, in Urfa province, on March 30, 2014. She was detained on December 20, 2016 and arrested on January 5, 2017. She was released on January 3, 2018.

I was born in 1974, the fourth of ten children, in Bozova, in Urfa province. My family was conservative. While I was still in my first year at high school, my family arranged my marriage. I now have four kids; one is in high school and three are at university. The heavy responsibilities I had to take on when young wore me out, but they also gave me many valuable life experiences.

My husband was a *mela*, and we were part of a conservative religious community. We had religious conversations with women once a week. Sometimes I mentioned Kurds in these conversations, like "Kurds are part of the *ummah* too, so why can't they exercise their rights? Doesn't our religion require that?" But the answers I got weren't sufficient. After a while, I stopped participating in those conversations. I worked with the Association for Human Rights and Solidarity for the Oppressed (MAZLUMDER) for a few years.

For the 2009 local elections, I regularly helped out with the campaigns at our DTP branch. Afterward I began to participate in party activities, and in 2010 BDP elected me to its provincial administration in Urfa—I served as the party's provincial vice chair. Urfa had a feudal and conservative structure, making it a formidable place to pursue our politics, especially for women. Women in every field, including politics, had to defy the patriarchal mentality, and they had to fight it within themselves too. So we had to struggle around the Kurdish question and for women's liberation simultaneously.

In 2013, after two years as the provincial vice chair, the Haliliye district congress elected me district co-chair. That year about 100 women attended a women's meeting we held in Halfeti—they told us about their difficult struggles, yet they showed remarkable self-confidence. Seeing so many women come together and speak up gave me strength and inspired me too.

My involvement in party activities caused problems with my family. They're very much assimilated into the system, and they'd always advised me not to rock the boat. One day when I was provincial vice chair, I made a condolence visit to a guerrilla's family. I was detained and arrested there. Of course, my arrest came as a shock to my uncomprehending family. "What kind of a woman goes to prison?" they wailed.

I tried to explain that I'd done nothing wrong, that I'd only been making a condolence visit. But they thought doing politics and going to prison were only for men. While I was in jail, my father phoned my husband. "It's because of you that my daughter is in jail," he accused him. "Why did you let her go to party headquarters? You should have beaten her to make her stay home." I kept assuring my family that it was my decision to attend party activities, but I couldn't calm them. Only over time did they start to respect me, but they still didn't actively support me when I ran for co-mayor.

In advance of the 2014 local elections, women friends and the election commission suggested that I run for co-mayor of Bozova. I welcomed that idea, but Bozova's social structure worried me. Most of its 57,000 people lived in villages. The district was very poor, and unemployment was high, so hundreds of families spent part of the year in Turkey's western provinces as seasonal workers. Many young people went to the western provinces to work at temporary jobs such as waitressing or construction. And others went abroad. Not only was Bozova poor, but women's problems were severe, and state policies and the tribal system had adverse effects. The responsibility that I was proposing to shoulder was huge.

For that same election, lots of party men applied to run for seats on Bozova's district council. But only one woman applied, a Kurdish-patriotic mother in her 60s. I tried to recruit more women candidates, and the women said they'd like to run, but their husbands and families wouldn't allow it. This patriarchal mindset, denying women the right to participate in politics, was common in Bozova. It was our biggest obstacle—and it was also present in our party. During my years in the party administration, I was often told, "You're a woman—stay out of it." Party women in other regions experienced similar problems, but some places were more challenging than others due to their strong patriarchal feudal structures.

I had an uncle who belonged to the Motherland Party—he'd previously served in Bozova as his party's district chair and then as the district mayor. When I was working for BDP, he used to say, "Why are you visiting Ankara and Diyarbakır? Why are you going to party congresses?" But when I announced my candidacy for co-mayor, he was the only person in my family who called to congratulate me. He even helped out with my campaign.

One day I was about to attend a dinner meeting in a village. My uncle was there and asked, "Are you going to sit and eat with us men?" Traditionally a solo woman wouldn't sit, have a meeting, or eat with men. I said yes. He said, "Then come and sit by me." I sat down next to him so as not to hurt his feelings. He was proud of me, but he also couldn't hide his feudal mindset. He found it all strange. Even though he himself was involved in politics, he had trouble accepting something new when it came from a member of his own family.

For our election campaign, the party let us open a women's office in its district building. That was important since women had no other accessible space to get involved in the campaign. During those weeks, we went out and knocked on every door in every village. That year, luckily, March 8 fell during the election season. For the first time ever in Bozova, we celebrated International Women's Day. The women were so enthusiastic, dancing *halays** in the demonstration arena and ululating. Their roars of *Jin jiyan azadî* (Women, life, freedom) reached a fever pitch of excitement. It's impossible to describe the thrill of holding that first women's event in Bozova—or the elation of so many women clamoring joyfully for freedom.

Election day was March 30, 2014. I got 12,800 votes, defeating the AKP candidate by 1,100 votes. Remarkably, Bozova people were so jubilant that they streamed into the courthouse and refused to leave. Their dream had come true—80 years of fear had been broken. In the first two or three months, visitors flooded the town hall.

Seeing that the people of Bozova had high expectations for us, we got to work zealously. We established a women's directorate

* *Halay* is a traditional folk dance commonly performed at political events in Kurdistan and Turkey.

and staffed it with twelve women, more than had ever worked in Bozova's municipal administration before. That was an important development in a district where patriarchal forces were so strong.

One of our first acts was to open the Bozova Women's Guest House. When women from the surrounding villages come to Bozova for a day to shop or see a doctor, they had no place to rest, breastfeed, or use the bathroom. To meet this urgent need, we opened the guest house.

Our women's directorate developed plans to create a women's solidarity center to offer counseling services for women. We formed a team and equipped the building. We named it the Mizgin Women's Solidarity Center* since it was "good news" for women. We intended to open it on November 25, the International Day for the Elimination of Violence Against Women.

We found out that the Mesopotamia Women's Cooperative, in Urfa city, was about to be closed, so we moved it to Bozova. The cooperative carried out important work under the leadership of about five women. Although the women didn't earn much income from the cooperative, they could socialize there, gain confidence, and experience women's solidarity.

The women's directorate also did outreach to the nearby villages. We met with village women to hear their problems and develop solutions collectively. We organized workshops for them on violence against women, women's health, and gender consciousness. Sharing experiences with them in these spaces empowered all of us.

In seven of the villages, we opened cultural centers with spaces for meetings, cultural activities, and condolence visits. These centers became the villages' common spaces, and they were open to women as well as men. We also opened that kind of center in Bozova itself. A building that belonged to the municipality was in ruin, so we restored it for public use as a cultural center, equipped with a library, classrooms, a movie theater, and a conference hall.

We created so many projects that sound easy on paper but took a lot of work to bring into existence. Our vice co-mayor, the one and only Mother Bedriye Kılıç, helped, and so did the two women on

* *Mizgin* means "good news" in Kurdish.

the Bozova district council. It was quite draining to try to persuade the men on the district council that we should hire a woman, and they judged prospective women workers by much stricter criteria than men. Despite those difficulties, we carried out important work for women, and everyone started to notice. Women became more visible in every aspect of life in Bozova.

A big problem in Bozova is that most girls aren't educated—they're married off at a young age. In the worst cases, brokers arrange the marriages—they send the girls to the western provinces to live in villages they've never seen with husbands they've never met. They're really not marriages at all—they're more like modern enslavement.

I worked hard to end this practice while I was working for the party and then as co-mayor. I investigated alleged cases. Some of the men, accused of being brokers, denied it and refused to answer questions. Rumor had it that in a single village in Bozova, more than 20 girls had been sent off to a western province through a broker. I went to that village and met a woman who had herself been married through a broker. She told me her husband had tyrannized her and forced her to perform heavy labor. He refused to let her attend the funeral of her closest relative. He forbade her to speak in her mother tongue. She later got a divorce.

A reporter from Jinha, the women's news agency, came to Bozova to investigate. She interviewed the mother of a girl who had been sent off to western Turkey—the girl came back because she couldn't take it anymore. She got divorced, but then they married her off to someone else. The daughter had a one-year-old child from her first marriage—the mother was raising her grandchild herself.

But many girls didn't want to share their experiences with the press. They couldn't freely express themselves in a patriarchal society. Meanwhile some families tried to defend the practice and said their daughters had married these men voluntarily. Since there are so many cases here—at least 200—we need a sociological study of this practice to reveal its underlying causes and its effects. And we need to look into whether it's an extension of state policies.

When we visited villages and held women's meetings, we'd warn women to be vigilant about brokers. We counseled them to claim their autonomy and make informed decisions about their lives. We always emphasized that they had free will.

All the projects we developed for women came to an abrupt halt in October 2016, when the government appointed a *kayyum* to run the Bozova municipal administration. At the stroke of a pen, all the district workers came under the authority of the district governor's office. We co-mayors were dismissed. The Mizgin Women's Solidarity Center was shut down one month before its scheduled opening.

Three months later, on December 20, 2016, I was detained in the Urfa precinct, where I'd gone to testify on another issue. I was in custody for 17 days. Often when people are in detention, their rights are grossly violated, but at that time a state of emergency was in effect, so it was worse than usual.* Women were taken in for interrogation and insulted, beaten, and tortured. In Urfa, more than 300 people were detained in one day. Some were taken to the gym because there was no more room in the precinct or security headquarters. After those 17 days, I was arrested by the court on January 5, 2017, and sent to Urfa No. 2 T-type Prison in Hilvan.

Back in 2011, I'd spent nine months in prison. Comparing my experiences then and now, I can say that prison life is much worse now, under the pretense of the state of emergency. The government claims to be repressing only opposition groups, but the 20 women in my ward come from very different parts of society, from all walks of life. They range from 50-something *dayes* [mothers] to doctors, lawyers, nurses, journalists, mayors, politicians, and students. Two co-mayors, Özlem Kutlu and Rabia Takas, have been released, leaving three co-mayors in the ward: me, Sevinç Bozan, and Sadiye Süer Baran. While the women here are constantly coming and going due to new arrests, releases, and

* The AKP government declared a state of emergency in the wake of the July 2016 coup attempt.

transfers, we try to empower each other as long as we're sharing the ward.

My first hearing took place on October 12, 2017. The next one will be on January 4, 2018.* We political prisoners know that our services, efforts, and sacrifices won't be in vain, and I call on women everywhere to continue the freedom struggle.

* Doğan was released in that hearing.

9

History Has No Love for Women Who Stop and Keep Quiet

Figen Yüksekdağ

Translated by Dilar Dirik

Figen Yüksekdağ (b. 1971) was elected as Van MP in June and November 2015. She was arrested on November 4, 2016, while she was also HDP co-chair. She received short-term prison sentences from several cases. Her main cases are still pending. She is currently in Kocaeli F-type Prison.

My story coincides with the stories of many women at similar intersections and situations. We live the same stories in different lives. We encounter the same obstacles, deal with the same problems, and walk the same paths of struggle. That creates a kind of kinship among our stories.

As I girl, I yearned for freedom—it was my main motivation to act. When I was about 14, I made my first conscious protest against curfews. I couldn't understand why anyone would want to lock a fun, active, curious, and fearless childhood inside, so defying that constraint was my earliest struggle. Next came my efforts to avoid lessons in the traditional "lady" role, which I had to endure until 17 or 18—I skipped them at every opportunity.

As with many girls, my main teacher in "womanhood" was my mother. It was she who warned me that if I studied too much, I'd go mad. It was she who swept me back into the house using a pomegranate tree branch. It was she who would have to answer to the men for all my wrongdoings. But once a woman understands the heavy fate forced on mothers, she rebels not against her mother but rather against those who would condemn her to the same role. The starting point of my political struggle, then, was my rebellion against confinement as a woman, against the crushing of my identity and personality by the male-dominated, conservative, and discriminatory life order.

At the same time, I yearned to get involved in real life, chafed to become a doer, if you will. I felt that people must fight injustice, must do something to achieve a good world, and that gradually turned into political consciousness and conscious action. When this basic sentiment comes up against an accumulation of intellectual fragments, a person inevitably searches for more. I found that "more" in socialism and the revolutionary movement. But in a family and environment like mine, where the hegemonic male and state ideology was deeply rooted and dominant, it was impossible for me to advance on a revolutionary, transformational path. Inevitably, I ruptured with them, early and severely. I made a radical break. My first days of freedom felt like a test I had to pass to enter the next chapter of my life with strength.

By the 1990s, when I entered the political struggle, the left had only partially overcome the traditional gender division of labor in its ranks—it essentially continued. Many women were fighting it fiercely. From the late 1980s, I must say, the feminist movement—although not yet under that name—had had a positive impact on the socialist movements and women.

This period saw serious new breakthroughs for the people's struggle and movements of the oppressed. In this new political atmosphere where the Kurdish freedom movement advanced, workers' strikes and movements shook the agenda, and student and youth struggles gained ground, women became part of organized resistances en masse, but made no equivalent leap with regard to gender oppression. Feminist campaigns and the collective revolutionization of Kurdish women upset dominant perceptions, but in western Turkey the left-democratic women's movement didn't complement their politics. In a way, the socialist movement reached a certain threshold, and it was at that moment that an organized, politically conscious, and systematic axis of women's liberation emerged. Around 1993–4, the Working Women's Union's Congress helped organize a united front of left-socialist women's groups. Here I too crossed a concrete threshold in women's politics and mobilization efforts.

Of course, walking the path of political struggle doesn't make for an easy life. You can try to prepare yourself for the challenges you might face, but it won't be enough to overcome them. I learned from experience that if you're going to try to walk, you have to be ready to get back up when you stumble and fall. Women's political struggle, it turns out, is as difficult to manage as living under the patriarchal traditional order and learning that hard truth is indeed part of our story. In absorbing this fact, you learn what it means to be doubly oppressed, to struggle twice as hard.

The political left where I matured didn't necessarily understand this problem. The form of male domination that we'd later call "refined" nonetheless continued to be rough and outright dominant in many ways, and by directing women's thought-world and consciousness, it covered up the fundamental contradiction and inequality that shaped our lives. Women were held back by the mentality that suggested that women's emancipation would automatically come with the emancipation of all working, laboring, and oppressed classes.

As such, many women who came up in the socialist movement, myself included, encountered concepts and practices that were painfully outdated. Compared to the backward makeup of society and the strictly male-dominated state, the space in which we moved was certainly the freest that was then available to women, but that relative freedom had limits, which left me feeling incomplete.

But in that period, I got involved in women's activities alongside my "main" and other duties. Today, if you ask me where I became complete, I'd say it was then. Not being able to march directly on the path of women's liberation with all my energy and consciousness had left a side of me unfulfilled, but then, I remade myself as a woman. I recreated myself by burning old bridges. And in doing so, I had to face the fact that I was missing something foundational: the thought and practice of women's revolution.

Getting involved in a political movement with an explicit women's agenda was critical for me. Among the landmarks of my development as a woman: I played a primary role in organizing campaigns, I worked in autonomous commissions and committees, and for a while I was the Working Women's Union (EKB) representative in Adana. The common belief at the time was that women would be empowered faster and more profoundly by working in general politics, in mixed-gender organizations, but that wasn't the case for me. In mixed arenas, women had to work two or three times as hard just to make themselves heard, let alone assert their will. Positive discrimination wasn't considered desirable. Whenever someone proposed it, others would invoke women's alleged lack of qualifications. In my case, challenging this masculine egalitarianism from the point of view of the oppressed and of women—who could achieve in life only by fighting tooth and nail—meant fighting relentlessly not only against the fascist power but also within our own parties and institutions.

Amid these difficulties, the women's liberation movement moved forward, sometimes gradually, sometimes by leaps and bounds. Since I took part in both the general political movement and the women's movement, I felt the contradictions and conflicts deeply. But that helped me grow. I've always considered my work in the women's sphere more valuable, despite the small steps and all the tension and isolation. It was valuable for me to learn that all personal development would remain incomplete and that all social progress and revolutions would lack substance until one looked at life and revolution through the prism of women's consciousness.

The late 1990s and early 2000s were critical in the development of Turkey's women's movement. During this period, feminist organizations and action units were established alongside women's platforms, and together they affirmed the historical meaning of March 8 and set the goal of getting it formally recognized as Women's Day. Together women struggled to put it on the agenda throughout society. March 8 events since then have been important venues for women's organizations to meet and share experiences, despite occasional conflicts and tensions among them.

The socialist women's front, in retrospect, could have achieved more benefits for the women's movement, but factionalism weakened us. Even as the women's liberation movement was trying to stand on its own feet, the male mentality continued to dominate the political arena to a great extent. I'd experienced the pressure of this mentality, yet I didn't regard it as urgently in need of redressing, and thus I helped allow the plague to continue in our midst for a while longer. Unfortunately, the male-dominated approach prevailed in socialist movements for a long time. These movements persisted in viewing social struggles and revolutions purely in terms of class and failed to recognize that women, the marginalized half of society, were the first slaves. In my opinion, their interpretation bent socialist theory to suit their will.

Within socialist movements, it wasn't easy for us to agree even on holding women-only rallies, to give a simple example. Every time we proposed one, a fight would break out, as some would demand that participation be mixed. "Nothing will come from rallies attended by women only," we were told. To overcome such objections within our own party ranks, we finally decided not to attend either mixed March 8 rally or the women's platform rally but rather to hold an independent women's rally with the participation of the EKB and some socialist groups. In the end, the resistance was broken, and the idea that women would hold women-only rallies and make decisions about Women's Day and women's agendas became a matter of principle.

With the campaign against sexual harassment and rape, we crossed an important threshold. Such personal attacks, particularly against political women, intensified in 2000–2001, prompting us to react. As the campaign expanded, our sense of gender identity evolved, we focused on women's liberation, and we made staggering confrontations with ourselves and with all sorts of male domination. It was a turning point in our lives, as we explored our womanhood with critical eyes, seeing our learned weaknesses but also our powerful potentials.

Years ago, when my mother finally accepted that she wouldn't be able to break my determination to engage in political struggle, she gave me a classical piece of motherly advice: "Fine, you're going to do it, but at least don't stand out in front." I replied, "Mama, I'm not standing in front at the moment, but when the ones who are in front now withdraw, then that's where I'll end up." For me the political struggle, aimed at transforming life in a revolutionary spirit, was a serious matter, and the question of whether to be in front was no dilemma at all. I told myself I'd be wherever I needed to be. That resolve may not be a deep life philosophy, but it always guided me. You don't always get to decide for yourself where to stand. Standing in front often manifests as movement work, part of our division of labor.

My own tendency to stand in front has always been directed by the movement's needs and even by necessity. Since I accept being in front as related to a purpose, I've never experienced it as a burden. But even in the absence of such demands, I'd still have done it without hesitating. Naturally I'd prefer to do what must be done without becoming the target of opponents' hatred, without bearing the brunt of friends' and comrades' unmet expectations. But well, that didn't happen. The winds of life and the movement pushed me from the forefronts of demonstrations and marches to the forefronts of the representation of a political line.

Unlike most men, women don't always calculate what position they think they might hold two years later. Not resembling men in this respect is a good thing, but women do need to consciously direct their own progress. Plunging into the jungle of men's realpolitik with a mere knife can be naïve. I know because I tried.

Having represented the Socialist Party of the Oppressed since 2004, my long journey took me to the general presidency of ESP in 2010 and to co-chair of HDP in 2014. My term as ESP general president was rocky but also saw progress, leading to revolutionary results for the party. Women's work and agenda ceased to be a sectional sphere of work and moved to the center of party politics. We established women's administrations and assemblies at every level, from the local to the center, parallel to the mixed-gender administrations. They radically transformed the party, in both structure and mentality. But some party administrators and members, unwilling to adhere to the new standards, seriously resisted the changes. The result was crises.

To overcome the male-dominated resistance, I became our new party's first chair. As we went through difficult stages, my duty was to ensure unity, carry the party forward, and despite all sorts of risks, entrench women's gains that we couldn't bear to lose. I had to spend some time in prison, but after I got out, I was elected president. In the next period, together with the socialist women's assemblies, we engaged in some tough struggles. Looking back, I can say that we succeeded, apart from some shortcomings and problems arising from us women and the level of our work. To overcome the male-dominated capitalist (and socialist) order in all its dimensions, women would need a struggle that affected all aspects of life. After all, the leap of placing women's will at the center of our party politics infused not only women's autonomous groups but also the whole party with women's mentality. It changed my life as well.

Since 2014, co-chairing HDP has doubtless been a valuable experience, as I followed the trail blazed by women before me. A whole book could be written about co-chairing, but the struggle for women's freedom, equality, and co-life undoubtedly constitutes a fundamental revolution. Of course, the Kurdish women's movement brought us to this revolutionary level, and we reached a new milestone of achievement: we formed a parliamentary Women's Group. If the path you've taken is the correct one, it'll lead you to your goal. For us, co-chairing was the correct path, and it took us forward without our needing to look back or to the left or right.

Being HDP co-chair was as unique and difficult for me as it was an honorable duty. It was an adventure, a never-ending struggle experienced "one by one and all together." Co-chairing isn't intended to mirror already existing equality but rather represents an aspiration to bring equality into existence in all forms. Only women know how hard this struggle can be. But no difficulty of co-chairing could be worse than not fighting for it.

While I was HDP co-chair, I was arrested. Four months later, the state revoked my parliamentary status, then my party membership and co-chairpersonship. In fact, the attack on my party began with the women in order to weaken our political will. It continues to this day. But the mission that the people and women have entrusted to us remains essential. So, the attempt to prevent us from fulfilling that mission and strip us of our rights is doomed to fail. We've never needed the seal of approval of the powerful. They can never control us—at most, they can control our physical location, as they do now. Instead of being outside, we're inside, that's all. Now I carry out struggle on behalf of HDP and women from prison, as do all the other women politicians here.

In June 2014 I took over as HDP co-chair from Sebahat Tuncel. On June 7, 2015, in the general elections, HDP overcame the 10 percent electoral threshold, enabling it to gain seats in parliament, while AKP suffered its first electoral setback in 13 years. AKP decided to make us pay for this political loss by targeting our party with provocations, blockades, attempted lynchings, and mass murders. It put hopes for peace "on the back burner" and threatened, "Without us, there will be chaos." Finally, it forced the November 1 re-elections, in which the AKP-Erdoğan coup planned to drag HDP below the electoral threshold. Even as their outrageous attacks and deep injustices battered our party and people, we pulled out another miracle: HDP gained 11 percent of the vote and 59 MPs, and consolidated its position as the third-largest party in parliament.

Van is one of our party's strongest constituencies. In June the people of Van elected me an MP—we won seven of its eight seats, with more than 70 percent of the vote. I ran in Van again on November 1. With great courage, Van issued a historic rebuff to the government, electing six HDP deputies with 60 percent of the vote, allowing us to preserve most of our representation there, even as the government threatened "to unleash the White Toroses on the streets."

A year later, on November 4, 2016, I was detained in Ankara. The AKP government lifted our parliamentary immunity and detained eleven politicians at once, among them co-chairs and MPs. Both the lifting of immunity and the detentions violated the Constitution. It was a coup operation against democratic politics, which began with the arrest of mayors and the appointment of *kayyums* to municipalities, and it reached a wider and more centralized level with the detention and arrest of MPs.

This political coup under the state of emergency meant that the government was moving Turkey openly and directly toward fascism, indeed to a monist dictatorship. But then, AKP had long ago dropped its pretense of being a civilian-elected administration. My own detention revealed a bitter truth: the co-chair of Turkey's third-largest party could be arrested after the door to her house was broken down.

As this latest imprisonment wasn't my first, the experience hasn't been particularly strange to me. However, this time, our people's freedom to vote and our party's right to be elected were arrested with me. This was the most important thing that I couldn't and wouldn't accept. Prisons are constructed to shatter people's will and spirit by confining their bodies. But sometimes, in the face of the greatness of one's will and spirit, that doesn't work. How will AKP suppress the will and spirit of 6 million HDP voters? Feeling the power of that, from the moment I entered jail, I ruled out the option of loneliness.

But the isolation we faced was very strict. Upon our arrival, one by one, we were placed in F-type cells, isolated and removed from one another. For a long time, we couldn't even hear each other's voices due to the distance. I was able to hear and talk to women who had been convicted in the Revolutionary People's Liberation Party-Front case—they were in nearby cells. F-type cells are spaces of severe isolation but also revolutionary solidarity, which is good to feel.

This was my first experience in an F-type cell. Every aspect of such cells, from architecture to regulations, is based on the logic of isolation and prolonged torture. Considering that political prisoners experience so much repression and torture in jail, the hardships that my elected friends and I endured are scarcely worth mentioning. But our imprisonment and every nonlegality perpetrated on us constitute an attack, beyond our individual personalities, on the inviolable democratic rights of the people.

Let me also mention some positive sides of imprisonment. If you don't bow down, you always see the sky. You realize deep in your soul that the phrase "Like a tree—alone and free" isn't just a line of poetry but life itself.* Your vocal cords develop, as you shout ever more skillfully. Your sense of hearing becomes acute. You specialize in discerning who called out to you and in listening to what they're saying. Since touchscreen smartphones are now things of your past, you learn to use smarter communication tools such as the "scream-screen," the "pencil-screen," and the "air-screen." As you throw balls (of holiday candy, pieces of cake, pepper, etc.) from one prison yard to another, you take justifiable pride in breaking the airlines' monopoly on the use of airways. In the evenings, you listen to women's voices singing fugitives' folk songs. Then you hear the songs of individual trees come together in the roaring of a whole forest.

Humor aside, the women prisoners here, myself included, are gaining new and valuable experiences. In the past we never walked very far apart anyway, but our paths have converged at this razor-sharp moment in history. I said we're a forest, but this place also becomes like the sea, as women flow into it from their own riverbeds and mix their waters. Sometimes you fit a whole forest or a sea in between four walls; and then you don't fit in those four

---

* Lines from a poem by the Turkish communist poet Nazım Hikmet:

"To live, like a tree—alone and free,
And like a forest—in solidarity"

walls any longer and burst out. This is how I describe the rich existential resistance of the women politicians whose paths have led them here and to prisons all over Turkey.

On the other hand, we're rediscovering ourselves and each other. Outside, we were women who always ran; here we're also becoming women who now speak about ourselves as a collective and as individuals.

When I first heard about this book project, I was happy that it would tell the tales of women who are constantly running and speaking out. I'm not sure how well I'll be able to account for the collective experience. But one thing I know for sure: history has no love for those who stop and keep quiet. And it definitely has no love for women who stop and keep quiet. I'm sure this project will present the plural voices of free women and the living history of women politicians, each of whom has made a mark in history.

After all, everyone in this country is likely to face prison at some point, just as they'll face death one day. So, I cannot say that I find my situation here too strange. If you view prison as a site of compulsory duty, it won't be unbearable. To me, the most valuable aspect of my imprisonment, which began on November 4, 2016, has been the chance to build close and deep relationships with women from all walks of life who have borne the heaviest burdens.

The power of women's comradeship knows no borders, walls, or obstacles. It's good enough for me to be a sentence in the story of women who cultivate freedom while in captivity and who then share that freedom lovingly and justly with others from Diyarbakır Prison to Kocaeli F-type. The ugliness of prison cannot overshadow this beauty. Finally, I salute, with heartfelt respect and love, all the women whose stories made it into this book as well as those whose stories are too big to fit in it.

10

Three Times Elected, Three Years Barred from Serving

Gülser Yıldırım

Translated by Çağrı Yoltar

Gülser Yıldırım (b. 1963) was elected MP for Mardin province in June and November 2015. She was arrested on November 4, 2016. She is currently in Kocaeli F-type Prison.

It was around 1:30 a.m. Someone was knocking on my door insistently, as if to break it down. They shouted to me to open up, they were police. "How do I know you're police?" I shouted back. Then, they brought in my neighbor to attest. That was when I opened the door. A pack of special operations police and undercover officers had surrounded my house. They hustled me outside in a rush. They didn't tell my husband and lawyer where they were taking me. They drove me to Mardin Airport. When we arrived, they picked up two other HDP MPs, Selma Irmak and Leyla Birlik, then helicoptered the three of us to Diyarbakır.

As we stepped off the helicopter, they separated us. They took me to police headquarters and put me in a cell. To my astonishment, I heard the voice of our party co-chair Selahattin Demirtaş: "Dear MP Gülser!" he called to me. "So they've brought you here too?" That was when I realized my arrest was part of a larger political operation. Co-chair Figen Yüksekdağ and four other HDP MPs—Ziya Pir, Nursel Aydoğan, İmam Taşçıer, and Sırrı Süreyya Önder—were also in custody.

Early the next morning, they took us to the courthouse separately and kept us waiting until the evening, when the processing was finally completed. We refused to give statements on the grounds that this was a political operation. They issued our arrest warrants through separate courts. At midnight they flew me, Nursel, Leyla, and Kurdish activist Ferhat Encü out of Diyarbakır on a noncommercial jet. The plane landed at an unknown airport. They put Ferhat and me in one vehicle, and Nursel and Leyla in another. Our second journey of the night began, the journey to prison.

They took me to Kocaeli No. 1 F-type Prison and, long after midnight, put me in cell A4-11. I was now alone with the cold isolation of an F-type prison, which I was encountering for the first time. At 8 a.m., after a grueling night, they opened the door to the prison yard. As I darted into the yard, shouts of "Welcome *heval!*" resounded around me. And that was how, on my first day, my first and last sense of loneliness disappeared.

Co-mayor Gültan Kışanak, who had been locked up in this dismal place a week earlier, took charge of welcoming us. The iron gates and the tall, barbed-wire-topped walls no longer had the power to intimidate. Women who had been convicted for membership in the Revolutionary People's Liberation Party-Front even made us a welcome cake. Such solidarity and camaraderie, along with the human values we believe in and our deep commitment to our people, make even prison life bearable.

Like they'd done with other friends, the prison authorities kept me in solitary confinement for three months. And they recorded my lawyer visits with a video camera.

I was born in 1963 in the village of Çalê (Çalı Kuyular) in Nusaybin, in Mardin province. I grew up in a hamlet of that village. The hamlet had 13 or 14 houses, amid green orchards and beautiful springs, and was surrounded by mountains and an oak forest.

As the eldest child, I'd help my father with chores in the orchards and my mother with the housework. When my brother was born, guns were fired to celebrate the good news. My father was a democratic man for his time—he didn't make me or my sister feel inferior because of our gender. But our family's general outlook overlapped with the traditional culture that considered boys more valuable.

After a normal day of arduous work, the nighttime would be ours. In the evenings of what we called *şevbihêrk*,* we'd play games together. My favorite was the contentious chess game *kışıle* (barracks). *Listika guslikê-hingulîsk* (a ring game) was also popular. To accompany our games, we'd read the Kurdish poet Cigerxwîn's poems. My enjoyment of my mother tongue dates from those days, as well as my commitment to preserving it.

Every so often mounted soldiers would raid our house and bellow at my mother, "Where is Zübeyir?" meaning my father. He'd be hiding somewhere, so they'd tear our place apart looking for him. Once we heard a rumor that if they couldn't find him, they'd take my mother away. So, the next time, she went to Nusaybin and stayed with my grandmother for a week. The point is, I was just a child when I first witnessed my father being a fugitive because of his Kurdishness. We longed to be together and would meet with him in secret. Once he actually was arrested, but after being impris-

* A Kurdish word that refers to nighttime gatherings that are sometimes accompanied with music.

oned for a while, he was released in a general amnesty. I spent my childhood in that atmosphere.

After the crackdown that began with the 1980 military coup, arrests and torture became part of life. In 1984, I married my uncle's son, and we moved to Adana province, where my husband entered the university. We lived in a students' house with his two brothers, one brother's wife, and a couple of other close relatives who were preparing for the university entrance exam. These young men had the duty to study and prepare, while my brother-in-law's wife and I had the duty to serve them.

Two years later, when I visited Çalê during the summer break, I found my whole family under political strain. My uncle had an arrest warrant out for him, so the authorities pressured the family to surrender him. And in 1986 my father was taken into custody, heavily tortured, and died a week later. I left the village carrying the weight of this pain. I visited Çalê again in 1988, with my 20-day-old baby, and this time the soldiers arrived to take me into custody. The moment they showed up was the last straw for my mother—she suddenly looked crazed. They put me in the car, and then she handed me the swaddled baby through the window, along with the rebellion in her heart. Then she put my grandmother in the car too. If she could, she'd have put the whole village in the car with me because she knew from my father's fate what it meant "to be taken." I'll never forget her rebellion that day.

The soldiers were stunned. At the Mardin police station, they pried my baby from my arms, blindfolded me, and led me down to a basement, where they interrogated me. I could hear my baby crying in the next room. The news of me being detained with my baby went public, and the authorities released me the next day.

After my husband graduated from university, which took almost ten years, we returned to Mardin to live. One day we made another visit to my beloved Çalê. We had many memories of good times in the village, as well as hard days, but now those memories no longer had a location. Çalê, like 4,000 other Kurdish villages, had been forcibly evacuated and destroyed.

Since my past was integral to my identity, I had to do something. In 1999 I got involved with HADEP's grassroots activities. Several other women and I established the party's women's branches in Mardin. We created many great programs with enthusiasm and devotion. We worked to raise women's consciousness and solidarity, starting with our own. The women's branches sparked a conflict over gender within the party, and it deepened with the further growth of women's organizing. Sometimes I held leadership roles in the party, and my priority was always women's activities. I tried to extend the work we'd done in the provincial women's branches to the district branches. Other party women welcomed this work eagerly. We reached a point where we had an opinion on every social issue.

I'd begun my political journey primarily because of my Kurdish identity, but the women's liberation struggle gave me the political consciousness to see life and history from a gender perspective. When we start viewing our social environment from this perspective, social roles that once seemed normal are revealed to be wrong and groundless. And we grow ever more determined to fight this manufactured patriarchal mentality and the problems it causes.

As our gender consciousness heightened, we party women built up a firm opposition to all kinds of oppression, to violence, harassment, rape, and femicide, considering them crimes against all women, and we set out to organize on that basis. We held autonomous women's meetings in the neighborhoods and organized events that attracted thousands of women.

One thing that bothered me from the women's perspective was the phrase *Filan jin wekî mêra ye*, or "That woman is like a man." It's intended to be a compliment, as if a woman has to be a "man" to be praiseworthy. Although I objected to it many times, I was still subjected to it. Party men would sometimes call me *birê min*, "my brother," to express their admiration for my efforts. They thought they were showing respect by masculinizing me. I replied that I considered it an insult and didn't accept it. When they saw a woman who did good work, took the right positions, intellectualized, and had a rebellious spirit, they'd communicate their admiration by disassociating her from her gender. When they did it to me, I'd say to my men friends, "Imagine that I called you *xwishka min* (my sister). Believe me, whatever that would mean to you, *birê min* means the same to us women." Once I explained it this way, they stopped.

The party's decision to adopt the women's quota met with a lot of pushback in the local. Some men friends would say, "If a woman is fit to do the job, we don't object to her, but why are you imposing a quota on us and forcing us to nominate someone just *because* she's a woman?" To be honest, I didn't know how to respond convincingly until in 2002 I attended a conference in Diyarbakır where women talked about the challenges they faced in their localities. There the women's quota came up, and we analyzed in detail the reasoning underlying it. By the time I returned to Mardin, I had a powerful answer ready: "We don't raise boys and girls under equal conditions. We don't offer them the same opportunities in our society. We tie women's feet together, but we leave the men's free, and then we tell them both to run. Who do you think will win the race under those conditions?" These few sentences were enough to make men friends drop their objections to the quota: "Okay, *heval* Gülser, we're convinced!"

We struggled with many such challenges. No change occurred spontaneously—every one of them was hard won. Overcoming social prejudices took tremendous effort, firmness, and courage. We led by working twice as hard as men.

In my city, Nusaybin, the women's quota wasn't implemented for a long time due to some resistance. Then in 2009 Ayşe Gökkan was elected mayor with 80 percent of the vote.

Besides fulfilling our regular duties, we women went all out for election campaigns. We'd troop from house to house explaining the party's general policies and the women's positions. Women active in the party had a hard time doing it all, what with housework and childcare responsibilities at home—the grassroots work alone required a great deal of time. My family showed respect for my party work, although that was the extent of their support.

As if all that weren't enough, the state constantly harassed us. Every press conference we held, every protest we organized resulted in an investigation. I was continually summoned to the prosecutor's office to give a statement. I was detained several times. In 2006 I spent four and a half months in prison, as officials followed orders blindly: "Whether it's a woman or a child, what needs to be done will be done."* After I got out of prison, I went right back to my party work.

At the time when the anti-KCK operation began, I was the district vice chair of DTP's Artuklu branch in Mardin. One night in February 2010, police raided our homes and detained about 30 of us, including the party's provincial and district chairs. They arrested almost all of us and threw us into prison. They packed 75 people into the women's ward at Mardin Prison, then added even more people as they arrested more. There was only one toilet and one sink, which we had to wait in line all day to use. Two or three people had to share each bed.

For the 2011 general elections, I was one of the MP candidates to be nominated from prison. Imprisoned candidates had to be represented by someone on the outside. Our Nusaybin mayor, Ayşe Gökkan, organized a strong campaign on my behalf. I was elected an MP by winning over 54,000 votes—but I never saw the inside of the parliament. I remained in prison until 2014.

Time and again we submitted petitions to the authorities protesting our horrendous prison conditions. Finally, they heard us—one day after the 2011 elections, a delegation from the parliamentary Human Rights Commission visited. We were ready to tell them about our problems and demand solutions. Since our ward was too small to squeeze them all in, we lined up chairs in the prison yard to seat them. Including the delegation members, we were about 100 people.

We opened the meeting and got right to the subject at hand. One prisoner said, "There are so many of us here, but we have no social activities." The commission's chair, an AKP man, responded condescendingly, waving his hand around the prison yard, "Is there any better social activity than this?" We tried to explain our problems, but this man hardly let us speak. He kept talking over us, opening his mouth at every opportunity to spout government propaganda. Finally I said, "Look, we hear you on television every day.

* Then-prime minister Erdoğan's response to the Diyarbakır uprising of 2006.

I was elected an MP, but to this day no one has ever heard my voice. So just stop now and let us talk, and you listen to us for a change."

That did it. I explained our problems and spelled out my critiques of the government.

After the delegation left, Mother Cemile, who was 76 years old, came over to me. "Now I can die without regret," she said. "I can only imagine how you'd articulate our issues if you got out of here and went to the parliament. I welcome the day you're free to defend the rights of our people." She leaned over and kissed my forehead.

That day proved once again that the best way to debunk social misconceptions—such as "Women can't do politics," "It's not her job," "Why are women doing politics, are there no men left?"—is through action. Women can eradicate the prejudices created and perpetuated by male domination through great effort and intense commitment, that is, through organized struggle. Sometimes I wonder what would have happened if there had been no women's liberation movement, if women hadn't risen up against patriarchy and labored to reclaim and elevate moral and political values, if society hadn't had the benefit of our work. Would families, of their own accord, have encouraged their daughters to become MPs? Likely not—in the traditional worldview, politics and leadership weren't women's spheres, and speaking up about social problems and expressing their will weren't things women did. Fortunately, Kurdish women are by now long-standing fighters for that change.

Two and a half years after I was elected MP, I was released, along with our party's four other imprisoned MPs, based on the Constitutional Court's Balbay decision.* Our campaigns for the March 2014 local elections were just getting started, and I quickly fell in step. Then in August came the presidential election. Thanks to a jam-packed schedule and breakneck work pace, we did well in both elections. Meanwhile in the summer of 2014, ISIS attacked

* Mustafa Balbay, an MP from CHP, was arrested during the Ergenekon trial. In 2013 the Constitutional Court freed him on the grounds that since he was an elected parliamentarian, his conviction was illegal, as it violated his rights to freedom and representation of the people.

Sinjar and Kobanê, and the women they murdered, abducted, or sold in slave markets became the great pain suffered by all women and the icons of our struggle.

It was in that atmosphere that the June 7, 2015 elections appeared on the horizon. We decided that HDP would enter the elections as a party. We won five of the six MP seats for Mardin, including me and another woman. HDP also achieved a great success throughout Turkey. But AKP rejected the people's will and held a re-election on November 1. In that contest too, HDP surpassed the electoral threshold to become the third-largest party in parliament. Once again, I was elected an MP—for the third time in a row! But even after three years, I had yet to serve. I'd spent two and a half years of my first MP term in prison. When I was elected for the third time, I was arrested again a year later. The will of the people, especially women, was scorned.

Before I close, I'd like to briefly share the work I accomplished in the week before my arrest. I was scheduled to participate in women's activities in Muş and Iğdır provinces. In Muş, our MP Burcu Çelik Özkan and I spent two days holding women's meetings in the neighborhoods. Then I went to Iğdır and for another five days visited villages and met with women, which gave me great memories. I made many home visits, where women let me sample the delicious breads they baked in sunken tandoori ovens. As I write, memories of my days there are flashing before my eyes. The deep friendship of those beautiful people who hosted us in their homes is unforgettable.

On my first evening in Iğdır, I saw on television that Gültan Kışanak, co-mayor of Diyarbakır Metropolitan Municipality, had been taken into custody. I sprang into action and issued press releases condemning this overturning of the will of the people of Diyarbakır. A few days later, back in Mardin, I too got detained, then arrested. Three parliamentary investigation reports were prepared about those press releases I'd written.

My experiences as a woman have shown me that the struggle for women's liberation can never be confined within four walls. We're physically imprisoned now, but millions of women are walking the path of freedom and knowing that I've made some contribution to that renders these walls and iron bars meaningless.

11

Being a Woman Is Hard, Even Dangerous

Gültan Kışanak

Translated by Ulrike Flader

Gültan Kışanak (b. 1961) was serving as co-mayor of Diyarbakır Metropolitan Municipality when she was detained and arrested on October 25, 2016. In February 2019 she was sentenced and is currently in Kocaeli F-type Prison.

A parliamentary commission of inquiry had been established to investigate the attempted coup of June 15, 2016, and I was to testify at a hearing. On October 25 I traveled to Ankara and told the commission how in 2013–15, when I was an MP for Diyarbakır and HDP co-chair, we'd tried to find a peaceful solution to the Kurdish question but had been obstructed. To understand the mentality that led to the coup attempt, I said, the commission needed to investigate the ways the government had sabotaged that peace process.

After the hearing, my friends in the HDP parliamentary group joked, half-seriously, "After that talk, they'll definitely come after you. You might want to stay here tonight. Don't bother going home."

"I know they're going to arrest me," I said. "That's why I wanted to come and pour out my heart to parliament one last time. But now I've got to get home. I've just come back from a trip abroad, and I've got so much work to do."

I finished my tea and hurried to catch the late flight home. As soon as I stepped off the plane in Diyarbakır, I was detained and taken to police headquarters. At around the same time, police also detained my fellow co-mayor Fırat Anlı and raided both our houses and the city hall.

All the HDP and DBP's provincial and district co-chairs in Diyarbakır were in custody. The party administrators had been detained 15 days before us. The police had planned to arrest us at that time too but had to wait because I was abroad. One police officer, assigned specifically to carry out the unlawful action, boasted, "We rounded all the others up first so they wouldn't cause any trouble when we brought you in." After the party administrators were detained, they were neither questioned nor brought before the prosecutor. They were released as soon as we were arrested.

That night in custody, I was held in a cell directly opposite the restroom. About 50 people, mostly men, were under arrest at the time and were taken to the restroom one by one. In other words, the toilet and sink were used continuously for 24 hours. I hardly slept a wink.

Five days later, Fırat Anlı, Ayla Akat Ata, and I were brought to the courthouse to see the prosecutor. The courthouse was empty—only the police, a few court workers, the lawyers, and us were there—but they made us wait in separate hallways and kept us there for a long time. Our lawyers had had to walk there because all the roads were closed to traffic.

The court finished its proceedings and adjourned to decide on the verdict. The headline "Kışanak arrested" was being broadcast over all the television channels. Around 1 a.m., we boarded a plane for transport to Kocaeli. I don't know where it landed, but we drove for a while and arrived in Kocaeli Prison in the morning. They took Fırat to F-type Prison No. 2, and Ayla and me to No. 1. Ayla and I were put in separate cells.

What I'm calling a cell was actually a small, empty room consisting of a toilet and a kitchen sink on the lower floor and three iron bunk beds upstairs. This was Ayla's and my first taste of an F-type prison. Until recently, women hadn't even been held in F-type prisons.

The room was filthy and covered in grime. There were no cleaning supplies, but then, I wouldn't have had the strength that night anyway. I hadn't slept in days. They gave me a mattress and a sheet. While I was in custody in Diyarbakır, my family had brought me blankets, and knowing that I'd be arrested, I'd carried one of them with me, thinking, *Prison will be even worse.* Now I pulled it over myself and fell asleep immediately.

After a while, I awoke to women's voices calling my name. "Welcome!" they shouted. "We know you're tired, but the hot water will be on soon, if you want to take a shower!" They were the prisoners in the next cell. They tossed some shampoo and soap over the wall.

I was so grateful. I shouted thanks to them and dashed to the bathroom, because the hot water would be on for only an hour. This was how my three months of solitary confinement began.

It took me some time to get used to the senseless restrictions and absurd formalities of an F-type prison. Five days after I arrived, they brought in some newly arrested women MPs, then Dersim co-mayor Nurhayat Altun and former Dersim mayor Edibe Şahin and put them in cells near mine. They took precautions to ensure that we couldn't see each other while coming and going to our meetings with our lawyers.

It was our bad luck that Kocaeli was experiencing its coldest winter ever. For two months, the snow stayed on the ground. The building was old and damp, made of iron and concrete. The doors and windows didn't close properly, and there wasn't much material inside to absorb the heat. In short, our first big complaint was the cold.

In February the cold ended, and so did our isolation. I joined a cell with two others, Nurhayat and Edibe. Spring hadn't yet come, but just being among friends and conversing with them was enough to warm us.

I grew up in Elâzığ without any awareness of discrimination against women, although my family was conventional. Men worked outside, while women did the housework and took care of children, the elderly, and the sick. They didn't dream of any other arrangement. The women weren't subjected to overt violence, but they submitted to lives confined to the household. Politically my family was democratic, leftist, and socialist, as was our whole neighborhood. In such an environment, no one questioned the way women's lives were constrained.

I attended university in Diyarbakır, and in 1980, while I was a sophomore at the School of Education, I was arrested. I spent two years (1980–82) in Diyarbakır Prison No. 5, where we experienced all the pain, resistance, and solidarity of those most horrific times. We were 60 or 70 people in a ward, including Duriye Kaya and Emine Hacıyusufoğlu, municipal councilors from Hilvan. At that time, I didn't really understand what a municipal councilor was. To us, these two older women were mothers: Mother Duriye and Mother Emine.

The rest of us women were younger, between 16 and 25. We tried to protect the mothers from beatings and torture, but it was hardly possible. The soldiers* even singled them out for insult and tortured them because they knew it would hurt us especially.

* Diyarbakır Prison in 1980–82 was militarized, so instead of guards, it employed soldiers.

At one point, the soldiers tried to cut our hair by force, saying, "This is a military prison. You have to obey military rules. Soldiers' hair is cut every week." But our refusal of haircuts became just another pretext for them to beat us. For the first three or four weeks of this torture, the soldiers didn't touch the mothers' hair. But they fought to keep the soldier's hands off of us, and sometimes they got beaten even more harshly than we were. One day the block warden ordered the mothers' hair to be cut, too. All hell broke loose. For days, we huddled around the mothers, even when the soldiers beat us.

Finally the soldiers said, "Okay, we won't cut your hair. But as soldiers, while we say our prayers at dinner, we remove our caps, so you have to uncover your heads, too." Mother Duriye and Mother Emine both wore headscarves. Mother Duriye started beating herself and lamenting in Kurdish, which created an uproar. The ward's resistance to this removal of headscarves continued for days, until finally the torturers gave up.

Whole books have been written about Diyarbakır Prison, but none by women. Over the years, I've been asked repeatedly why I don't write about it. Maybe it's an issue of womanhood—it's not so easy for women to talk and write about the hardships they've been through. But all women have the right to know that despite the atrocities of Diyarbakır Prison, not one single person from the women's ward confessed to anything. It's not because women were so heroic or were tortured less: rather, it was because of the solidarity among us and its therapeutic effect. Sakine Cansız played a decisive role in establishing that solidarity. And the women in our ward were all so close-knit that the soldiers couldn't get to us. In the 1980s we weren't thinking about our prison experience from a women's perspective but rather tried to explain it in terms of fascism and colonialism. Yet even as we assessed it theoretically, we were in fact affirming our identity, body, and dignity as women.

I first became aware of women's issues at Elâzığ Closed Prison, where I was transferred after Diyarbakır Prison. I was the only political prisoner there, and I was quite nervous at first, and the others kept their distance. Almost every day fights would break out over some petty issue—pans and pots would fly through the air, along with insults and threats. It took me a few months, but amid all that turmoil, I finally found a way to connect with some of the women, and the ward calmed down somewhat. Other prisoners later admitted they'd staged some of the fights just to scare me.

I met a mother from Malatya who had confessed to a murder so that her son wouldn't go to prison. She'd wash clothes from the men's ward to earn pocket money.

I met Sebahat from Bitlis, whose life had been wrecked by her husband. Police found marijuana in their house, and her husband sent her a message, saying, "They don't punish women. Say the drugs are yours." Sebahat, a 17-year-old who didn't speak Turkish, believed him and told police, "The marijuana is mine." She was arrested and sentenced to years in prison. Her husband, scot free, married another woman two years later.

I met Nermin from Tokat, whose father abducted a married woman, and the woman's relatives raped Nermin in revenge. What followed was a tragedy, too painful to recount.

Listening to these stories, I realized how hard, even dangerous it is to be a woman. Their tragedies introduced me to women's issues in a profound way.

After my release, I enrolled at Ege University in İzmir to study communication, intending to become a journalist. When I was in Diyarbakır Prison, no one had cared to hear our voices. I resolved to be a journalist and report the truth. In my third year I did an internship at the newspaper *Güneş* (*The Sun*). One day the paper sent me to cover an event at Konak Square, where women were being offered free makeup and skin care sessions. Women lined up to have their makeup done. I took a photo of the women waiting in line, focusing my lens on the woman having her makeup done. I wrote the story and handed it in. It was published on the front page, "thanks to the photo of a beautiful woman," our department chief pointed out proudly, holding it up as an example to the others.

In general, media coverage of women was abysmal. When I compared the stories of the women in Elâzığ Prison that I'd heard with what was published on the third page of newspapers,* I saw

* Stories about violence, particularly violence against women, are commonly published on the third pages of Turkish newspapers.

how biased "objective" journalism was, how it supported male domination—even in news stories reporting on murders of women.

I finished my degree in 1990 and moved to Istanbul, where I worked for the weekly newspaper *Yeni* Ülke (*New Land*). In 1992 I helped found Özgür *Gündem* (*Free Agenda*), which began publication with the slogan, "The truth must come to light." The staff in Istanbul were quite experienced. I was assigned to be the correspondent in Adana. All the newspapers had representatives in Adana, but I was the only woman. Sometimes we'd meet up at the Çukurova Journalists Association, which felt like a men-only space. I had self-confidence, but I still wasn't comfortable. If I had something to say about our problems, I'd say it and then leave—and they were happy about that.

A year later I returned to Istanbul. At *Özgür Gündem,* women held administrative positions. The editor-in-chief was Gurbetelli Ersöz, I was the editorial director, and Yurdusev Özsökmenler headed the news desk. Our goal was to increase the number of women working at the newspaper, assign women to cover important stories, and provide support to women reporters. These efforts became the cornerstone of women's journalism in the tradition of a free press.

In the 1990s, the newspaper received many photographs of people who had been violently brutalized. Some of them were sent to us so we'd investigate and expose the atrocities. Others were sent by the perpetrators themselves to instill fear in us and even to threaten us. Among them were photos of sexual violence and of women who had been tortured. We published some photos of brutalized men, but we never even thought of publishing photos of brutalized women.

I think the newspaper printed only a small fraction of the images of sexual tortures that prisoners experienced in detention. Instead we reported on the legal actions taken against sexual harassment and rape tortures in custody, as documented by İHD and by some women lawyers. Generally, women didn't want to speak to the public, so we took care to protect the victims and not expose them. However, now that I think about it, the traditional perception of "honor" may also have played a role in our response. In 1994 the newspaper office was bombed, and all those photos along with the entire archive were destroyed.

Until 2002, I worked at newspapers that followed in the tradition of a free press. During that time, I also participated in women's activities whenever I had the chance. After 2000, I got more involved in them. I read more books to increase my understanding of feminism and the global women's movement. I attended talks and discussions at Amargi* and participated in discussions there. DEHAP's women's branches organized ideological discussions with the autonomous women's institutions that were founded at that time. I made every effort to be part of those too.

In 2004, several women in our party were elected as mayors, and women mobilized to support the model projects that they initiated. I went to Diyarbakır and contributed to the work of its Bağlar district administration. Bağlar mayor Yurdusev Özsökmenler was my old friend who knew a lot about women's issues. Bağlar had previously been governed by one of our parties, but they'd undertaken hardly any programs for women. Our task was to break the old understanding of municipal responsibilities and restructure the administration so it could enact new policies. It wouldn't be easy, as the administrative structure, personnel, budget, priorities, and preferences were all shaped by the patriarchal mentality.

First, we established a team that, under the leadership of Mayor Yurdusev, carried out women's programs with passion and zeal. Rojda Balkaş, a municipal councilor, was appointed vice mayor. Çağlar Demirel took charge of establishing Kardelen Women's House, which provided counseling and legal services. We created the Bağlar Women's Cooperative to encourage women's entrepreneurship. Between our neighborhood meetings, gender awareness trainings, cultural events, vocational courses, and health screenings, we managed to reach 10,000 women in just one year. At the end of that year, we held a women's festival, where smiling women packed the hall.

None of it was easy, of course. Our greatest difficulty was getting funding, since the prevailing mentality of the municipal staff was that money spent on women was "wasted." In their view, a munici-

---

* Amargi Women's Academy was a feminist collective founded in Istanbul in 2001. Until 2015, it published a trimonthly journal on feminist theory and politics.

pality's tasks were to collect garbage, build and maintain roads and parks, and ... that was it. That distorted outlook ignored the municipality's responsibilities to the people, especially to women and disadvantaged groups. We had to find outside funding for some of our activities, while others were financed by the municipal budget.

As preparations for the 2007 general elections began, I became a candidate for MP from Diyarbakır, at the suggestion of party women friends. The campaign was truly invigorating, and the women friends standing by my side gave me strength. I articulated our positions in women's campaign offices and at women's meetings. In every neighborhood or village, women welcomed us and were just as elated as I was. For the first time in 13 years, the Kurdish people's dream of once again sending MPs to parliament seemed within reach. Women, for their part, were thrilled to meet with women candidates. While I was visiting a village in the district of Lice and talking to some women, I asked one little girl, "What do you want to be when you grow up?" She answered, "I want to be a woman MP candidate from the Thousand Hopes Alliance." This was so encouraging! Girls were now growing up with dreams of entering politics themselves, not just voting for men.

The hard work of the campaign staff, especially the women, bore fruit. Our candidates won 22 parliamentary seats, eight of them held by women. Our DTP had the highest rate of women MPs among all the parties. After the election, we formed a parliamentary Women's Group.

During our first days in parliament, the hot topic in the media was our clothing. According to parliamentary bylaws, women had to wear a "dark skirt suit." So we all showed up in the proper skirts, giving rise to some news reports that implied, *Oh, so they actually know how to dress up,* with the undertone that women didn't deserve to be in parliament. I hadn't worn a skirt in years, and on the first day I hobbled into the parliament taking tiny steps like a penguin. The memory still makes me laugh. After some struggle, this bylaw was changed, and the skirt requirement ceased to be a problem.

Based on the number of our MPs, our party had the right to two group vice chairs. Our party bylaws specified that one of them had to be a woman. We elected Van MP Fatma Kurtulan as our group vice chair. If I'm not mistaken, Fatma was the first woman group vice chair in the history of the Turkish parliament.

Women also took active roles in the parliament's standing committees. I was elected to the planning and budget committee. At its first meeting, I realized that I was the only woman among its 25 members. Regardless of what topic we were discussing, I'd always try to explain its impact on women, and on their needs, in addition to giving my general assessment. At first, the men found this annoying. They'd sneer, "At every turn, you insist on adding women." I'd point out that it wasn't a question of "adding women" but rather of taking women into consideration at all.

Being the only woman on that committee exposed me to the familiar torments of male domination. At various times, men tried to silence me, or they relegated me to talking last, or they warned me to "wrap it up now," or they just didn't listen when I spoke. But I always carried on, thinking, *I'm here on behalf of women, so I have to speak out.* Even in committee meetings that lasted all night, I stayed until the end as the only woman to voice our concerns.

We women MPs were determined to make effective use of the parliamentary rostrum. We'd give speeches on every subject, from foreign policy to economy, from energy and environmental policies to human rights. The men weren't accustomed to this either. The patriarchal mindset limits even what a woman MP can do and say by telling women they "don't understand." But we pushed back and spoke up on every issue, especially the ones that were supposedly beyond our mental grasp.

One of our primary demands was for the establishment of a gender equality committee in parliament. We finally persuaded the ruling party to form this committee. Women MPs from all the parties came together and agreed on the name: Committee for Equality Between Men and Women. However, while the draft law was being debated, AKP's men MPs moved to change the name to the Committee on Equal Opportunity for Women and Men.

We objected. As DTP group vice chair, I went to Minister Nimet Çubukçu and asked, "You previously agreed to 'equality.' Why is it changed?" A man MP sitting next to her interjected, "What do these women want anyway?" Then AKP MP Burhan Kuzu, head of the constitutional committee, taunted, "They're saying that up to now, they've given birth to children, and now it's time for men to do it. How else will we be equal?" Apparently, he was joking, but it wasn't funny. In fact, it all drove us to the brink of giving up. This patriarchal mentality that assumes that men have the right to dominate women also willingly submits to the hierarchy of domination: the instruction to change the name to "equal opportunity" had come from the top, since equality was allegedly "against nature."

In 2011, in anticipation of the forthcoming general elections, DTP's Central Election Commission conducted a study of local political dynamics, province by province, and also met with people and took suggestions. In Siirt, the commission decided the party would run only one candidate, but it was difficult to apply the women's quota in a place with a single candidate. We received a report from Siirt stating, "If the women's quota is to be implemented, we want our party's co-chair to be the candidate." So, I became the MP candidate for Siirt. During the campaign, I visited the town center and the districts as well as all the villages, one by one, meeting people everywhere. The people's political consciousness was very strong. For about a week, an AKP MP also campaigned in Siirt, spewing ugly propaganda against me: "She's both a woman and an Alevi, so it's a sin to vote for her." Fortunately, the public ignored him.

We lacked resources and faced other obstacles, but our biggest problem was that we were participating as independent candidates. Citizens who were illiterate had a hard time finding the name of an independent candidate on the ballot. *Koçers* [nomads] had moved up into the highlands and couldn't easily come and vote. Still, the election results were outstanding. The city that had given us 24,000 votes in the 2007 elections gave us more than 54,000 this time around.

Clearly Siirt had undergone a social transformation. No Alevis lived there except those who came as civil servants, but in 2011 the people not only elected an Alevi woman as MP but did so with a record number of votes. This success belonged to the women's movement and our party workers, who had carried out the campaign with extraordinary diligence and personal sacrifice.

Here I'd like to point out something we noticed and that women need to watch out for. When a woman attains a politically important position, society starts to see her as genderless. The restrictions traditionally imposed on women no longer apply to her. She can meet with all the men notables of a village, and they'll listen to her very carefully, but they still won't listen to the women in their own households. She can sit at the table with men, and they might even give her the seat at the head of the table, but they still won't let other women do that. She may choose not to wear a headscarf, but if a man's daughter-in law wants to take hers off, he'll disapprove it. And so on. All the political women friends who have held positions, especially as MPs and mayors, have experienced this paradox. In a sense, these men are prepared to acknowledge the position of a woman official but not her identity as a woman. It's important for all political women to understand this point, because if they don't, then they might well become elitist. They can fall prey to the misconception that *I'm alone in this position because I'm uniquely successful* instead of *I'm alone because other women have been hindered.* If women fall into this trap, the next step will be that they become politicians "like men."

DTP had set out in 2005 to advance democratic politics and achieve major gains for women. But in 2009 the state attempted to incapacitate the party through a series of detentions and arrests, and in December it shut it down altogether. In February 2010, a congress founded BDP, which took over the party tradition and elected Selahattin Demirtaş and me as co-chairs.

For many years before me, women friends have struggled, grinding down the roughest aspects of the patriarchal mentality, and achieving critical advances for women. Their achievements have been my anchorage. I always felt this great support while I was carrying out the difficult duties of a co-chair.

Within the party, women significantly pushed back the patriarchal mentality, but in politics you're in constant contact with institutions and organizations that it has shaped. And that reality was frequently reflected in the party. The media persisted in referring to me as the "vice chair," while the government refused to recognize me as a co-chair, citing as its excuse the fact that co-chairing was not legally recognized.

Our practice of co-chairing attracted particular interest abroad. A delegation from Sweden came to Diyarbakır, and we, the two co-chairs, welcomed them together. After I made a short speech on political developments in Turkey and our party's policies, I gave the floor to cochair Selahattin, who delivered a somewhat lengthy assessment. Afterward a woman in the visiting delegation said, "You say you have a co-chair system, so why didn't you share the speaking time equally?" Women's rights to speak and to have equal representation are important, so her remark had merit. But we couldn't have developed a model of shared governance simply by "sharing" everything. The important thing was to achieve transformation toward a democratic mindset and to organize women well enough to safeguard the principle of gender equality. Only on that basis could co-chairing serve its purpose. I served as co-chair until March 2014, when I was elected co-mayor of the Diyarbakır Metropolitan Municipality.

For the March 2014 local elections, BDP decided to run woman candidates in the three metropolitan cities of Diyarbakır, Van, and Mardin. The decision wasn't much disputed—the party bylaws required it. It might not be obvious from the outside but having the women's quota in place significantly strengthens women's hand. When we can say, "The party bylaws require it," no one can openly object. By 2014, no one in the party overtly challenged the women's quota. Everyone knew that the women wouldn't give it up. Still, sometimes men tried to block women candidates, even indirectly by raising such classic challenges as "Do we have a suitable candidate? Governing a metropolitan city is difficult—can a woman really manage it?"

Later, when the party committed itself to co-mayoring, it put an end to grumbling about the women's quota. Within the party, districts that had already applied the women's quota welcomed the co-mayoring system, while other places raised objections like "Where did this idea come from? Is it really necessary? It'll just cause confusion." These challenges were usually raised by individuals who were preparing to be candidates. The party administration, especially the women's movement, decisively put an end to them.

When the party announced my candidacy as co-mayor for Diyarbakır, men with a patriarchal mindset didn't target me explicitly as a woman. But certain people did complain that I wasn't originally from

Diyarbakır, and that I am Alevi. These were in fact excuses of male domination.

Our supporters, especially women in the party, ran a vibrant campaign. We won the election by a large margin, and Fırat Anlı and I were elected co-mayors of the Diyarbakır Metropolitan Municipality. It was a historic vindication: a woman who had survived Diyarbakır Prison No. 5 in the 1980s, in the wake of the fascist coup, was elected co-mayor 34 years later. It was a remarkable achievement both for democratic politics and for the women's liberation struggle.

Diyarbakır is considered to be the center of Kurdish politics. Electing as its co-mayor someone not privileged by a hegemonic identity—male or Sunni—and not supported by an economic or tribal power, revealed that the political arena had changed. The power of organized women and a democratic change in society had created this concrete result.

As soon as we took office, we got to work on the five-year strategic plan and the budget for 2015. To determine our programs for women and to achieve our goal of undertaking all municipal activities from women's perspective, we needed women to participate significantly in all public meetings and forums and bring their demands to the fore. Additionally, we needed to establish a strong administrative unit in the municipality to carry out women's activities, with a separate budget and the authority to plan and execute its own measures. Without such a unit, we wouldn't be able to do the work we envisioned. Previously, municipal activities for women had been carried out under the department of social services. But now we established the directorate of women's policies, bringing all women's activities together under one roof. The directorate would carry out its work in collaboration with branch offices for the prevention of violence against women, for women's economy, and for women's education and research. It set up a women's shelter called the Women's Life House, and a halfway house to serve women who didn't need full shelter. It set up a domestic violence hotline to help victims of violence access municipal resources. We expected the women's directorate to be a model for other metropolitan municipalities.

We tried to hire more women for the municipality's general administration, but we couldn't reach our goal. Women's lack of self-confidence had as much to do with it as misogyny. But then, almost all the municipal services were traditionally seen as "men's work." We worked hard to break the sexist division of labor, but I can't say we were successful. We tried to hire more women bus drivers in public transportation, but their number remained limited. We hired women for the fire department, but after a while they insisted on returning to office jobs. Women hired for the cleaning unit mostly applied for indoor duties. We couldn't encourage women to leave their jobs in tree nurseries for parks and recreation services. To break the sexist division of labor, we needed long-term, comprehensive activities that would raise women's self-confidence and change their outlook. I'd like to emphasize that we never had any difficulty finding women technical personnel or engineering technicians. But women in technical positions have to be more forceful in claiming the products of their labor and be bolder in taking responsibilities, and we need to encourage them in this direction.

Our experiences have shown that if women are to carry out municipal services from their perspective and to find democratic-ecological solutions to urbanization problems, they need to step outside their offices and go into the field and take responsibility in the relevant administrative units.

We held meetings that brought all the women in the municipality together to strengthen women's solidarity and encourage strong communication between women employees and elected representatives (co-mayors and councilors). This practice gave rise to a women's assembly. The assembly talked about women's problems and how male domination affected women's work—and out of those discussions it developed ideas for solutions. Other goals were to prepare a Local Equality Action Plan, to make data collection processes gender-based, and to prepare a gender-sensitive budget.

Unfortunately, I was able to stay in my position only for 19 months. After that, as we all know, the *kayyum* period began.

Immediately after we were elected in March 2014, a new geopolitical process started in Turkey and the Middle East. War, violent clashes, and migration deeply affected local governments. In August, ISIS attacked Sinjar, and Yazidis had to leave their homeland in huge numbers. Many fled to Diyarbakır. It was shocking for me to listen to Yazidi women describe the atrocities they'd experienced. We used all available means to support them to overcome their trauma. Then in September, ISIS attacked and overran much of Kobanê. Again, many residents fled to Diyarbakır.

Late in 2015, Diyarbakır was shaken by curfews, violent clashes, shootings, migration, and destruction. Turkish armed forces reduced to rubble our districts of Sur and Silvan, deeply wounding all of us. A lot can be said about what happened there, but witnessing firsthand that "war harms women and children the most" was an indescribable agony, all the more when the heavy burden of responsibility sat on my shoulders as co-mayor.

Being human and remaining humane isn't easy. You'll be tested 1,000 times.

12
"Are Men Going to Walk Behind a Woman?"

Leyla Güven

Translated by Mediha Sorma

Leyla Güven (b. 1964) was DTK co-chair at the time of her arrest on January 31, 2018. Even so, on June 24, 2018, she was elected MP from Hakkâri. She went on a hunger strike that threatened her life, so she was released and treated. She was arrested again on December 21, 2020. She is currently in Elâzığ T-type Closed Prison.

On March 24, 2016, while the political genocide operations were underway, I was unanimously elected DTK co-chair. (As I write, I also bear the duties and responsibilities of the Hakkâri MP, although I'm in prison.) On January 24, 2018, as I was returning home from DTK headquarters, someone called out to me, "Good evening, Ms. Güven," at the entrance of my building. I didn't know him—I thought he might be a neighbor. "Good evening," I said, heading to the door.

"I'm from the Counter-terrorism Office," he said. "We're here to arrest you."

I said, "'We?' You're by yourself, and you don't have a vehicle."

"My colleagues are on their way."

We stood at the door for half an hour, when a Ranger-type armored vehicle arrived. Two women officers took me for a health check and then to police headquarters.

The holding cell was full of action. Dear Nurcan Baysal was there—she was released two days later.* Ten days later they took me to the courthouse, where I was to give my statement. When I said I'd give it in my native language, the prosecutor refused even to see me and referred me to the court to decide whether to arrest me.

Since the case concerned Afrin, I was sure I'd be arrested. After a few routine questions, the court did decide to arrest me. At around 8 p.m., I was taken to Diyarbakır Prison. I didn't feel out of place, since I'd previously spent four and a half years in the infamous Amed Dungeon. Thirty women welcomed me, all joyous and bright as buttons, women who couldn't be "disciplined." They weren't surprised to see me. No one sighed wanly, "Ah, how I wish you hadn't been arrested." Instead, they said, "Huh, we were expecting you sooner. How on earth did they let you run loose this long?"

As we were chatting, I surveyed our ward, which consisted of a kitchen, a bathroom, and a toilet. Nothing had changed in the three and a half years since I'd left. The trashcans, bathroom buckets, bread baskets, and so on were all where they used to be. The only thing that had changed was the people. And of course,

* Nurcan Baysal is a Kurdish journalist and human rights advocate from Diyarbakır.

they pranked me, the way they always prank newcomers. I suppose they were wondering if I'd fall for it. Yes, I did—even though it was my second time in prison, I still fell for it.

At this writing, we're approximately 50 women staying in two adjacent wards in Diyarbakır Prison. There are about 30 in my ward, more than in the past. I'm the oldest, but the average age is quite low. We're here as three generations of Kurdish women. What brought us all together is the fact that we're motivated, passionate, and vigorous.

Like all political prisoners, we've established order in our confined world. We never miss a reading session, the only activity permitted to us. According to an old saying, "What gives meaning to a place is those who inhabit it." We remember that as we try to give meaning to this place that constrains us.

Sometime after I got arrested, I received my indictment. It included all my DTK activities and all the statements I'd made—they were now considered criminal. The file's five folders were stuffed with nothing but statements and activities that any democratic civil society would regard as perfectly normal. As I read the indictment, I realized the full extent of my past work. My praxis wasn't that bad after all!

I'm a Kurdish woman who was uprooted centuries ago and exiled to the barren lands of central Anatolia; a Kurdish woman who could, however, never be assimilated, who went looking for her past, and whose search for her roots led her to the women's liberation struggle.

I was born in Cihanbeyli in Konya province in 1964, the youngest of seven children. Our well-off family lived in a village of 500 houses. My mother called the shots at home. She was a wise woman who spoke through her deeds. She'd deliver babies, give injections, and set broken bones. She could sew well; her cooking was legendary; and the carpets she wove were so lovely, they were passed from hand to hand. When it came to animals, she was all but a veterinarian. People from neighboring villages would trek to our village to see her. Her healing methods dated back to Neolithic societies and were effective. She was a vessel of the natural world to her core. Thinking back, I realize she was a philosopher. She's 94 now. None of her children has her skills.

When I was 17, my family married me off to a cousin. My husband and I moved to Germany, and we had two children. After a while, I divorced him and returned to Konya to raise the children on my own.

I started a new life in Konya. To provide for my kids, I got a job at a survey company, where I worked as the Konya regional manager. Meanwhile, I also got involved in party work. At HADEP's 1994 congress, I was elected to the party's provincial administration. I was one of only two women in the provincial party. The other was married and couldn't invest much time, but I threw myself into it. I was raising kids, paying for their education, and at the same time doing party work.

Needless to say, working for the party went against my family's wishes. With their traditional perspective, they kept raising classic objections such as "You're a woman—what are you doing working at the party?" "You've got children, you're a divorcée. People will talk." "What are we to do if you get arrested?" They pressured me to quit my party work. I'll never forget the day my older sister said to me, "I'll jump out the window if you get involved in the party." I said, "Go ahead then, jump now," since I had no intention of giving it up. I was fighting to stand on my two feet and show everyone that women could make it on their own.

I got involved in party work because I wanted to do something about the injustice and unlawfulness to which Kurds are subjected. Frankly, I originally thought, *Yes, I'm a Kurd, but I'm not oppressed. But Kurds in the east and the southeast are suffering. We need to support them.* When I visited Diyarbakır for the first time in 2000, I cried the whole time and kept asking, "Why did they tear us away from this beautiful land?"

In 1996, I met Selma Irmak, who holds a special place in my heart. *Heval* Selma was my first mentor in HADEP. She taught me everything. With her support, I set up a women's commission within the party and got even more deeply involved. We held meetings where we brainstormed: *What else can we do to help build the party in Konya?* At the office, we strategized till dark, then continued at home in evenings. One day, those of us on the women's commission decided to get drivers' licenses. Ten of us passed the driving test and got our licenses. "See," we said, "we can do anything if we put our minds to it!" We always aimed to outdo ourselves.

In 2001, I decided to make party work my profession. My children were grown, and there was nothing keeping me in Konya anymore. I gave away all my furniture, packed a suitcase, and traveled to the party headquarters in Ankara's Balgat district. The HADEP congress that year elected me to the central administration of the women's branches and to the Party Council. I was assigned to the city of Adana, where I worked for three years. For a while, I oversaw party activities in the entire Çukurova region.* Fatma Kurtulan, head of women's branches at the time, used to say, "Wherever there's a problem, let's send Leyla. She'll go fix it."

Party women cared a lot about local elections, especially with the women's quota in place. For the 2004 local elections, the party nominated me as the candidate for mayor of Küçükdikili, a town in Seyhan in Adana province. I challenged the sitting mayor, a man from the center-right DYP. On election day I beat him, and that was a big deal.

That year nine of us party women got elected as mayors. Once we took office, the public and our respective communities kept their eyes on us. Everyone wondered, *Will these women be able to handle it? Can they succeed?* Since our party had no MPs at the time, mayors were the ones who represented Kurdish people in Turkey's politics.

When the European Parliament held a conference for elected women mayors, they invited us. As far as I can recall, 18 women mayors were present, and nine of them were from our party. We made presentations on our activities. Our EP hosts were astonished and asked, "Do you have a lot of money? Or are you from wealthy tribal families?" Yurdusev Özsökmenler, mayor of Bağlar district, explained that neither was the case. The EP people were perplexed. How could a woman who didn't have much money or come from a rich tribe get elected mayor?

---

* The large fertile plain in southern Turkey that covers the provinces of Mersin, Adana, Osmaniye, and Hatay.

Back in Turkey, we participated in a project organized by KA.DER, which supported newly elected women mayors and councilors and sought equal representation for women with men in Turkish politics. We explained our ideology of women's liberation and gave them examples from our experiences with autonomous self-organizing. When it came to decisions regarding women, we explained, women made them, and no man, not even the party chair, was permitted to interfere. They had trouble believing us. When we told them about our efforts to end domestic violence, a CHP mayor piped up, "Oh, there's no domestic violence in my town! Our women are liberated." That same day she got a phone called and was shocked to learn that a man in her town had struck his wife on the head with a propane tank. As a matter of fact, these organizers were oblivious to what women were going through. In their perception, apparently, violence against women was a problem only in eastern Turkey—it didn't happen in the west. How wrong they were.

The chair of the Ataturkist Thought Association,* who was also participating in KA.DER's project, couldn't hide her astonishment either. She admitted how prejudiced they'd been against us Kurdish women. As we continued to meet, we realized that women who lived in western Turkey weren't aware of our experiences or struggle—perhaps they didn't want to be. We invited them to visit the cities where we'd won elections, to see for themselves. When they came, we showed them lots of things. Such get-togethers with other local government officials helped diminish the prejudices against us.

To combat violence against women, we offered gender trainings, both to people in the neighborhoods and to municipal staff. In 2005, I was drawing up a collective labor agreement between the Küçükdikili municipality and Turkey's Public Services Employees Union. I was looking for something meaningful to add concerning women. We didn't have a single woman on our municipal council,

* A large secularist Turkish foundation that advocates for the ideas and principles of Turkey's founder, Atatürk.

and I didn't have anyone to discuss it with. So, sitting alone, I jotted down my ideas and came up with a list of four items:

1. A staff member who takes a second wife will be fired without compensation.
2. If a staff member commits violence against his wife, his salary will be given to the wife.
3. If a staff member doesn't let their daughter go to school, scholarships previously awarded to their son will be discontinued.
4. All municipal staff will have paid holidays on Newroz and March 8.

The next morning the union representatives arrived. I shared my list with them, they accepted all my items, and we added them to the collective agreement. The municipality signed it in a press conference.

When I read the articles aloud, everybody, especially the municipal staff, was astonished. The whole town discussed them for days. The women MPs of Adana province from AKP and CHP came over to my office, trailed by a pack of reporters. "We're so grateful for you!" they said. "You did what we couldn't do in parliament." Mainstream media channels invited me to appear on their TV programs. Newspapers ran the headline "Men Who Take a Second Wife Are in Trouble."

I honestly didn't expect to set off such a big reaction. Reporters asked me, "How did you come up with those ideas?" I responded that we, in the women's movement, had a strong position on all such matters, that we didn't recommend women without gender awareness for such positions, and that Kurdish women had made significant advances but paid a heavy price for them. The second article, the one that imposed sanctions on municipal staff who committed violence against their wives, was later added to collective agreements in other municipalities.

Still, prejudices against women were so deeply rooted that it wasn't easy to break them down—it required enormous work, every day. Outside our town, for example, there's a railroad crossing. When a train approaches, the municipal workers on duty lower the barrier to prevent accidents. One day when the barrier was down, a driver tried to slip underneath it—and had an accident. The commander of the gendarmerie station investigated the scene and interviewed the eyewitnesses. "Things like this are inevitable when you have a woman for mayor," he remarked. An employee working there came and told me what he'd said. I couldn't make sense of it—the commander blamed a woman mayor, instead of the man who tried to drive under the closed barrier? It was like a bad joke.

Our municipal staff were so accustomed to the one-man top-down rule of the authoritarian patriarchal order that when I told them I wanted to hear their ideas, they were shocked.

Here's another episode. Küçükdikili municipality had a road grader, but we didn't use it much because the responsibility to maintain the town's main roads lay with Adana Metropolitan Municipality. A woman from our party had recently won the mayorship of Dersim, and she told me they needed a grader for winter snow removal. I discussed it with the municipal councilors, who agreed to lend Dersim our grader. I called in the grader operator and told him we were loaning the vehicle to Dersim for a while and that he could drive another vehicle. Of course, I also asked him if he needed anything.

He looked at me in a state of shock and said, "Okay," and left the room.

I heard later that he went directly to the worksite and said, "Guys, what's with this mayor? Why did she ask me? I'm just an employee. If you're the mayor, you do whatever you want. Yeah, she doesn't know how to do this job because she's a woman."

In 2009, after serving as Küçükdikili mayor, I ran for mayor of Viranşehir, in Urfa province, at the suggestion of women friends. The AKP candidate came from a big tribal family and was a village guard.* He built his entire campaign around the fact that his opponent was a woman. His discourse was along the lines of "Are you willing to walk behind a woman? I'll accept no such thing." Meanwhile my campaign was run predominantly by women—

* Village guards (*korucu*) are a paramilitary group that the Turkish state recruited, mainly from pro-government Kurds, to aid its security forces' military operations in Kurdish-populated cities. The Turkish state has deployed village guards since 1985 in its fight against the PKK.

which was a first, both in Viranşehir and in Urfa. We won the election by a landslide. It was like a revolution. Urfa, which had for so long been ruled by a patriarchal culture and feudal values, was being reborn with women.

Eight months after the election, the state began the political genocide operation known as the anti-KCK operation. I was arrested on December 24, 2009, along with more than 20 former and sitting mayors. I spent four and a half years in prison and was released in July 2014.

After that I started working on the party's local government commission. I believed I'd be useful in that field thanks to my experience as a mayor. We were looking for ways to empower women through local governance and projects to carry out. Women had already made phenomenal achievements in local government, but they weren't enough. We wanted to do more.

For the general elections of June 7, 2015, I ran for MP from Urfa. Our campaign's objective was to reach as many women as possible. We'd leave not a single village or city neighborhood unvisited. In Urfa city, where Arabs and Kurds lived together, women and their political will were all but invisible. Even when a woman went outdoors, she'd walk three or four feet behind a man, covered in a traditional outfit.

When we held meetings, both Kurdish and Arab women showed up. What they liked most was that before we started, we'd say, "Men, step back. Women, please move to the front." They'd blush but step forward proudly. We asked them what problems they were facing, and they talked about second marriages, bride exchange,* child marriages, bride price, and violence against women. They wanted us to initiate projects to combat those practices. And they asked us bluntly if we were strong enough to take on feudal landlords and wealthy tribes.

One day at a campaign event, a woman asked, "Ms. Leyla, our men are going after the Syrian women who fled to our city because

* Called *berdel*, this arrangement refers to exchanging daughters for concurrent marriages between two families.

of the war in Syria. They're taking them as their third or fourth wives. They pay for young girls and marry them. What are you going to do about this if elected?" It was tragic. The horrors of the Syrian war were causing tremendous suffering for women.

The election result was a huge success. Our party won four parliamentary seats for Urfa, two of them held by women. It was an incredible success to achieve equal representation in a city where women were still so repressed. But then the government ordered a re-election, in complete disregard for the will of the people and women. In the run-up to the re-election, our party was subjected to intimidation and violence that we all know too well,* and the number of MPs that our party won in Urfa went down to three. I lost by a very small margin.

Since 1994, I've carried the multiple identities of woman, mother, Kurd, and feminist. As a woman, it wasn't at all easy for me to enter the world of politics, identified as it was with maleness. I worked harder than all my friends to turn the disadvantages of being a woman and a divorcée into advantages. I had to prove one way or another that I could stand on my own, enter the lion's den of politics, perform better than men as mayor, and stay clean as a whistle in municipal governance, a space fraught with corruption. It was an uphill climb, but my faith in the struggle and in our values enabled me to stand strong, indeed, to pursue success all the harder in the face of adversity, which became a way of life for me. Like many women friends who achieved in this arena, I acted in full awareness that women's liberation and the liberation of the Kurdish people's language, culture, and identity were essential. Women actively participated in election campaigns, they interrogated candidates about their plans, they made up 90 percent of those who visited town halls, they were prioritized in municipal staff recruiting, they rose to prominence in higher management positions in municipalities, they opened women's centers, they participated in governance, they benefited from urban services—all

* The election was preceded on October 10 by the deadliest terrorist attack in Turkey's history, when two suicide bombers killed 102 people attending a peace rally in Ankara.

these were accomplishments that the Kurdish women's movement achieved in a brief time. We believe in the ideology of women's liberation, and we tried to share with the public the fact that no society can be liberated until women are liberated. It's to that idea that we owe our accomplishments.

13
"A Lion Is a Lion, Woman or Man"

Mukaddes Kubilay

Translated by Ebru Öztürk

Mukaddes Kubilay (b. 1955) was elected co-mayor of Ağrı on March 30, 2014, with 50.91 percent of the vote. She was detained on December 22, 2016 and later arrested. She is currently serving a sentence of eight years and seven months in Sincan Prison.

I was born in 1955 in Bazîd (Turkish Doğubayazıt), in Ağrı province, the fifth of 13 children. I went to school in Bazîd, married in 1974, and moved to İzmir, where my husband worked as a teacher. I got into trading to contribute to the family budget. In the early 1990s, when DEP was established, I got interested in politics. I worked for DEP, then for HADEP's Bornova district organization. I served two terms as the provincial party head in İzmir.

I returned to Bazîd, and in 1999, I ran for mayor on HADEP's list. For the very first time in Kurdistan, three women were elected mayor: me in Bazîd, Ayşe Karadağ in Derik, and Cihan Sincar in Kızıltepe. That achievement was huge, not only for the party but also for Ağrı, which had never seen a woman mayor. Credit for my victory belongs to the women who went all out for my campaign—they wanted to participate in governance that would create women's programs. Once they entrusted me with office, I had the responsibility to represent that political will.

Our electoral success inspired women who had previously been silenced, whose opinions had been ignored, and who hadn't been allowed to articulate their needs. We held frequent meetings, both in the neighborhoods and in the town hall. At women's neighborhood meetings, about 300 would show up and share their demands and needs and suggestions comfortably with their elected women representatives—the mayor and several councilors. Equally important, they expressed themselves in their mother tongue. For the first time, women felt that they were listened to, and their ideas were taken seriously. Their enthusiasm invigorated our work.

Normally, these women's lives were restricted to the four walls of their homes. They rarely went outdoors except to visit family and relatives. Once we heard about their serious problems, especially in education and health, we wanted to develop projects to address them, but the municipal budget was limited. *Where can we get some funding?* I wondered.

Sometime later I attended a meeting of mayors in Van province. Among the dozens of mayors present, I was the only woman. A delegation from Italy's Ancona municipality was there, and I introduced myself to Ancona's deputy mayor, a woman. She looked surprised that a woman could be elected mayor in a region where the feudal structure seemed so dominant.

As we talked, she asked me about women's conditions in Bazîd, and I told her about the women's projects we were proposing but lacked funding for. She said, "If you design a project for women, the Municipality of Ancona will be happy to fund it."

Back in Bazîd, we swiftly developed a proposal for a women's health and education center and sent it to the Ancona deputy mayor. Her municipality accepted it, and we signed the protocols. Within a year, we built the center and named it after Ayşe Nur Zarakolu, a fighter for women's rights and human rights.* The center proved very popular—it served as a women's counseling center and provided education and health services to 150 to 200 women daily. In fact, it was the first public space in the city that served women. The center made their dreams come true.

Later, women told us at neighborhood meetings that they wanted to participate in economic life. So, we established a Women's Cooperative that encompassed, among other things, a carpet workshop, a textile workshop, a restaurant offering local cuisine, and a hair salon. About 70 women worked in these units, both as managers and as laborers, and they shared the income equally. Other local people admired their work, which boosted their self-confidence.

Women also requested an educational center for teenagers. We inaugurated the Orhan Doğan Educational Support Center, where about 500 young people received tutoring, especially students preparing for the university entrance exam. We also awarded scholarships to university students in financial need.

Every year in Bazîd we organized the Ahmedê Xanî Festival, a celebration of arts and culture.** It featured movie screenings, theatrical performances, and concerts, as well as panels and discussions. Women took an active role in organizing it, and we included women-themed activities in the program. Booths offered local foods, clothes, and crafts, adding meaning and color. The Women's Cooperative showcased its products there.

---

* Ayşe Nur Zarakolu (1946–2002) was a Turkish author, publisher, and human rights advocate. She co-founded the notable Turkish publishing house Belge. Her publications frequently brought her into conflict with Turkish press laws.

** Ahmedê Xanî (1650–1707) was an important Kurdish poet and scholar who wrote the classic Kurdish love story *Mem û Zîn* (*Mem and Zin*). He lived for most of his life in Bazîd.

Although women in Bazîd normally didn't go out at night, they never missed festival events. In fact, because the festival concerts went on into the evening, husbands would complain that their wives were coming home late. The wives would shush them, saying, "Mayor Mukaddes was there too." Then the husbands would come to the town hall and jokingly complain: "Mayor, we don't dare say anything to these women anymore!" I told them I stood with the women and they had to be treated fairly. After more jokes and chitchat, they'd finish their tea and leave.

At one neighborhood meeting, the issue of domestic violence came up for the first time. Once the ice was broken on this subject, women had so much to tell that the meeting went on for hours. Some women said they wanted to work outside the home, but their families didn't allow them. Others wanted to participate in party work but weren't permitted. Women were overwhelmed with housework, they were forbidden to go to school, they were under pressure to get married, and so on—all familiar problems. I explained that these were cases of oppression and violence. They said, "Yes, we know, but that doesn't solve anything. Mayor, you should have a meeting with the men."

It was a great idea. We sent out invitations, and a group of women and I met with the men who accepted. We told them that violence against women was unacceptable. They insisted that what they were doing wasn't violence. We went back and forth for a while, and I don't know whether we really persuaded them, but by the end, they at least said they were convinced. We'd made a first step in transforming a mentality.

One story will illustrate what we accomplished. When I was first elected, some of the local tribal chiefs didn't want to accept that a woman was now mayor. "What are we supposed to call her, 'Lady Chief'?" they moaned. "No, a woman can't run the municipality—she should stay home." I paid no mind to such statements and carried on with my work, developing Bazîd's first women-centered projects as well as municipal services for everyone, taking special care to distribute them equally. We improved the district's infrastructure, even in neighborhoods that hadn't voted for us. We strove to be transparent. The tribal chiefs who had said, "A woman can't be a mayor," looked around at our accomplishments and apologized. Abashed, they used a Kurdish expression, *Şêr şêr e, çi jin e çi mêr e,* "A lion is a lion, it doesn't matter if it's a woman or a man," and thanked us for our work.

Over my five-year term, we changed Bazîd significantly. Then came the 2004 elections, and women persuaded me to run for another term. I faced competition because the party decided to hold a primary, and eight men friends presented themselves as candidates too. The party directed all of us to maintain courtesy and abide by ethical rules.

The party said that all the candidates were to campaign jointly. The men, however, didn't comply. Instead, they visited houses individually, trying to win over voters for themselves.

One day a group of women friends came to my house and demanded, "Why don't you run a campaign for yourself?"

"All the candidates are supposed to visit the neighborhoods together," I said. "That's the right way."

At the neighborhood meetings, however, women were unequivocal: "We want to reelect Mayor Mukaddes. She got us through hard times, she's never abandoned us, she stands by us every day, and we love her work. We don't want anyone but her." As a result of the Kurdish women's struggle, the women of Bazîd were now politically conscious and knew what they wanted. Thanks to them, I won the primary by a large margin.

In the general election, I was elected mayor of Bazîd for a second term. I served out that five-year term too, and then in 2009 I went back to İzmir, where I worked as the provincial party head, then was elected a party councilor.

In 2014, as local election campaigns were getting underway, I was a BDP councilor. At the urging of women friends, I decided to run for co-mayor of Ağrı city.

Back in 1999, our party had won the municipal elections in Ağrı, but after a while the mayor had been arrested, and municipal leadership passed to another party. The next two elections were troubled by allegations of rigging. So, in 2014 our party bent over backward to avoid any trouble. The polls closed, the ballot boxes were opened—and it became obvious that BDP had won. AKP immediately objected. The votes were recounted, but the result was the same. For a week, appeal followed appeal. In all the other districts, the election results were finalized, but not in Ağrı. They recounted the votes eight times, and the result never changed, we'd clearly won. But AKP never conceded. In the end, the provincial board of elections decided to hold a new election.

For the re-election of June 1, 2014, the people mobilized. Even those who hadn't previously voted for BDP were repelled by the gross injustice and voted for us this time. We received even more votes than before, winning 19 of the 31 city council seats.

For the first time in Ağrı, a woman would serve in city hall. My co-mayor and I had a responsibility to govern transparently, with a participatory and democratic approach. It was also our duty to consider women's needs in delivering municipal services and to design projects that would serve them as well as all citizens. Co-mayoring was a manifestation of the principle of women's equal participation in local governance.

We encountered problems getting women's projects underway. Co-mayoring wasn't understood well in Ağrı, and the patriarchal mindset resisted considering women's needs in planning urban services. While developing our projects, we had to fight this mindset. Ultimately, we established a women's directorate in our administration, which enabled women to come to the town hall and express their needs comfortably.

Our goal was to build a participatory, transparent administration that manifested the political will of women as well as men. But AKP couldn't tolerate that will. In 2016, a *kayyum* was appointed to govern Ağrı, and the first thing it did was shut down the women's directorate and fire its women employees. In so doing, it left women almost without air to breathe.

On December 22, 2016, I was visiting my daughter in Torbalı, in İzmir province. That morning at about 6:30 a.m. there was a knock at the door. I opened it. It was the police, saying they were there to detain me and search the house. I told them it was my daughter's house, so they couldn't search it. They showed me a document that they claimed was a search warrant for the house, but it didn't say that, as I pointed out. They waited outside the door for about an hour.

Meanwhile the prosecutor's office issued a new search warrant. The police searched my daughter's house until 2 p.m., then took me into custody. I was held at the Torbalı police station for a day. The next day they took me to Ağrı, where I was detained for five more days. My cell was cold and dirty. I wasn't feeling well and was shivering; I asked for a blanket, but they wouldn't give me one. There had been a blanket in the cell when I first arrived, but they removed it. At the end of the fifth day, they let me see my lawyer. The police wanted to take my statement. I told them I'd exercise my right to remain silent and make a statement only at the prosecutor's office. While I was in custody, the police subjected me to psychological abuse, saying my husband had undergone heart surgery, even though my husband didn't have heart disease. They were trying to unnerve and demoralize me.

On December 26 I was taken to court, arrested, and committed to Ağrı Prison. It had no ward for political prisoners, so they were going to put me in a ward with ordinary prisoners, but I refused it. The next day they transferred me to Sincan Prison. The friends who greeted me there were so warm and spirited that I almost forgot we were in a prison.

Women have a remarkable ability to create livable spaces in all conditions, and I soon adapted. While I was on the outside, I'd never had time to read books. In here, I've concentrated on reading. I read a lot of books.

M indictment charged me with involvement in political party activities. At my first hearing on April 25, 2017, I told the court that it was my constitutional right to participate in party activities. I added that democratic politics was possible only with strong local governments in which women participated. As of this writing, my legal process continues.

Women are the essential dynamics of democratic politics and a democratic society. Even when they lock us up, we continue to struggle with the same will and determination. As long as we believe in ourselves and organize, we'll overcome hardships.

14
Nobody's Daughter-in-Law

Nurhayat Altun

Translated by Dilek Hüseyinzadegan

Nurhayat Altun (b. 1964) was elected co-mayor of Dersim on March 30, 2014. She was arrested on November 17, 2016 and sentenced to ten years in prison. She is currently in Kocaeli F-type Prison. Her case is pending in the Supreme Court of Appeals.

I collapsed onto the bed. We'd been on the road for two days, I was exhausted, and I fell asleep right away. I awoke to people shouting slogans and banging on doors. When the same thing happened again in the afternoon, I realized I was hearing protests. All day I tried to get a cup of tea. I asked the wardens, "Do you give tea?" "No." "Hot water?" "No." "Can I get a teakettle from the commissary?" "It's closed." "How about drinking water?" "Drink from the faucet," they said.

Their answers were short and clear. During the transfer they'd allowed me to bring 100 liras, so when the commissary finally opened, I was able to buy cleaning supplies—but only the most urgent. I wouldn't get a hot cup of tea for days. The wardens didn't answer my questions and resolved none of my issues. I thought, *You don't know us, you're prejudiced against us. Once you get to know us, your attitude will change.* I was right—after a while, their behavior did change.

But for now, I was alone. The sound of a door startled me. I strained to hear voices in the hallway, hoping to recognize a voice. A guard delivering our mail yelled "Gültan!" and I thought, *Oh! She's in this ward!* The second day, while I was returning from a lawyer visit, I passed a door, and someone yelled, "Nurhayat, welcome! How are you?" I recognized the voice. "Sister Gültan," I cried, "we're here! Edibe [Şahin] is here too, in another ward." Just knowing that someone familiar was down the hall made me feel much better. I went out to the prison yard to see if anyone else might call out my name. I heard Ayla [Akat Ata]'s voice. Hearing friends' voices made me forget that I was alone.

I didn't have a radio, a TV, a newspaper, a book, nothing. Not even a watch—the prison authorities took mine when I was admitted. Not knowing the time of day was very frustrating. I tried to tell time by following shadows on the walls and coordinating them roughly with the scheduled meals and inmate counts.

Someone had left a newspaper's two-page book review section in my locker. I read it again and again. One day Gültan shouted, "It snowed so much in Dersim, the roads are closed!" That was the only current piece of news I heard. Thinking that I'd soon be put in the same cell with others, I didn't buy a TV. But gradually it dawned on me that solitary was going to continue for a while, so I bought one. Once you realize that solitary confinement is a deliberate tactic, you can proceed accordingly. Still, I kept wishing for someone talk to.

About a week after I arrived, the authorities gave me the books I'd brought from Elazığ. I was delighted to see them—it was as if a friend had arrived in my cell. They gave me my watch too, so I was really blissed out. A book and a watch! My life was transformed!

As long as I live, I'll never forget the bitter cold of those isolation days. Not only was the cell freezing, it was also very damp. The prison yard was blanketed with snow. One day the gate to the yard was iced shut, so when they came for the morning inmate count, they couldn't open it. I poured boiling water over the gate to open it. The space where we met with lawyers was warmer than the cells, and thankfully the lawyers visited often, so I could warm up a bit during their visits. That was how I passed the winter. Toward the end of February, they moved me into Gültan's cell. With two of us together, it was warmer. It was also getting warmer outside.

I'm the youngest child of a family from Dersim who were exiled to Kayseri. I was born in Kayseri in 1964, and after that my family moved to Ankara. I grew up in Ankara's Tuzluçayır neighborhood, which was majority Alevi. My family was leftist and democratic. My older brother went to high school with Hüseyin İnan,* and they even lived in the same house for a while. Hüseyin İnan had a big impact on my family. I remember when Deniz and his friends were executed** and when Mahir and his friends were murdered;*** everyone in the neighborhood was devastated, sobbing over their newspapers.

My childhood passed in that kind of environment. I was already familiar with political topics when I was in the fifth grade. Not only my family but my entire neighborhood was politicized. It was

---

* Hüseyin İnan was a young Turkish revolutionary leader in the early 1970s.

** Deniz Gezmiş, Hüseyin İnan, and their comrades in the People's Liberation Army of Turkey were executed by the state in 1972.

*** On March 30, 1972, Mahir Çayan and nine other leftist militants were killed by soldiers in Kızıldere, a village in Tokat, in an event known as the Kızıldere Massacre.

a neighborhood of revolutionaries. İbrahim Kaypakkaya's family* were our neighbors—our families knew each other. When İbrahim was arrested, his family told us about the torture he'd endured, how he'd been forced to walk barefoot in the snow. That must have made a big impression on me. One morning when I woke up, there was snow outside, up to my knees. I took off my socks, went out, and walked barefoot on the snow. My mom saw me and yanked me back inside.

I attended Tuzluçayır High School, where students often held boycotts, like one protesting the Maraş Massacre.** We barricaded the doors with our desks. One time, soldiers arrived and opened fire on us high schoolers with real bullets, pocking the walls with bullet holes and smashing windows. We threw ourselves onto the classroom floor. After a while, military and police entered the school, the families arrived, the teachers negotiated, and they sent us all home.

The 1980 military coup took place when I was a junior in high school. They arrested a lot of people from our neighborhood, our circles of friends, and my family. I had to quit school.

Life after the coup was hard. We made a lot of prison visits.

In 1990, while working at the Ankara Metropolitan Municipality, I was also spending time at HEP's offices. At some point I worked in HEP's Ankara provincial administration. When HEP was shut down, I got involved with DEP's Ankara provincial administration.

After DEP made women's commissions official in its bylaws, we set out to organize a women's commission in every city. But in those days the party had no autonomous women's activities in its agenda. Mostly we party women followed the party program, working on events tied to the general political agenda. In fact, the women's commissions were administered by a man in the party executive—there was no Central Women's Commission yet. Leyla Zana was the only woman MP in parliament. The party's Central

* İbrahim Kaypakkaya was a Marxist-Leninist revolutionary executed by the state in 1973.

** In 1978 the neo-fascist Grey Wolves massacred Alevi Kurds in the city of Maraş.

Executive Committee had only two women members, Aynur Gürbüz and Melike Alp, and the Party Council had a few women. But women were well organized in the cities and districts where we had women's commissions. In some districts we organized neighborhood meetings, and most of those who attended were women. One time, our man party administrator of women's commissions had to open a district meeting by saying "We women." As women working in the cities, we objected: "Why are women's commissions administered by a man?" Answer: there were no women in central party positions. At that time, women were participating as party members, not as women.

During the DEP period (1993–4), I was working at the municipality and attending party events. In 1994 Melih Gökçek, an AKP member, became mayor of Ankara, after which I and many other city employees were let go. On December 4, 1994, the office of the newspaper *Özgür Ülke* (*Free Country*) was bombed.* Its staff, unfazed, simply prepared to start a new newspaper. I thought I'd be useful in accounting and management, so I started working for the paper.

Many of my memories of newspaper work are about things we lacked. The bomb had destroyed all the equipment, computers, desks, everything. The newspaper had been financed only by subscriptions, so it had serious financial issues. And here I was working in the accounting department. We couldn't afford even to cover our journalists' basic expenses. Some days we couldn't pay for their transportation, so they had to walk to news sites. Usually the cashbox was empty, and I'd keep my face stern so nobody would ask for money. I wasn't dour or unhappy; we just had no money.

Zülküf, a man in management, would bring me a shopping list. Paper, printer, toner, utilities, fax, rent, kitchen supplies—the list went on and on. "We don't have any money for toner!" I scolded him. "How did you run out so quickly?" He snapped back, "Well, I didn't eat it!" The newspaper had to come out every day, so Zülküf would borrow money to cover everything. But then the creditors

* *Özgür Ülke* was founded on April 28, 1994, to cover the Kurdish-Turkish conflict, after the state shut down a similar newspaper, *Özgür Gündem*. *Özgür Ülke* was itself shut down on February 2, 1995, and its issues confiscated.

would show up at the door. Sometimes I hid and had others tell them that I was away from the office.

Years later at a women's conference, I found myself sitting next to a friend I'd known at the paper, Mukaddes Alataş. She announced at the top of her voice, so everyone could hear, "Don't be fooled by this woman's laughing face! Back in the day, she never even cracked a smile!" We burst into laughter, agreeing that the most important thing was that the newspaper came out.

While I was at the paper, I got involved in the party's women's activities. As our gender consciousness rose, our women's activities escalated. In 1998, I think, we decided to publish a women's journal, so we rented a room in Taksim. We had only one computer. But we started publishing *Özgür Kadın* (*Free Women*), a monthly. HADEP's women's branch helped with sales and distribution. I worked at that journal for about two years.

I spent many years as a member of HADEP. As the women gained more power in the party, we started restructuring women's organization within it. We added a 25 percent women's quota to the bylaws. In Ankara the Party Council assigned me to work in the Marmara region. Around the time the international conspiracy forced PKK leader Abdullah Öcalan's extradition to Turkey, protests erupted everywhere. At the party's Tekirdağ branch, people went on a hunger strike. Police arrived and detained 16 people, including me. We were arrested and taken to Ümraniye Prison. The wards were filled to capacity, so they turned Ümraniye's rooftop into a ward for 46 women prisoners. I spent three weeks there, then was released on probation, then was acquitted.

After my release, I went back to party work. The 2000 party congress had decided to establish women's branches. The women in the Party Council established a Central Women's Branch and chose Fatma Kurtulan to be its first head. Among the Central Women's Branch members, I remember, were Hande Çağlayan, Ayşe Gökkan, Emine Ayna, Fatma Nevin Vargün, Yasemin Andan, Filiz Oğuz, and Sevahir Bayındır.

Next we needed to appoint more women to the party's Central Executive Committee (CEC) and give them more active roles there. Four women (Fatma, Sevahir, Filiz, and I) were appointed. Because of the women's quota in the bylaws, men couldn't object, but the meeting to decide on assignment distribution was an acrimonious ordeal, grinding on till morning. Our enlightened, democratic, revolutionary men friends argued against women taking active roles in the CEC, saying, "You have to travel from city to city, it's a tough job. Women can't do it." When the dust settled, Filiz was party treasurer, Sevahir was deputy secretary general, and I was vice chair in charge of public relations. Fatma was already on the committee as head of the Central Women's Branch.

As women took active roles in the party administration, some people needed time to adjust. When party leaders were assigning tasks, they'd assign men to places with larger communities, and women to smaller ones. Men would quickly fill up the general chair's schedule with their issues, elbowing the women aside. Only after the head of the Central Women's Branch insisted, were women included in some of the programming. Sometimes men friends tried to undermine women's events by postponing them or invoking some planning concern or some other excuse. It was arduous to establish some equilibrium in the central party, and even after we gained some acceptance, we had to remain vigilant and keep pushing forward.

Having a woman as party treasurer made things much easier. Before that, the party would have plenty of funds for general events, but somehow when it came to women's events, the treasurer would say, "We're short of money, so women will have to come up with their own budget." But with the new treasurer, we overcame that problem. Besides, the bylaws specified that a portion of the party budget had to be allocated to women's branches.

Even after we overcame many practical issues, a true change in attitude took much longer to achieve. At party headquarters and at CEC meetings, when we proposed "femicide" as an agenda item, some men took issue with the term. "What femicide?" they demanded. "Just how many women are murdered anyway?" One time when the party chair Murat Bozlak needed to go abroad, he appointed me as his proxy. The men lost their minds, apoplectic that he'd chosen a woman when, after all, a number of men were available for the job.

One of the toughest cities for women was Urfa. The party was going to hold a provincial convention there, so someone from the central party had to go there in advance to get the preparations underway. I informed the provincial party chair, Ziya Çalışkan, that I'd be doing it, and he alerted the district party administrators and all active staff, saying, "Our vice chair will be coming to the meeting. Be sure you attend."

On the day of the meeting, I arrived early at the convention building. People were trickling in, and I sat down to wait for everyone else to take their seats. An elderly man ambled over and sat down beside me. After a bit, he turned to me and asked, "Whose daughter-in-law are you, my dear?" I shot back, "I'm nobody's daughter-in-law." The hall was almost full now, and the meeting was about to start. The same old man called out to the provincial chair, Ziya, "Where's that general vice chair, the one you said was coming?" Chair Ziya responded, "She's sitting right next to you." The man jumped to his feet, looked at me anew, and roared, "What? It can be a woman?" People in the room laughed out loud. All of us women were facing attitudes like this. But after a while, people got used to having us as administrators.

Women's efforts clearly bore fruit in the 2002 general elections. During the run-up, the party drafted its candidate lists. In past years, it had nominated women to run in unwinnable districts and men to run in winnable ones. It was almost an unwritten rule to put men at the top of the list. In 2002, however, this attitude changed. Many women were listed in winnable districts, even at the top. If I remember correctly, Aysel Tuğluk became a top-of-the-list candidate from Siirt, same for Sevcan Bozlak from Diyarbakır, Sevil Erol from Mersin, Yurdusev Özsökmenler from Antep, Filiz Oğuz from Van, Handan Çağlayan from Urfa, Ferah Diba Ergül from Ağrı, and myself from Batman. Each of these friends got more than enough votes in her district to win—in Batman, I got 76 percent. But because HADEP's total national vote didn't surpass the 10 percent threshold, we couldn't take seats in parliament as MPs. In fact, we had to stand back and watch as men from other parties, who had received fewer votes, went to parliament.

It had been laborious to recruit so many women as candidates and put them at the top of our party lists. Now those in the party who didn't want to change the men-first mentality could invoke the failure of "the people" to vote for our party as an excuse to de-emphasize women as candidates. "People won't vote for a woman candidate—when we run women, we lose elections" was an often-heard argument. Some even blamed the party's failure to surpass the electoral threshold on women's candidacies. Nobody said that out loud, officially, but some sniped informally. And those who had said, "We'll lose unless I'm the candidate," while the lists were being drafted were the same people who now blamed women. But all this was just a reflection of the patriarchal mentality that saw politics as a way of achieving personal glory. Neither the people nor the party supported this argument.

Moreover, their argument was undercut by the fact that in the districts where women were at the top of the list, they'd in fact received the most votes. Our encounters with the people led us to conclude that in the 2002 elections, our support was the most enthusiastic our party had had so far. I traveled to every city in my region with DEHAP chair Mehmet Abbasoğlu. Wherever we went, the people were so excited to see us, they'd stop the bus and insist that we visit the smaller towns and villages too. As a result, I finally made it to my own district, Batman, in the last two weeks. In Batman, the people didn't see me, an Alevi woman candidate, as an oddity. They were exuberant, and their morale was high.

What had tipped the scales was women's efforts. The women candidates were well known to the people. They'd previously traveled to the cities and districts for meetings and had helped with organizing efforts. They'd developed strong bonds with the people. Those who had once warned, "We'll lose with a woman," were now joking, "Oh no, there's no stopping the women now!"

After the 2002 elections, one friend made the following assessment:

> Everything was great, especially that women were at the top of the candidate lists. It was a very enthusiastic campaign; you all gave great speeches. It was so empowering to see women on top

of the campaign buses. The results were also great. But why did all you women candidates wear black pantsuits the whole time?

It's true, we did all wear black, navy, or dark brown pantsuits during the campaign. This showed that we hadn't sufficiently questioned the formal aspect of politics, namely, its masculine appearance.

At the party's postelection convention in 2002, some of the party assignments changed. I was elected as general party treasurer. The party had grown, and its activities had expanded, and we'd just carried out a massive election campaign. But we weren't getting any aid from the state treasury. The party was in financial trouble. My first step as treasurer was to impose austerity on, among other things, transportation. I asked people to take a bus instead of flying to places when it took less than eight hours to get there.

One day one of the men vice chairs needed to go to Izmir. He asked our administrative assistant to book him a flight. That friend told him, "The treasurer has a memo forbidding that—we'll buy you a bus ticket instead." He stalked over to me. "Izmir takes nine hours by bus," he said. I said, "Nope, it takes eight hours." He said, "Then let the party give me the price of a bus ticket. I'll make up the difference for plane fare out of my own pocket." My refusal to pay for the vice chair's plane ticket was unheard of. But once we had a rule, everyone had to follow it, regardless of their preference; that was women's way.

I had worked fervently in party politics for a long time and served as treasurer for about two years. After that tough assignment I wanted to take a break from party activities. I felt like experiencing the civil society side of things. I wanted to reconnect with my family's roots in Dersim and immerse myself in Dersim socially and culturally. There was a Dersim Association in Ankara, a diverse group of people who came together due to the shared fact of being from Dersim. The association appointed me vice president, noticing that I had administrative experience. The association's activities became very meaningful for me, and I learned a lot there.

Those were the years (2013–15) when calls for peace were made, and the Peace Assembly was established.* I participated in the Peace Assembly activities as part of its secretariat. At some point I also worked with DTK.

In advance of the 2014 local elections, the party decided to implement the co-mayoring system in all municipalities. This was a new thing, and to fill all the positions, we'd need a lot of women candidates who had party experience and were known to the public. Some women friends asked me to run for co-mayor in Dersim. Due to the women's quota, women candidates had previously been in Dersim's lists, and they'd won elections there. They'd gone on to do good work. The public had learned to trust women and was confident that women weren't interested in lining their pockets. There had been a woman mayor for the last two terms, so a woman co-mayor candidate didn't stir much controversy.

But I can't say that people fully grasped the concept of co-mayoring. At a neighborhood organizing activity, a group of women told me, "We've always voted for your party in the past, but we won't in this election." "Why not?" I asked. "Because you have this man candidate," they said. "We want a woman candidate." I tried to explain that in co-mayoring there was one candidate of each gender. They were confused. "But which one will be the official mayor?" I tried again, explaining that co-mayoring was a collective approach to governance that would strengthen democracy.

Another time, while I was handing out leaflets in a market, I met a woman who made a similar remark. "I've voted for your party in the past," she said, "but not this election. Why didn't you nominate a woman candidate?" Our provincial chair Engin Doğru was standing with me, and he knew her to be an avid supporter of our party. I explained that for this election we were nominating a man and a woman together as candidates to make a collective, hence stronger administration. She thanked me and walked off with our leaflet. After a few steps, she turned back. "I'm not sure

* Founded in the late 2000s by human rights activists, journalists, labor unionists, and others, the Peace Assembly serves as a platform for joint action to bring a peaceful solution to the Kurdish question.

I quite understand. Are you the candidate, or is it your husband?" Engin and I laughed. "Come to party headquarters, and we'll talk some more!" And we continued leafleting.

The patriarchal and bureaucratic mindset is deeply ingrained; it won't be eradicated quickly. People kept asking, "But who will be the official mayor?" Then after we won the election and got to work, people saw what we were doing, and their attitude changed quickly.

Dersim doesn't have a large population, so people hung around the town hall a lot. One day an old man walked through the door. "What's the matter, Uncle?" I asked. "Do you need something?" "No, I was just passing by and thought I'd have tea with the mayor," he said.

Whatever their issue was, people would now stride into the building thinking, *They'll solve it here.* They saw the municipality as a place where solutions were created. Whether their problem involved unemployment, poverty, education, or housing, the first place they thought to ask for help was here.

In Dersim, two women mayors had already served for two terms, so women's leadership had a track record. The Women's Counseling Center that they established now handled women's activities. To institutionalize our programs, we founded a women's directorate at an administrative level. Instead of waiting for women to come to the center, we'd hold events in neighborhoods. The health team was always in the field, providing information about women's health issues and checking people's blood pressure and glucose level. Women's meetings were held regularly in the neighborhoods, where we'd talk about the needs of the neighborhood and about women's demands. Sometimes men would complain, "Is she the mayor for women only? Why can't we go to these meetings?"

Economically, Dersim was once a thriving place, with agriculture, husbandry, and beekeeping. Integral to its social fabric, people shared what they had as part of their faith. But the forced village evacuations in 1993–4 displaced so many people that its economy collapsed. To find solutions, we organized meetings with the women employees and took their suggestions. One was to create a community garden. There was an empty lot close to the city center. Women went to see the owner and got his approval to use it for a garden. Then they gathered original seeds from the villages to cultivate organic produce.

Men who were looking on said, "Women can't do it. In a few days, they'll give up and turn it over to us." When women heard that, they dug in their heels and worked even harder. Credit where credit is due—a few younger men criticized the other men's regressive attitudes and came to help. But from sowing to irrigation, women took care of everything. They'd stop by the garden first thing in the morning to tend it, then rush to get to their regular jobs at 8 a.m. The head of our women's directorate, Ayten Kordu, made an extraordinary effort. The women relished having contact with the soil, doing collective work, and harvesting organic produce.

At first, some people got the wrong idea and complained, "The municipality should give us a garden too" or "The municipality should grow and distribute the produce!" As we talked it out together as a community, we overcame those attitudes. Meanwhile, the women working on the garden developed solid friendships. It became a great example of a sustainable, self-managed economy.

Apparently, some people in Ankara were bothered by what we accomplished in Dersim. So in 2016, the Turkish state arrested us and appointed *kayyums* to run the municipality, invalidating the people's will, women's will. They all but robbed people of air to breathe.

I knew they were coming. When they started detaining co-mayors, I guessed I'd be next. At around 6 a.m. on the morning of November 16, 2016, my doorbell rang. I got up and opened the door. They read me my rights, then came in to search the house. They took my copies of the journals *Demokratik Modernite* and *Rewşen*. They also seized my small tape recorder. It'd been a gift from Ismail Beşikçi.* Back when I was working for *Özgür Kadın*, I visited him in Bursa Prison, and he gave it to me, saying, "For your interviews." This precious keepsake had great sentimental value for me. I tried to explain, but they didn't listen.

* İsmail Beşikçi (b. 1939) is a sociologist who pioneered Kurdish studies in Turkey. He has written dozens of books defending Kurdish people's rights, for which he has spent many years in prison.

They took me to the police station at 8 a.m. I'd been under the impression that DBP was the chief target of this arrest operation, but at the station, I saw that they'd detained leaders from all the democratic institutions in Dersim: provincial chairs, municipal councilors, and union representatives, people not only from DBP but also from the Labor Party, ESP, and HDP. Clearly, they'd arrested everyone they could get their hands on in order to suppress any and all democracy in the city.

The operation had clearly been planned in advance. For our health exams, instead of taking us to the hospital, they brought the doctor to the police station. The doctor asked, "Do you have any health issues?" and then left, having checked that box. Then they took us to the jail.

We'd refused to give our statements at the station. They told us, "Fair enough, you'll be questioned by the prosecutor anyway." At noon they drove us to the courthouse in a van. The prosecutor took our statements one by one. I was thinking that they'd probably release us after that, but when my turn came, he said, "I have a couple more questions, but I'll use SEGBİS for those." When I heard that, I realized they'd already decided to arrest us. When I returned to the jail, I told my friends, "Brace yourselves, we're all going to Elâzığ." The police didn't even wait for a judge's orders. As the prosecutor's questioning was underway, they arranged for a bus to take us to Elâzığ. We could all see it waiting in the courtyard.

Our questioning continued late into the night. Early the next morning, three of us were taken to Elâzığ Prison: me, our municipal councilor Cemile Altaş, and the co-president of the Municipal Civil Servants Union, Şükran Yılmaz. After a body search, they put us in a cell. The walls were tiled, and it had a toilet and a shower. It was an old bathroom that had been turned into a prison cell. There were two bunk beds, with two old mattresses, both filthy. We told the prison authorities we couldn't stay there. They told us that there was no other place, and no clean beds or blankets.

There was no tea, no hot water. It was cold, and we were shivering. We kept asking for blankets, and they finally brought us two. At around 10 p.m., they brought in our friend, Mayor Edibe Şahin. Four women, two mattresses, two blankets, no sheets or pillows of any sort; we passed the night half awake.

By morning, the women inmates in the other cells had heard about us. We communicated by shouting. We asked for pen and paper and petitioned the administration, "We want to be transferred to the women's ward." The administration didn't say no but didn't take us there either. They were just stalling. In late afternoon, the friends in the women's ward pounded on the doors and yelled, "We want our mayors!" We shouted back, "*Jin jiyan azadî!*" That night they took us to the women's ward.

It was crowded, and again there weren't enough bunk beds. The women improvised bedding on the floor and slept there, letting us use their beds. We protested, but they wouldn't hear of it, insisting, "You're exhausted."

We stayed in Elâzığ for a week. One morning the courtyard door opened, and they told us that Mayor Edibe and I were to be transferred right way. Friends threw things together to meet our most urgent needs. At about 6:30 a.m., the guards escorted us out of the ward. The women sent us off chanting, "*Jin jiyan azadî!*" We didn't know where they were taking us.

Police officers in military gear were lined up along both walls leading to the exit, a narrow pathway down the middle. They were wearing helmets and holding up shields, as if they were going to strike at any minute. But we two women walked between them, holding our heads high and carrying our bags, pretending they weren't heavy. *Why this show of force?* I wondered. *What are they afraid of? Two women who were mayors, or all the women and people we represent?* But it'd have been useless to voice my thoughts—they were acting on orders from higher up.

We exited through the prison gate. As soon as we reached the transport vehicle, they handcuffed us, and we climbed in. "Now that we're in the transport van," we said, "do tell us where we're going." An older military officer replied, "Kocaeli Prison." We'd left without breakfast. A soldier gave us a package of cookies and some juice. "Your rations," he said.

After a while, we stopped at a gas station, where the soldiers would use the restrooms. We saw a small convenience store. We had 100 liras each—all they'd let us withdraw from our prison accounts. "We have money. Can we get breakfast here?" we asked. "You can't get out," they said. So, we waited in the vehicle. When they returned, the officer in charge handed us two pieces of pastry. "I saw that they were warm, so I got you some," he said. "We have money, let us pay you," we said. He wouldn't take it. We were famished—the pastry was delicious.

It was a long drive. We stopped for restrooms only twice before we reached Ankara. That evening they took us to Sincan Prison and put us in the temporary waiting room overnight. The next morning at 7 a.m., we got underway and arrived at Kocaeli around 11 p.m. They uncuffed us, and we grabbed our bags and entered through the gate. They took us into different rooms and body-searched us. Then they processed our admission. They asked many detailed questions, down to our mothers' maiden names. "Married or single?" they asked me.

"Divorced."

"How many children?"

"One."

"Your ex-husband's home address?" I was at a loss. How was I supposed to know his address? I decided to make a joke out of it: "I got over him—why don't you?" Smiles broke out on everyone's faces. I managed to forget some of the exhaustion of the long trip.

We walked down the hallway, and they separated me from Mayor Edibe. I stepped into an empty cell. They locked the iron gate behind me and left. There was just a bed inside. I understood then that I was to be held in solitary confinement. I'd spent once a week in solitary at Sincan Prison, so this would be my second time. I was so very tired. *So this will be my world now,* I said to myself. Walls, iron bars, iron gates, and me. Then I added, *I don't care how cold you are. I'll beat you.*

15
Women Should Handle Finances

Sara Kaya

Anonymous Translator

Sara Kaya (b. 1970) was elected co-mayor of Nusaybin, in Mardin province, on March 30, 2014, with 80 percent of the vote. She was detained on August 28, 2015 and released three months later. She was detained for a second time on January 13, 2017 and arrested on January 26. She was sentenced to twelve years and is currently in Tarsus T-type Prison.

This is actually my third arrest. I was first detained on August 28, 2015, about a year and a half after I was elected co-mayor of Nusaybin. I was held in custody overnight, then taken to court and released. The prosecutor objected, and two days later I was arrested. My detention had no legal basis whatsoever—it was entirely political.

They sentenced me to Mardin Prison. When I stepped into the ward, I was thrilled to see so many beautiful women of different ages all together. I felt like I'd arrived at a women's group meeting instead of a prison.

Shortly afterward I was transferred to Sincan Women's Prison. They shut me up in a cell with nothing but a bed and a blanket. I had to steep tea in a plastic container. I had no contact with the other prisoners. That strict isolation lasted 40 days. Then I was allowed to communicate with women in the other wards, who shared things I needed from their storage. I was deeply touched by their generosity. After three months, I was released.

In 2016 the interior ministry removed me as co-mayor. Nusaybin, like other towns, was going through a painful time, subjected to armed clashes and curfews. There were endless house raids and arrests. On January 13, 2017, police raided my house, but that night I happened to be at my sister's place because my father was sick. The police found me at my sister's and took me to the station. Police stations, as you may know, are where criminal cases are brought in, and brawls erupt all night long. They put me in the cell just across from the bathroom, so it was impossible to sleep, night or day.

On top of that, it was cold, and my cell had no heater, and the windows were broken. I froze for 14 days. I got a little sleep by pulling on four or five pairs of socks, plus a sweater and a parka. I never changed my clothes during the detention. They took me away once, to the police headquarters to fingerprint me.

The day I was to appear in court, they handcuffed me behind my back. First, they brought me to the Counter-terrorism Office. At the entrance to that building, there was a staircase of about 15 steps. As I was leaving, cameras flashed in my face. It was like they were staging a movie scene: *Here's the mayor, handcuffed, walking downstairs with a woman officer holding her arm. She smiles bitterly.*

They took me to the courthouse, and at the prosecutor's office, I reported their poor treatment of me so that it would go on the record.

By creating that spectacle, the authorities were trying to humiliate an elected official and frighten the public. Detaining me at the police station rather than at police headquarters, served the same purpose. Moreover, the police station's window directly overlooked the town hall where I'd worked, as if to send me the message, *We can drag you from that building and lock you up here anytime.* Clearly, they still didn't grasp that we were indifferent to positions of power or office titles.

As I expected, the court issued an arrest warrant for me on January 26. I was to be incarcerated in Mardin Prison again. I wanted to get there as soon as possible because this detention was chilling my bones to the marrow. I remembered the warm, friendly welcome that I'd experienced earlier at Mardin Prison. It was 11 p.m. when I arrived there for my second stint. The building was even older now, and the conditions inside were worse than before. But after all those days of icy cold, the kindness and affection of my comrades warmed my heart. We chatted, smoked, and drank tea until late. I was exhausted by the time one of the friends said, "Your bed is ready."

Mardin Prison had a huge, cold room that we called the Mortuary Room. It chilled you as soon as you entered. I saw that they'd made my bed in there. Of course, as a newcomer, I didn't feel I could say anything about it. Older mothers often stayed in the Mortuary Room when they were going through menopause, since cold air is good for alleviating menopausal stresses. Some elderly mothers were in there, and they said, "Mayor, seriously, whoever stays in this room leaves after a day or two. We hope you don't." "Of course I won't leave," I assured them, my teeth chattering.

But the windows in the room were open, and snow was blowing inside. I felt like I was sleeping outdoors. I had four blankets, three or four pairs of socks, my parka, and a hat, but it was useless. It was impossible to warm up. After a week, friends moved my bed into another room, and my mortuary adventure came to an end. Later when I passed by that room and poked my head in, the mothers would joke, “We won't let you in here in summertime!”

Twenty days later I was transferred to Van T-type Closed Prison. I boarded the plane like a passenger and sat by the window with two soldiers next to me. It was February 14, Valentine's Day. When the flight attendants came by and passed out heart-shaped chocolates, I thought, *Everything is so phony*. The search for truth comes at a heavy price.

I arrived at Van Prison at the end of that taxing day. I'd been up since 5 a.m., and they didn't complete my check-in until 9 p.m. About nine women guards surrounded me, intending to strip-search me. I wasn't having it. After a long argument, they took me to the ward.

Van Prison felt strange, after Mardin's awful physical conditions. The building was new, the furnishings were new, everything was new—yet the cold, the bane of my existence, found me there too. Here it was that infamous bitter cold of the Serhat region.* I glanced out at the prison yard. It was a small outdoor space with low-pitched windows, blanketed in three feet of snow. Mardin at least had a spacious yard and less snow.

The snow didn't melt. March 8 was approaching, but the yard was still filled with snow and was iced over. Some other prisoners and I asked permission to have a shovel to remove the snow. The authorities denied our request. We didn't have any salt. All we had was our hands and our strength. We looked at each other and said, “Let's go,” and got to work. We broke the ice with our hands and removed it in chunks. And we celebrated March 8 in the yard.

Even today, after enduring that harsh climate, I'm still not warmed up. I hope I'll be released soon so I don't have to spend next winter in that piercing cold.

When a person is in prison, they think more deeply about life and freedom and struggle. That's why I don't consider my time here as a loss. The one thing that pains me is not seeing my children. I have two daughters and two sons, all very young. But sometimes their letters amaze me—what they write is so deep and mature. They

* Serhat is eastern Turkey's border region and includes the cities of Iğdır, Kars, Ardahan, and Ağrı.

remind me once again that children in this country are forced to grow up too fast. I'm thinking not only of my own children but of all the children who've gone through similar experiences. It's not that I try to follow the conventional mother role. It's that I bear on my shoulders the heavy responsibility to leave a livable and free future to our children.

Reader, by now you may be wondering, "So how did Sara Kaya end up in prison?" I'll tell you frankly that my story isn't much different from those of other women friends. All our stories are about journeys to truth and freedom.

I was born in Nusaybin, in Mardin province, the fourth of eight children—six girls and two boys. I finished high school and in 1992–3 attended a school in Diyarbakır to prepare for the university entrance exam, since there was no such school in Nusaybin or Mardin. I attended Dicle University in Diyarbakır and graduated with a degree in civil engineering.

Determined to stand on my own feet, I went back to Nusaybin and got a job in the municipal administration. The other employees were all men—I was the first woman ever to work there. The environment was utterly permeated by the patriarchal mentality, and I was working in accounting, one of the most difficult municipal departments. Patriarchy perceives money as power and uses it to keep women under men's thumbs. It's a formidable weapon. For me as a woman, this was the most challenging field. But I comported myself proudly and stood tall. To enhance my professional knowledge, I studied business management at the College of Open and Distance Education. Ultimately, I succeeded in overcoming the patriarchal mentality in the accounting department—I rose to become its head.

At one time Nusaybin's women citizens never set foot inside the town hall, but once they finally did start coming in, my presence as a woman employee there made them feel more comfortable, so they came more often. In time, the accounting department became a place that only women visited. Men would send their wives to follow up on matters pertaining to their family business.

I'd like to share with you an unforgettable memory. One day an older man who had retired from the municipal administration came in and said to me, "I'll buy you a gold twist bracelet if you pay me half the pension I'm owed." I joked, "Oh, you know how we women are fools for twist bracelets!" Then I got serious and said, "Look, you worked for this municipality for years. You're entitled to that pension." I was sad that he wasn't getting it. I told him he should make a formal claim to his pension and look out for his rights under all circumstances. Although the administration didn't have much money in its budget that month, I made sure it paid his pension in full.

I worked in the accounting department for 15 years. As a woman administrator, I learned—and helped others learn—how not to let money corrupt us. You may be wondering, "Wasn't it hard, Sara?" Of course, it was very hard. But the hardest thing of all was to challenge the mentality that "women don't understand financial matters." I was determined to replace it with "women should be the ones to handle financial matters."

At the urging of friends, I ran for co-mayor in the 2014 local elections. Nusaybin was by then accustomed to women leaders, as Ayşe Gökkan had been mayor since 2009.* We ran a good campaign, and I won with 80 percent of the vote. I was very familiar with the town hall as a workspace. For me, co-mayoring wasn't a sinecure but a duty, one that I was confident I could perform.

I got down to work right away. My administration prioritized projects that encouraged women to express themselves, participate in social life, and achieve financial independence. Nusaybin was already a town where women felt powerful. Mayor Gökkan had established a women's cooperative, and it had helped lots of women become financially independent. I tried to strengthen and advance the commune-cooperative projects that she'd initiated.

We also developed a new plan for a women's market called Jiyana Bê Sînor (Life Without Borders). Women, constantly faced with obstacles, yearn for "a life without borders." The wire fences that separate Nusaybin from Qamishli, just across the Syrian border, made us yearn all the more for a borderless life. Thirty-eight

* Ayşe Gökkan (b. 1965) is an outspoken Kurdish journalist, feminist, and politician, currently imprisoned.

women applied to participate in the project. We built wooden booths for them. Sadly, the women's market never got underway, because the state revoked the people's will.

Another project that we thought was meaningful was White Rose Park. In earlier times, before wire fences and mines separated Nusaybin and Qamishli, people used to boat along the Jaghjagh River. The shoreline was known for its white roses, so Nusaybin was called the "Town of White Roses." By the time I became co-mayor, one area had been cleared of wire fences and mines but was being used as a garbage dump. We wrote a proposal to remove the trash and plant white roses there, in accordance with the town's history. We called the project "We Plant Roses Not Mines, Life Not Death," and sent our proposal to the district governor's office and other relevant institutions. They unfortunately denied our request, and we couldn't implement it. Instead we distributed the white roses to families for planting in their own yards.

In 2015–16, Nusaybin went through daunting times. While we were working to create a democratic municipality, the state put us under curfew and kept it in effect for a long time. During that curfew, armed forces destroyed the streets and neighborhoods where I was born and raised. It was very hard to witness. I felt like I was being stripped of my breath as well as my past.

The result: prison. Apê Mûsa once said, "Of the destruction I was the witness, now I am the accused." And here we are as his descendants.* I have so much to tell, but how can I fit it all into a few pages? When our hearts are full to overflowing, is any amount of paper enough to tell it all? Still, I feel most acutely on my shoulders the heavy responsibility of leaving a livable and free future to our children.

---

* Musa Anter (b. 1920), known as Apê Mûsa, was a Kurdish journalist, author, and activist. He was assassinated by Turkish agents on September 20, 1992.

16
"This Woman Is Tough as Nails"

Sadiye Süer Baran

Translated by Suna Parlak

Sadiye Süer Baran (b. 1968) was elected co-mayor of Pasûr (Turkish Kulp), in Diyarbakır province, on March 30, 2014, with 60 percent of the vote. She was arrested on January 5, 2017 and released in 2019.

The story of one of us is the story of all of us. I will try to tell my own to contribute to the story of all of us.

I was born in 1968 in Kızıltepe, in Mardin province. My family is originally from Mardin's Avina (Sürgüç) district. I spent part of my childhood in Şenkaya, in Erzurum province, where my father was exiled. Later we settled in Mazıdağı, back in Mardin.

When I was still young, my family arranged a marriage for me. We had four children. My husband was arrested in 1995 and was sentenced to twelve years and six months in Midyat Prison. I and my children moved in with my in-laws in Bismil, in Diyarbakır province. My mother-in-law was traditional and protective of me, so we argued a lot. I can still hear her yelling at me, "Oh look! *Ev jinik hesin bi sarî dicû!*" which means "This woman is tough as nails—she can't be beaten!"

Two months after my husband's arrest, I was detained, severely tortured, then released. I visited my husband in prison, and he and his friends there tried to give me strength and raise my spirits. Thanks to their efforts, I slowly recuperated. But it wasn't easy for me to shake off the effects of torture. I kept getting lost in my thoughts, like *Why are women always threatened by womanhood?* Between the state's pressure and attempts by my in-laws to control me, I began to search for freedom.

In 1997 I heard that HADEP had opened a district branch in Bismil. Without telling my in-laws or anyone else, I went to HADEP's building. I was nervous that if something happened to me, I'd be tortured again. But when I arrived, I saw that the person answering the door was as nervous as I was because, due to the ongoing pressures, not many people, least of all women, were visiting the party headquarters. The man who welcomed me was a nice elder named Mehmet Kaplan, who seemed to want to get to know me.

When I introduced myself, he got excited. "Oh! You're Mele Veysi's daughter," he exclaimed, "the Communist mufti! Both your father and your father-in-law are good friends of mine." We fell into a deep conversation.

Later that day, as I left, I noticed that one of the notorious "White Toroses" was following me. I sprinted to the nearest safe place, my sister's house. Out of breath, I told her I'd just come from the party and was being followed. She said, "What are you doing? Your husband is in prison, and you have four children!" She told me not to go to the party anymore. But I'd already taken the first step, and that evening I made my decision. I'd join the party to help make sure that my children wouldn't experience the same injustices. From then on, I went regularly to party headquarters and took part in women's activities.

For a long time, I hid from my mother-in-law the fact that I was going to the party, knowing she'd disapprove. She always said, *Çawa jinik qiloçê xwe li qiloçê mêra xe*? or "How can a woman bang her horns against a man's horns?" But when I saw other women daring to bang their horns against men's, everything changed. I helped created a women's commission for Bismil and would later serve as head of the commission and then the women's branch.

Fortunately, my two sisters-in-law helped me participate in politics. When I came home late in the evening, I wouldn't knock on the door. I'd tap softly on their window, and they'd stealthily let me in. They even read the newspapers and magazines I brought home. Over time, the rest of my extended family came to appreciate my political work.

In the 2004 local elections, I was elected a municipal councilor in Bismil. Soon afterward I was arrested for referring to the PKK leader Abdullah Öcalan as "Dear Öcalan" at a press conference. I was released a month later. Then I worked as DTP district chair in Kağıthane, Istanbul. I continued my work in HDP and HDK.

In 2014, I ran for co-mayor of Pasûr (Turkish Kulp), in Diyarbakır province. In the 1990s, Turkish security forces had burned down Pasûr twice. It's one of the places where Kurds suffered the most onerous forced migration and extrajudicial murders. There were still 2,500 village guards in the town center, so we had to campaign with caution. Nevertheless, we developed a full campaign program. We visited every family in the district, one by one. We prepared a special program for International Women's Day. The district hadn't seen such events in years, but when March 8 arrived, women poured into the demonstration arena decked out in all their fine colors. Their mass participation boosted our morale. That day,

Pasûr's women, who had suppressed their screams for years, walked the streets proudly.

Our campaign energy spread throughout the district. In the March 30, 2014, elections, I got 60 percent of the vote. No woman had ever been elected co-mayor, or anything close to it, in Pasûr.

At first, the men who normally came to the town hall looking for solutions for their problems didn't meet with me. But over time, my personal involvement in municipal projects altered their behavior. Soon women too began to show up, especially to share their needs and problems—including family matters—with me.

Our district had no venue where women could undertake projects, so our first major task was to establish a women's center. We built a beautiful center with a conference hall, a sitting room where visiting village women could rest, a children's playroom, and a room for counseling services. To commemorate the 1990s suffering of our district, we named the women's center after Zozan Eren, a nurse who, along with her husband, was pulled out of their car and killed while traveling from Diyarbakır to Pasûr. To this day, their bodies haven't been found. Zozan was a Mirabel of Pasûr.*

We built a day care center where women working outside the home could leave their children. It served about 30 children. We named it after Selma Yavuz, a child who died when an object she found on the highlands exploded. We also wanted to honor the memory of Mazlum and Mahsun, brothers who had lost their lives by stepping on a mine in the highlands, so we named a park after them. A lot of unexploded ordnance remains from the war, both in the highlands and in the rural areas around the district. It has already cost the lives of many children in Pasûr and still poses a grave threat.

Young people also had needs that the municipality could meet. In the 1990s, a hotel had burned down, but the charred ruins remained in place. We cleared the lot and built a nice youth center

* The three Mirabel sisters opposed Trujillo's dictatorship in the Dominican Republic and were assassinated on November 25, 1960. They've since become a global symbol of feminist resistance to authoritarian patriarchal regimes. The anniversary of their murder is commemorated as the International Day for the Elimination of Violence against Women.

there, with a library, exercise rooms, a live theater, and a cinema. By naming the center after Vahit Narin, who had been killed during the hotel fire, we kept his memory alive too.

Of course, the appointment of *kayyums* obliterated the district's historical memory as well as all these municipal services for women, children, and youth. When the political pressure started coming down on the municipalities, Pasûr got its share. In August 2016 I was detained, then released on probation and forbidden to travel abroad. But two of our councilors, Zeycan Zengin and Zülküf Zengin, were arrested. To replace our arrested councilors, the Interior Ministry appointed two *kayyums*. One of them was Muhsin Çiçek, who was a village guard.

Because I was on probation, I had to report to the police station every week to sign in. I did so, but they still they raided my house as well as the town hall on December 24, 2016, and detained me. I was in custody for eleven days. In the cell right across from mine, they held a man who was accused of drug use and rape. They didn't bring me any food or water for two days. When, two days later, they finally did arrive with food, I refused to eat for five days to protest their treatment. Health and sanitation conditions in detention were terrible. Even to visit the restroom, I had to make a request, and they'd give me permission only hours later.

The political operations against us continued relentlessly. Hence, on January 5, 2017, when I was arrested by the court, it didn't come as a surprise. In court I said, "I'll continue to struggle for democracy and peace whether I'm in or out of prison." That night the police in Pasûr kept me in detention for so-called security reasons. The next day I was helicoptered to Diyarbakır. Dozens of soldiers were squeezed into the helicopter with me—it was a form of sexual harassment.

We got to Diyarbakır E-type Prison. When the gate to the ward opened, dozens of women between 20 and 25 greeted me. We hugged tightly. Their friendly welcome melted my tension away—I was so relieved. It was customary for people in the ward to play a welcome prank on newcomers. The women played a prank on me, and I must admit I got pretty upset before I realized it was a joke. Seeing that I got so tensed up, they cut it short.

On January 19, I was transferred to Urfa No. 2 T-type Prison. While I was waiting for the authorities to process me, the officers treated me poorly. They tried to take off my shoes. They forcibly removed my coat. They handed me some plates and utensils and said, "This is state property. You have to return them when you leave." The same rude treatment continued during fingerprinting. Only when I protested did they change their attitude.

There were 27 of us in the ward at Urfa Prison. Inmates came and went, but our number always remained between 20 and 30. During Mother's Day week, the door opened, and an elderly mother with the bluest eyes entered wearing a purple headscarf. Getting arrested had been her Mother's Day gift. The 65-year-old *daye* [mother] had some serious health problems, but she was very strong and didn't say a word about her pain until it became unbearable.

Our ward was very colorful. The detention-and-arrest craze that had been going on nonstop for a whole year brought in people from all segments of society—Peace Mothers, journalists, doctors, nurses, students, lawyers, mayors, and party leaders. As I listened to their stories, I thought, *There is so much to fight against.* In fact, the common themes of the stories were "being a woman" and "believing in democratic politics." Sharing the ward brought us closer together. Despite our differences in language, religion, and ethnicity, we had much in common. I learned from Çiğdem, Dilek, and Ceren about the Turkish revolutionary movement. As we got to know each other in the ward, the walls that were supposed to divide us crumbled.

On April 7 my son Azad came to see me in prison. He went through all the visitation procedures but was detained at the meeting room door. He was arrested and sent to Siverek Prison on the grounds that his five-year prison sentence had been approved, after he was released on probation. The authorities deprived us of our chance for a face-to-face meeting.

There are five separate prosecutions against me. At the first hearing of my arrest case, I wanted to defend myself in Kurdish. They postponed the hearing to September 20, 2017, on the grounds that there was no Kurdish translator. At the next hearing, municipal councilors from AKP and Muhsin Çiçek, who had been appointed to the council as a *kayyum*, were to testify as witnesses because their complaints were one of the reasons for my arrest. What was I supposed to do—welcome the *kayyum* appointment with flowers? But despite all the political prosecutions against me, and despite all the pressures to stop our political struggle and break our will, I'll continue to sing a song that I used to sing when I was a kid: *Herne pêş!* Always forward!

17
From Prison to Parliament

Sebahat Tuncel

Translated by Emek Ergun

Sebahat Tuncel (b. 1975) was co-chair of DBP. She was arrested on November 6, 2016. Multiple lawsuits have been filed against her in prison, resulting in more than one prison sentence. She was imprisoned in Kocaeli F-Type Prison, although is now temporarily in Sincan Prison due to the Kobanê case.

I was born in the city of Malatya in 1975. When I was about five, my dad went to Germany, and the rest of us moved in with my maternal grandmother, who lived in Konakpınar village in Gürün, in Sivas province. That beautiful village is the setting of my childhood memories. One day if I get a chance, I'd like to go back and see again the place where I grew up boiling *gummi gundeliae* with my grandmother; gathering wild rhubarb, meadow saffron, sorrel, knotweed, and wild spinach; and playing with sheep. And I'd like to revisit the Behram Highlands, where we spent summer months.

When I was nine, my dad came back from Germany. I didn't want to return to Malatya, but we did. When summer break was over, my grandfather came and picked me up; I cried the whole way. Our new home would be in Balaban village, in the town of Yazıhan, in Malatya, where my father's family lived. I never really knew them before then. My paternal grandmother spoke Kurdish, and I kept saying, "Grandma speaks alien." But as I grew up, I came to understand that I was the alienated and assimilated one.

There I got to know my paternal uncles and aunts. My mother, father, and older brother went to work in the fields, and I stayed home and took care of the housework, looked after the children, and prepared meals for them. As I got older, I started helping in the fields as well. At the end of the day, after everyone had their meal, I'd rest and read books. I loved reading. When I look back, I realize how much that period contributed to my formation as a person.

My brother and I worked in the village in the summers and attended school in Malatya in the winters, where we rented a place. My paternal aunt Güler stayed with us. Then she passed the university entrance exam and got into Istanbul Technical University to study forest engineering. Her university life opened a new chapter for us. At the time, I was in eighth grade. When Aunt Güler came home for summer break, she'd talk about the Kurdish question and the rights of the Kurdish people. Our family already had a leftist, socialist awareness and an oppositional stance toward the system. After all, we're Kurdish Alevis. We practiced our ethnic identity and religious faith culturally but approached the Kurdish question from that general oppositional perspective. As my aunt continued at the university, we discussed these issues more often, which continued into my high school years.

I attended university in Mut, a district in the city of Mersin. After I graduated, I went to Istanbul and got a job with a construction company as a topography specialist. It was a male-dominated field. I worked there during daytime, and in the evenings and on weekends, I participated in neighborhood activities in Esenler district, organized by HADEP's local women's commission. If it had been up to me, I'd have joined the youth branch, but the party said, "No, the women's commission needs you more." So, I traveled around various neighborhoods in Esenler with Fatma Koçak (we called her Fadik), who later went on to become an editor at Jinha, the all-women news agency. The two of us kept busy—every month we distributed 60 copies of *Kadının Sesi* (*Women's Voice*) magazine, and every week we sat down with three or four new families and got to know them. That period was crucial for my personal growth. The articles in the magazine and our discussions of women's issues helped form my gender consciousness. That process brought me further into both the Kurdish people's struggle and the women's struggle and gave me ideological and political depth.

Women's search for liberation is an uphill struggle. We can't easily shake off the patriarchal mentality, habits, and patterns that have penetrated deep into the marrow of our bones. Too many women aren't even aware of what we're up against. Understanding and articulating male domination's impact on our subjectivities and our lives is a vital first step. I used to identify as a socialist, but as I got more involved in the women's struggle, I learned to question the gendered nature of the reality in which I lived.

Initially, as I said, I wasn't that excited about joining the women's commission. But over time, working there helped me confront my own gendered views. I can say that by organizing women's activities in the neighborhoods of Esenler and sharing in the love and solidarity I found among women there, my consciousness was rapidly raised. Dear Öcalan's analyses regarding women's liberation and his proposition that "no society can be free unless women are free" also played a constructive role.

As I sought to overcome the mental paradigms and habits of male domination, I found myself relating to women from a new perspective, especially the women in my family. I realized that women faced deep-rooted problems in the context of the family. The feminist movement's principle "the personal is political" helped call attention to family-bound realities like abuse, rape, and violence that had long been deemed private and hence weren't discussed as political matters. I became aware that this system of abuse was an integral part of women's domestic lives and that we had to put an end to it.

Women can begin to overturn this system first by opposing it, then by collectively organizing an opposition to it, and by expanding our solidarity. The personal is indeed political, but "it's impossible to win in any area of life without winning in the political arena"—that's another fundamental principle that has guided me and that will continue to do so.

Our organizing work in Esenler yielded results, as every day more neighborhood women joined our activities. I decided to take my own commitment further, first becoming chair of the Esenler women's branch, then Esenler district chair. By offering trainings for women and children's activities, we encouraged more neighborhood women to come to HADEP meetings. They did, bringing homemade cakes, which helped create a warm and intimate ambience. During that time (1999–2000), women in other places, too, were surging into the party in ever greater numbers. Male colleagues joked, "Women have changed the party's name to 'tea party'!" But seriously, women's hard work impressed the men. In addition to a large International Women's Day demonstration in Istanbul, we organized town-based March 8 celebrations. So many women came to Esenler's March 8 event that women from other organizations asked, "What, did you invite your party's whole Istanbul base?"

Of course, none of this came about on its own. Our women's branch worked very hard to make it all happen. We assigned each activist to a particular neighborhood. She'd make house visits for at least two days, then file a report on them with the party administration. One-on-one conversations were a very effective form of communication. And we learned a lot from the women we visited.

In addition, women made strong showings for protests and grassroots activities around current political agendas. Women were becoming politicized.

During that period, Kurdish-language education was a topic of public debate. We organized a campaign in which families filed petitions with the Ministry of Education saying, "We want our children to be educated in Kurdish in schools." About 30 mothers from Esenler filed these petitions. One night they got detained. The fathers took their children by the hand and brought them to Esenler's party headquarters. Fortunately, our building had a large meeting room. We took care of the children there while their mothers awaited court appearances, after which they were released.

It wasn't just in Esenler—our party and its women's commissions were gaining strength in many places. But in 2003, the government shut HADEP down, so we continued our work in its successor, DEHAP. Women in DEHAP wanted to strengthen women's influence within the party, so we raised HADEP's previous 25 percent women's quota to 35 percent. At the party convention that year, five of us—Türkan Yüksel, Pınar Işık, Zeynep Boğa, Şükran Gürbüz, and me, all very experienced in women's organizing in Istanbul—were appointed to the Central Women's Branch. I was elected provincial head of Istanbul's women's branch too. I held both positions at the same time.

During this period the Kurdish women's movement was becoming more engaged with the Turkish women's movement. Our popularity was on the rise, the women's liberation struggle was having an impact on general politics, and DEHAP's women's branches, with their powerful organizing work, attracted the attention of many women's groups. We were able to find common ground with feminist and socialist women's groups on gender politics. We participated in a feminist campaign to amend the Turkish Penal Code. We came together for events around March 8 (International Women's Day) and November 25 (International Day for the Elimination of Violence Against Women). We held joint conferences and seminars calling for an end to all discrimination and violence against women. Around this time, Gülbahar Gündüz, a member of our women's branch, was kidnapped and sexually assaulted. We co-organized protests about her case in alliance with the Turkish women's movement. We also undertook joint events to demand "peace, not war."

After HADEP failed to surpass the 10 percent electoral threshold in the 2002 general elections, we searched for a new approach to politics. In DEHAP we debated ways to restructure, connect with the public more effectively, improve local democracy, and strengthen the women's struggle. We thereby opened a new chapter in Kurdish politics. Several of the DEP MPs, who had been arrested in 1994, just then got out of prison and were involved in the debates. The upshot was, we decided to go for a new political formation that would be defined by democratic, ecological, and women-liberatory perspectives. First, as DTH, we held local public meetings and elected delegates. Then in 2005, as a result of all that work, we founded DTP.

We also revisited the party's women's structures. At a well-attended women's conference in Ankara, we decided to support raising the women's quota to 40 percent, instituting the co-chairing system, and replacing women's assemblies with women's branches. DEHAP's Central Women's Branch had 30 active members. The provincial and district women's branches also had dynamic structures. It was difficult to transfer that buildup into DTH and DTP. The transformation process was arduous but revising the party program and bylaws to incorporate the 40 percent women's quota, instituting general co-chairing, and establishing women's and youth branches as autonomous self-organized units became the new motivation for women's work.

The higher women's quota gained acceptance, and so did autonomous self-organizing. After all, for many years the party's women's organization had carried out its own activities without depending on the general party organization. But when it came to implementing general co-chairing, we encountered resistance. No party in Turkey had ever done that before. At that time, Turkey's Law on Political Parties required any given party to have only a "single general chair." Some in our party pushed back, warning that co-chairing wasn't legal and could cause the party to get shut down. Nobody opposed co-chairing in principle—they just resorted to saying, "It can't be done." The women's assembly pushed the issue forward anyway, hashing out the details of how the congress would elect general co-chairs, how they'd officially be positioned in the party organization, how we could overcome co-chairs' illegality, and so on.

But we didn't stop with theoretical deliberations; we resolved to charge ahead and apply co-chairing in practice, then address problems as they came up. Our first woman general co-chair, Aysel Tuğluk, had to endure the stress of the new process and manage the complications that emerged. At the time, I was active in the women's assembly. We worked hard to make the process go smoothly. The patriarchal political style caused a lot of perplexity. Our woman co-chair was often referred to as a "vice chair." Finally, just as we were correcting this error within the party, the media and press kept using the term "vice chair." For a year we spun our wheels, trying in vain to get people to use the right term, but then we gradually started making headway.

Today co-chairing and co-spokespersonship are legal and common in many institutions in Turkey. This is a big achievement for women. But the idea is still not well internalized politically, and people still experience difficulties implementing it.

Once co-chairing was in place in our party, our next step was to move forward to co-mayoring: we'd run candidates for co-mayor in the 2014 local elections. But here too we encountered obstacles. Many were of our own doing: we neglected to make all the necessary arrangements, we didn't prepare a women candidates' list, and the whole party structure hadn't yet adequately internalized co-chairing. Clearly, both women and men had to reexamine themselves and their societal roles from a gender-liberatory perspective. But I must underline that when you're creating something new, it's impossible to foresee every problem that will arise—you have to put the idea in practice first, then overcome hurdles as they arise. Eventually, this experience paved the way for us to make greater achievements down the road.

In November 2006, DTP called a meeting at the Bağcılar town hall, in Istanbul. To surpass the 10 percent electoral threshold in the 2007 general elections, the party decided to run independent candidates. But as the meeting was underway, police raided it and detained ten people, including me. At the time, I was the spokesperson for DTP's women's assembly. I was arrested and sent to Gebze Prison outside Istanbul.

There they put me in the ward with Azime Işık, older sister of member of the women's assembly Çimen Işık. During a visit, Çimen informed me that the women's assembly was thinking about nominating me as a candidate for MP from a district in Istanbul. I said I didn't know if a nomination for an imprisoned person would be appropriate, but it was a matter for the women's assembly to decide. Shortly after that Türkan Yüksel, who had taken over as women's assembly spokesperson after my arrest, came and notified me that the assembly had indeed decided to nominate me, but it wasn't clear yet which district. I thought they were just proposing a symbolic candidacy.

A few days later, some lawyers turned up to get my signature on documents required for a candidacy, and the full reality hit me. I was going to be a candidate for Istanbul's third district, an area where the party had a strong organized presence and good prospects. In fact, DTP seemed a shoo-in to win there. But I thought there was no way to run an election campaign from prison, so I said we shouldn't risk it. The party's decision, however, was final.

Later, I learned that my nomination had been much debated. In fact, a group of provincial party administrators had objected to my candidacy and gone all the way to party headquarters to demand that the third district's provincial chair be the candidate instead of me. After all, they argued, I wasn't well known and was incarcerated to boot, and so I was in no position to run an election campaign, and the party would lose a parliamentary seat that it was otherwise sure to win. However, the women's assembly insisted, and the administrators had to step back. Those who opposed my candidacy concentrated their efforts on campaigns in the first and second districts. It was mainly the district organizations that ran my campaign. The women's movement in Turkey also gave support, and the women's assembly managed to organize a strong campaign in my district.

The friends in prison supported the campaign by establishing our own election commission. We worked very hard. We wrote leaflets, sent letters to newspaper columnists to inform them about the candidate, held newspaper interviews, and so forth. We really did end up running a campaign from prison. I'd like to take this opportunity to thank all my women friends in Gebze Prison. Ours was an exceptional campaign that made history.

As the election results came in, we followed the tally with great excitement. When we saw that I'd won, we jumped for joy and started celebrating. I was elected an MP with 93,000 votes. I guess people get more creative in dire, even impossible, times. But the real credit belonged to DTP, the women's movement, and our people. This victory was the accomplishment of an organized people and the women's liberation struggle.

Thanks to that immense work, as an elected MP, I got out of prison. Women welcomed me, out in the open air, with exhilaration. The women's movement had broken new ground, and by electing a woman inmate as an MP, they enabled me to get back to women's grassroots organizing. My legal process continued, and I was ultimately acquitted in that case.

Another important source of support had been an alliance of young academics who backed our candidates. The alliance's campaign slogan was "Thousand Hope Candidates." After the election, we organized "Thousand Hope" themed meetings with those academics, many of whom were women, and I met with them periodically throughout my term as MP. We established a bridge between parliament and academia. I prepared and filed parliamentary inquiries on themes on academia's agenda, particularly issues of ecology, women's liberation, and labor rights. Later, during the state of emergency, most of those academics were dismissed from their jobs for signing on as "Academics for Peace."*

Of DTP's 22 MPs, eight of us were women—a gender proportion of 36 percent. We were veterans of the women's struggle, of the streets and demonstration arenas, and now as MPs we used the parliamentary rostrum on behalf of women. We brought women's

* Academics for Peace was founded in 2012 to support Kurdish political prisoners' demands for peace in Turkey. In 2016, members signed the petition, "We will not be a party to this crime!" after which they came under attack by the Turkish state.

liberation onto the general political agenda, increased the visibility of the organized women's struggle, and continued our strong ties with the women's movement while in the parliament.

Women's greater visibility in the parliament was an accomplishment of the Kurdish women's movement, which continued to play a major role by enabling us to be elected as deputy speakers and group vice chairs, and by increasing our numbers in parliamentary committees after 2007. I also salute the rising women's movement for the establishment of the Committee on Equal Opportunity for Women and Men and the signing of the Istanbul Convention.*

When DTP was shut down in December 2009, we collectively shifted over to BDP. After DTP managed to get into parliament with independent candidates in 2007, the electoral threshold of 10 percent stopped being an obstacle. But the government remained unwilling to remove or lower the electoral threshold. It wanted to obstruct BDP's participation in the 2011 general elections. The Supreme Election Council vetoed eight people's candidacies, including those of Ertuğrul Kürkçü, Hatip Dicle, and myself. Upon protests, they revoked this decision. In the 2011 elections, we won 31 MPs and once again formed a party group in the parliament. This time around, eleven MPs were women. Two of them, Selma Irmak and Gülser Yıldırım, had been nominated and elected from prison, but they couldn't join us for a long time because the state didn't release them, in violation of the constitution.

Even though BDP made a small party group with little experience in the parliament, it was the main opposition to AKP—which went down well with the public. The election results also meant that the people approved the electoral alliance. So after the elections, we expanded our dialogues with those parties as well as civil society organizations, local forces, and individuals to explore the basis for a common struggle.

A team of five MPs—Sırrı Süreyya Önder, Levent Tüzel, Ertuğrul Kürkçü, our general co-chair Gültan Kışanak, and me—got the ball

* The Istanbul Convention binds European states to prevent and prosecute violence against women. Turkey, the first country to sign the convention in 2011, withdrew in 2021 following a presidential decree by Erdoğan.

rolling. We held intense discussions with women's and youth organizations, ecological movements, Alevi associations, anticapitalist Muslims, leftist and socialist parties, publishers, professional associations, opinion leaders, and academics—in short, groups and individuals who stood for democracy. We drew on our experiences with election alliances and democracy platforms and adopted the principle of "socializing the political and politicizing the social." We found an acute need for a new political vision grounded in labor rights, women's liberation, freedom for all ethnic groups and religious faiths, and ecology. To bring their struggles together in a common platform, we created HDK.

This new political vision met with a positive response, and so in 2013, with the next elections approaching, HDP emerged on the political scene. Fatma Gök and Yavuz Önen were HDP's founding co-chairs. A few months later, the party's first extraordinary congress elected Ertuğrul Kürkçü and me as the general co-chairs. At the second extraordinary congress, in June 2014, we passed the torch to Figen Yüksekdağ and Selahattin Demirtaş. I continued my work at HDK and took the position of HDK co-spokesperson for a while.

On May 28, 2016, DBP* held an extraordinary congress that elected Kamuran Yüksek and me as general co-chairs. During this period the AKP government cracked down on DBP municipalities. First, it removed 22 co-mayors from office and appointed *kayyums* in their places. When our co-mayors of Diyarbakır Metropolitan Municipality resisted such unlawfulness, the state arrested them on October 25. On November 4, it expanded the political operation to include HDP general co-chairs and MPs. On November 6, as I was standing in front of the Diyarbakır courthouse to protest those arrests, I too was arrested and sent to Diyarbakır E-type Prison.

During the political operations, I learned, they'd already prepared an indictment for me. They used my participation in the protest as an excuse to arrest me. After all, what other explanation can there be for arresting the general co-chair of a political party that held regional power and controlled 106 municipalities?

* DBP is the regional sister party of the national HDP.

The AKP-Palace government had drawn up its "Collapse Plan" to eliminate democratic politics well in advance.* It targeted democratic, ecological, and gender-liberatory politics both locally and nationally. It annulled DBP control in 96 municipalities and arrested co-mayors and town councilors. Along with elected officials they also arrested thousands of DBP and HDP members.

I spent my first night in Diyarbakır E-type Prison in a ward with two politically independent women. They prepared some food for me, then I took a shower and went to bed. In the morning, I was told that there were two wards for political prisoners, one with 36 inmates and the other with 21. They took me to the second one. Its bed capacity was actually eight. I'd been there before. In 2012, with permission from the Ministry of Justice, Aysel Tuğluk and I'd visited this prison to help end an open-ended hunger strike, and we'd talked with women inmates in that big ward. This time I was here as an inmate myself.

On my first day, the ward's women welcome-pranked me. They pretended they didn't know who I was and played their roles so well that I fell for it, although I knew about welcome pranks from Gebze Prison. Still, they fooled me. Then around midnight, before I had a chance to meet everyone, the authorities notified me that I was being transferred to another prison. I said goodbye to those who were awake and left. They put me in a noncommercial plane and at about 3:30 a.m., I arrived at Çorlu Airport. I was taken to Silivri Prison No. 9, together with Nihat Akdoğan, HDP's Hakkâri MP. And now here I am in Kocaeli F-type Prison.

While we're in prison, we aren't just trying to bear problems—at the same time, under the difficult conditions of imprisonment, we're building communal living spaces. We're forging the most beautiful relations of comradeship and feeling the most intense love for and determination with the other inmates. We're experi-

---

* Palace refers to Erdoğan's newly built gigantic presidential residence and office. The "Collapse Plan," developed in 2014 by the Undersecretariat of Public Security, plotted out the attack on Kurdish cities in advance in "every minute detail, including city sieges, ambulance and firefighter instructions, restrictions on freedom of the press, the repression of social opposition, arrests and the escalation of detentions," then went on to execute the plan. See HDP, *Cizre Report*, released on April 17, 2016.

menting with the possibilities of free thought and free life despite the restrictions of these cold, gray places. We're developing new strategies to cope with the hardships of these places of constant struggle. While the outside world makes cheese sandwiches in toasters, we're trying to cook them on radiators. When flowers bloom on concrete walls, we go to great lengths to protect them so that they don't get plucked away during searches. We befriend bees and beetles who have lost their way. We distill beauty from difficulty in defiance of fascism and tyranny. In other words, we're living a life in prison.

18
Imprisoned for Providing Services

Servin Karakoç

Translated by Susan Benson-Sökmen

Servin Karakoç (b. 1986) was elected co-mayor of Ahlat Ovakışla, in Bitlis province, on March 30, 2014, with 42 percent of the vote. She was arrested on October 31, 2016. She was released in February 2022.

On October 10, 2016, police detained me in front of my home in Tatvan, saying, "You have to give a statement." The next morning my co-mayor and two MPs from Bitlis were detained the same way. In all, nine people from Bitlis were taken into custody: co-chairs, MPs, and party executives. Under the state of emergency, the police were allowed to detain us for 21 days without making any formal charges.

The detention cell had no windows, and our watches were removed, so we lost our sense of time. Each of us was held separately, in solitary confinement, for 17 days. If any of us tried to call out to one another, the guards would bark, "Talking is forbidden!" By isolating us, they were trying to instill despair in us. There was one toilet and sink, used by both men and women. They weren't cleaned regularly, so they were filthy and stank. They didn't even handle our routine health checks properly.

Among those detained in the anti-Gülen operation were our neighborhood's imam and my primary school teacher.* Our neighborhood imam now became the jail's imam. He'd recite the call to prayer (*azan*) five times a day, and the men would perform the prayer.

On the 17th day, they brought a woman detained in the anti-Gülen operation into my cell. I thought, *Finally, someone I can talk to!* But all she did was cry and pray.

On the morning of the 21st day, they took the four of us—two co-mayors and two MPs—to the prosecutor's office. A large crowd was waiting outside the courthouse, and the sight made me forget all about my solitary confinement. Almost half the town had turned out. Applause and jubilant ululation erupted as we strode toward the courthouse. Even more people were packed into the first and second floors.

The police took us to a room, then evacuated everyone else from the building. They kept us waiting at the prosecutor's door until noon for no reason. Our lawyers speculated that they were delaying deliberately because they were waiting to hear the verdict in the

* The anti-Gülen operation was the mass detainment and arrests of alleged followers of Fethullah Gülen. The AKP government claimed that Gülen, exiled leader of a religious movement, was behind the 2016 coup attempt.

case against Diyarbakır co-mayors, Gültan Kışanak and Fırat Anlı. The lawyers believed the verdict in our case hinged on that. If they released Diyarbakır co-mayors, they'd release us as well.

Evening came. Around 8 p.m., the officers took us into the on-duty court, which issued our arrest warrants. As our arrests were processed, a senior official from the police department came over to me and said something like "Your leader Gültan has been arrested. You must take that as a message." He meant, the same was in store for us. And he added, "Sorry, but we have to arrest you," then thanked us for our service.

I was arrested on the evening of October 31. At 2:15 a.m. the next morning, I arrived in Bitlis E-type Prison. When the door to the ward opened, the women inmates, sleepy and confused, stumbled downstairs. They'd heard about my detention, but because so much time had passed, they'd assumed I was released. It was wonderful to drink tea again after 22 days. And even better, it was smuggled Ceylon tea!

On the morning of November 5, the guards told us, "Get ready. In half an hour, you're being transferred." They were going to take us to Sincan Prison because Bitlis had no ward for political prisoners. On a cold December day, two student inmates and I were handcuffed, put in a prison transport vehicle, and driven for 17 hours to Sincan. They made us spend the night waiting in the observation ward. In the morning, they put us in the political prisoners' ward. After introducing myself to the others, I settled into my cell.

On the second day, my cellmates and I decided to tell the others about our detention by singing *dengbêj*.* Hanım Yıldırım, co-chair of the Ağrı provincial branch of HDP, began by singing an *uzun hava*.** She lasted about 20 minutes—not bad. Second to perform was Özlem Demir, co-chair of the Ağrı provincial branch of DBP. She sang a ten-minute melody recounting her experiences.

* *Dengbêj* is the Kurdish oral tradition of musical storytelling, which transmitted Kurdish heritage across generations, in times when it wasn't possible to publish written materials in Kurdish.

** *Uzun hava*, literally "long air" or "long melody," is a Kurdish folk music genre distinguished by its free rhythm and quasi-improvisational melodies.

Then it was my turn. I began around 9 p.m. At 1:30 a.m. I was still describing the tenth day of my detention. They said, "It's late, let's go to bed, you'll finish tomorrow." The next evening, I started at 8 p.m. At midnight, I was still telling the 18th day of my detention. We took another break and decided to continue the following day. On the third day, I began singing *hay lo, hay lo** at 8 p.m. and was still going strong at 10 p.m. Friend Özlem joked, "This is enough to make a saint swear! Get to the part where you go to prison already, so our misery can end!" With that, I had to stop, so I finished on the third day. By the way, my mother was a talented *dengbêj*, so I owe my talent to her. It's a very useful skill, both inside and outside prison.

I was born in 1986 in Kêrs (Kırıkkaya), a village of Ahlat, in Bitlis province. On January 15, 1993, Turkish armed forces evacuated and razed Kêrs, forcing my family to migrate. We settled in Tatvan, also in Bitlis. Going through certain experiences politicizes people. Toward the end of 2008, I joined DTP. Between 2009 and 2012, I served two terms in the party's district administration, carrying out women's projects in Tatvan. In 2011, I felt the impact of the detention craze known as the anti-KCK operation, criminalizing our party's activities. At trial they sentenced me to six years and three months of imprisonment. The Supreme Court of Appeals overturned the verdict.

In 2014, I was serving on the party's Bitlis provincial election commission. As that year's local elections neared, we planned our campaign, but I was curious about what was happening in nearby Diyarbakır. How many party members had applied to be nominated as Amed's co-mayor candidates, and who might be chosen? Then we went into a meeting and toward the end I asked, "How many candidates do they have for Amed?" Someone said there was none yet. That alarmed me. In my usual humorous way, I rose and said, "If you'll excuse me, friends, I'm leaving." "Where are you going?" they asked. "I'm going to sacrifice myself," I replied. "I can't let Amed be without a candidate!" We all laughed.

* A Kurdish expression of woeful lamentation.

Of course, when I later became co-mayor of tiny Ovakışla, people constantly teased me, asking, "How does it feel to dream about the metropolitan municipality, only to end up in a small town?" It became a standing joke. Then, when my friends saw that it was getting to me, they started referring to Ovakışla as a "metropolitan municipality."

All joking aside, we got down to work immediately. After all the people, especially women, had high expectations from us. Being the only elected woman in our municipal administration, I had a hard time at first. Since the problems that women experience are commonly known, I don't need to discuss them in detail here. But I did encounter some serious misogyny. People said things like, "Municipal government is men's work—what do women have to do with it? Ah, she'll get bored after a few months." Or "How can a woman who grew up in Tatvan understand us?" My village, Kêrs, was only 15 minutes from Ovakışla, and as everyone knew, it was the only village in this area that was razed and evacuated. Still, people raised issues about me that they'd never troubled men officials with. But I overcame these prejudices in a short time. Dedication, hard work, and perseverance turned out to be enough.

What was hardest for me to get over was a certain childhood trauma. In Ovakışla, the town hall and the police station faced each other. At first, every time I walked by my office window, I'd find tears streaming down my cheeks. A childhood memory had left the deepest mark on me. One snowy January day, my family and I had been kept waiting all day long in front of that police station, on top of a tractor. I worked hard to get over the trauma of that day. The best method, I found, was to work harder and be with the people.

Small towns have a hard time funding municipal services—it's a serious problem. The budget is limited, and employees are few. Here's a story about that. At the center of Ovakışla was a cemetery, much neglected. We decided to build a brick wall around it, so we purchased a truckload of bricks. The day the truck arrived, I noticed that it was standing in front of the town hall for hours. "Why aren't the bricks being unloaded?" I asked. Someone replied, "Mayor, we need to hire workers." The municipality had only office staff. I called two town councilors and asked them to come over.

While I waited for them, friends came by, and I climbed on top of the truck. "I'll pass you the bricks—you stack them," I said. "Mayor, this is a shame," they replied. "You get down, we'll do it. It's men's work." I ignored them and handed them a few bricks, and they had to begin stacking them. Across the road some men were sitting in a café. They got up and came over to help. In 10 or 15 minutes, we emptied the truck. After that day, we took care of all town services collectively, in solidarity.

I didn't rent a place in Ovakışla. Instead, I spent my two years as a guest of the locals. Every afternoon I'd visit a family, and we'd dine together. Then I'd spend the night with them. Ovakışla is a welcoming, warm town. I can say that it was a true pleasure to work there. Its livelihood depends on the production of potatoes, sugar beets, and dry beans. The citizens are hard-working, and the economy is strong. As the municipal administration, we supported the development of organic farming and raised awareness about organic production and ecological sustainability.

Despite our limited resources, we tried to support women. For example, twice a year we'd award scholarships to women college students. That alone was a significant contribution. One day, upon hearing about it, a man came to the town hall and started raving about his son's talents. At first, we didn't understand why he was saying that, so we just listened. Finally, he concluded, "Yes, he's a young man, but he's also more of a woman than most women. He works harder than his sister at home. He does all the housework. Give him a scholarship too!" I guess you could call it the multiplier effect of a small act of positive discrimination. But then, we could also call it the effect of women's solidarity on men.

19

One Woman Became 80

Yıldız Çetin

Translated by Ruken Isik

Yıldız Çetin (b. 1974) was elected co-mayor of Gürpınar, in Van province, on March 30, 2014, with 60 percent of the vote. She was arrested on May 1, 2017, and was sentenced to prison, then was released because she'd served longer than the sentence.

As my co-mayor friends were getting arrested one by one, I knew I'd soon be arrested too, but in the meantime, I'd carry out the duties that people had chosen me for, no matter what. I was detained on March 26, 2017, in a raid on my home. I was held in police custody for six days. At my court appearance, I was released on probation, but the prosecutor appealed, and the court issued an arrest warrant for me. In the middle of the night, dozens of police raided my friend's house in Van, where I was staying. My eleven-year-old daughter Havîn was there as well. I asked the police to wait and let her father come and pick her up. They refused, so I had to leave her behind. Havîn was crying out loud after me. She was impossible to console, but they wouldn't even let me try. As a mother, I couldn't forget her cries for days. Havîn's screams haunt me to this day.

I spent that night at the police station and was transported to court in the morning. I was arrested on May 1 and brought to Van T-type Prison. This was the first time I'd been arrested, let alone imprisoned. At the entrance of the prison, they searched me, using a stressful method called a "detailed search," which targeted human dignity. At the ward, women friends welcomed me warmly, which helped me relax a bit. There were other elected friends as well. It didn't take me long to get used to life in prison.

I was born in 1974 in the Otluyazı (Xulik) village, in Ahlat, in Van province. I finished elementary and middle school in Ahlat. Later, I studied nursing at Bitlis Medical Vocational High School. After graduation, I settled in Van and worked as a nurse at the University of Van. I'm the mother of three. In 2009, I was elected as a city councilor for Van on the DTP list. I served as a city councilor for five years, working on the women's activities.

In the city council, I served on the gender equality commission, where we prioritized gender awareness training, since it was necessary to raise consciousness first. We included the municipal staff in those trainings.

We established the Van Municipal Center for Research and Application on Women's Issues. We carried out surveys to assess women's priorities, demands, and problems, then gathered the information in a database. Based on the data, we organized women's activities. For example, we learned that women wanted to turn their labor into earnings and become economically independent. So, we gave priority to vocational courses and manufacturing workshops, initiating rug and textile workshops and jewelry design classes at the Rojin Center for Women and Life. Since employed women needed a safe place to leave their children, we also opened a daycare at the Center.

In 2014, on the recommendation of women friends, I ran as a DTP candidate for co-mayor of Gürpınar, a town in Van province. From the time the Gürpınar municipality was established in 1956, no party from the DTP tradition had ever won an election there. We realized that previous administrations had done no work for women. In fact, among the 300 employees at the town hall, only one was a woman. And she was there only because she'd been transferred during a bureaucratic reshuffling.

In order to extend municipal services to women and initiate women-oriented programs, we first established the women's directorate and hired women employees. Drawing on my previous work in Van, we conducted a survey in the town center and surrounding villages to assess women's needs and using that information, created a database. To respond to those needs, we established the Women's Center. In addition to providing counseling services, we established a tomato paste production unit, a milk collection center, a carpet weaving workshop, and a textile workshop. We also started classes on computers, Kurdish, English, and the Quran. We opened a sports center for women and founded cultural centers in the villages.

We established the Xavasor Women's Cooperative. Our women's activities improved so much so that we had 20 women working in the town hall, and another 60 in the cooperative. The number of women working in the municipality rose from one to 80.

We founded the Muharrem Taş Health Center to provide health services. Muharrem Taş was an 18-month-old boy who had died in 2014 because during a heavy snow, he couldn't be taken to the hospital in time. His father had to carry the child's dead body in a bag on his back from their village to the nearest town.

After the AKP government appointed *kayyums*, all the women's projects were handed over to the Women and Democracy Association.* The Muharrem Taş Health Center was turned over to the *müftü* office (the local religious affairs agency). The cultural centers were shut down.

I'd taken on the duties of co-mayorship knowing well the difficulties of working in an area dominated by 5,000 years of patriarchal mentality. And just as I expected, I encountered many difficulties. But together with women friends, we gave reality to our women-centered vision. We didn't give up, and we didn't hold back. The wellspring of our creativity and resistance was women's solidarity.

* Founded in 2013, the Women and Democracy Association is a pro-government neoconservative women's rights organization. President Erdoğan's daughter, Sümeyye Erdoğan, is its vice chair.

20

"Is Sir Chiefwoman In?"

Zeynep Han Bingöl

Translated by İlkim Karakuş

Zeynep Han Bingöl (b. 1960), was elected co-mayor of Karayazı, in Erzurum province, on March 30, 2014, with 88 percent of the vote. She was arrested on December 9, 2016. She is currently imprisoned in Sincan Prison. Her case is still pending.

I was born in 1960 in Karayazı, a town in Erzurum province. Karayazı was small and conservative, with a strong feudal culture, and most girls there wouldn't be sent to school. I finished primary and middle school and wanted to continue my education, but how? The town didn't have a high school. That year I and some friends who also had finished middle school pestered the principal to have a high school opened up. He set about the task. September came, but the new high school wasn't ready. We sat in front of the building every day, as if we were protesting. Finally, it opened in January, and I started high school. In junior high, there were 20 boy students—I was the only girl. That's how I became the first girl to graduate from Karayazı High School.

The year I graduated, 1979, Turkey was in great turmoil, amid unsolved political murders, the Maraş Massacre, and constant clashes. Then just as we seemed to be getting through it, the society suffered the inexplicable cruelty of the 1980 military coup.

I come from a family of revolutionaries, so we were targets of this cruelty. As members of my family were arrested, my mom suffered breakdowns due to heart and nerve disorders. The burden of maintaining our family shifted to my small shoulders, although I was only 20. I took charge of the household chores as well as the daily care of my two siblings, ages four and 13. And I had to keep the family going financially, managing our main source of income, the 20 cattle we owned. I had to handle all these duties at once. Between the atrocious coup and the heavy burden of the family, I got stronger as I struggled through those hardships.

To take on the role of breadwinner, I opened an accounting and letter-writing office to help people with official applications. As I did the chores, farming, and husbandry at home, I wrote letters for people and helped them navigate their official affairs at my office. Listening to people's grievances, trying to figure out where and how they should apply for help, and writing their letters through all these dealings, I built strong relations with people in Karayazı as well as in the surrounding villages. I started my business to financially support my family, but struggling to survive as a woman was also crucial to me. While conversing with people who came to my office, I'd try to persuade them to send their daughters to school. I can say that I helped some women, if only a few, gain access to education. In later years, some of those women would visit me. Words cannot begin to describe the thrill I felt when that happened.

I worked as an accountant in Karayazı until 1988. I also worked at the community training school's knitting workshop. I can say that I contributed, at least a bit, to women's employment and socialization. In 1989, I left my family home and moved to Varto, in Muş province, where my father owned some land—he'd abandoned it over 30 years earlier. I started farming the land, raising field crops, cultivating fruit trees, and growing vegetables. I lived alone for three years. I supported myself by working at Varto community training school and doing some more accounting work.

In 1992, I got married and moved to Ankara, where I continued my accounting work. During those years I also worked at İHD. And I served as a Central Disciplinary Committee member for DEP.

Later I returned to Karayazı, and I found that not much had changed in the intervening years. The rich were richer, and the poor were poorer. Control of the municipality changed hands between two local families, switching back and forth seasonally. They were interested in increasing their families' wealth, not serving the people. Meanwhile the people, eager to see their town urbanized, had given up on living in harmony with nature and subsistence economy and had become prisoners of a new system. In the villages, formerly pristine creeks and rivers were now polluted with sewage and devoid of fish. They were hotspots for disease. Streets became oceans of trash, and you couldn't find a single tree to shade yourself. Turkey was ostensibly a developed country with a presumably growing economy, but everything was worse in Karayazı, my hometown. There were no services or resources.

With all this in mind, and at the encouragement of women and my social circle, I ran for co-mayor of Karayazı in 2014. Four other women ran for the municipal council in a campaign that represented women's purple color in the election process. We won with a record-breaking 88 percent. For the first time ever, Karayazı had a woman co-mayor.

I encountered the expected hardships but nothing I couldn't overcome. The people had had enough with the former administrations' governance mentality and had faith in our political vision. They embraced co-mayorship as part of that vision, but we still had a way to go before everyone internalized the philosophy and governance style of co-mayorship.

One day as I was leaving Co-mayor Sait's room, I ran into an old man. He asked, "Is Sir Chief in?" Smiling, I said, "We don't have chiefs here." He turned and walked away, seemingly pensive. Then he turned back and asked, "Is Sir Chiefwoman in?" "We have neither chiefmen nor chiefwomen here," I explained. "We have *hevserok*—co-mayors. One is me, and the other is Mehmet Sait." I opened the door, and we went into Sait's office. Sait and I listened to the old man together; he had tea and left pleased.

Our real struggle was to get our staff on board with women-oriented projects. They didn't really want to change their established ways. Before we came into office, the municipal administration had only two women employees. The town hall didn't even have a separate women's bathroom. Those two women had avoided using the bathroom as much as possible and used the men's bathroom only when they had to. It never occurred to the men in charge to have a women's bathroom installed. So, our first task was to build that. Over time we increased the number of women employees from two to eight. By adding women town councilors, employees, and me as co-mayor, we finally made women's presence felt in the town hall.

Erzurum province is infamous for its cold weather. In wintertime, the water pipes in houses freeze. Our district had a *hammam* [Turkish bath], but it served only men. We wanted the *hammam* to allocate one or two days every week for women, but our men colleagues constantly came up with excuses not to. Women came to the town hall every day to demand access to the *hammam*, to no avail. Seeing how crucial this was for women, I and our women town councilors went to talk to the *hammam* manager. We asked him to designate one day for women's use. Finally, our request was accepted, and women could at least take a hot bath despite the frozen pipes.

We started a women's directorate in the administration to run women's activities. Women who had never before set foot in the town hall now dropped in, saying, "Co-mayor, I came to have a cup of tea," even when they had no formal business there.

I was detained on December 6, 2014, at my home in Karayazı. Co-chair Mehmet Sait Karabakan was detained as well. We were held in custody for three days in Erzurum police headquarters. On December 9, we were arrested and transported to Erzurum Prison. After being processed, I was taken to a ward. Twenty-seven people were crammed into a ward meant for four. I knew most of them already. There were municipal co-chairs, town councilors, and party officials from Ağrı, Van, Iğdır, and Erzurum. We spent that night chatting and joking. Then six of us lay head-to-toe in three bunk beds. You couldn't roll onto your side, or else your feet would touch your friend's face.

On December 14, I heard the guards say, "Get ready to be transferred." They didn't tell me where I was being taken. At the airport, I found out that they were taking me to Sincan Prison in Ankara. When we arrived, they first put me in a so-called temporary room since it was a weekend and they couldn't book me. As soon as I walked in, I was stunned to see Serpil Köksal, HDP's Ankara Mamak district co-chair. She was just as surprised to see me. She'd been arrested the day before, along with İbrahim Binici, HDP's Ankara provincial chair, and Kazım Genç, the party's other Ankara Mamak district co-chair.

They told me it was impossible to get the guards' attention from this room. When the time came for Serpil Köksal's medication, she couldn't get anyone to hear her. My arrival was convenient in this sense, because when the guards brought me in, she asked for her medication and so was finally able to get it. I came down with a migraine due to the lack of air and my exhaustion from traveling. We kept pounding on the door, but nobody responded. As day turned to evening, my migraine worsened. It receded a bit only after I got an injection in the hospital later that night.

On Monday I was taken to a regular ward, where there were six young women. "Why did they bring you here?" they asked. "We have scabies." Thankfully, they were careful, but I wrote a request for a ward change. The authorities moved me to a new ward five days later, putting me in with another familiar face: Mukaddes Kubilay, co-mayor of Ağrı. Like me, she'd just been arrested. Our ward had nothing. We were told that the prison commissary was closed for an end-of-year inventory, so we couldn't even get a cup of tea for days. After a while, though, we were able to establish a regular prison routine.

After the tumult of those first days, I was able to process my feelings about being imprisoned. The unjust arrests, the overturning of the people's political will, and the intolerance for women's representation stirred many emotions. As I gazed at the familiar faces around, I saw that the current that we were pitting ourselves against was strong. But essentially, these political arrest operations just indicate how frightened male power is of women's resistance. In Karayazı five elected women—the four councilors and I—had initiated significant changes in the municipality and the district. By arresting all five of us, the authorities were attempting to break women's struggle. But their attempt will be in vain.

21
"They've Turned It into a Women's Municipality"

Zeynep Sipçik

Translated by Gülay Kılıçaslan

Zeynep Sipçik (b. 1986) was elected co-mayor of Dargeçit district, in Mardin province, on March 30, 2014, with 62 percent of the vote. She was arrested on March 28, 2016. She is currently in Sincan Prison.

On March 28, 2016, I was driving from Mardin to Dargeçit, accompanied by Leyla Salman, Kızıltepe's co-mayor, and Yüksel Oğuz, a Dargeçit town councilor. Near Midyat, the police pulled us over, detained us, and took us to the Midyat police station, saying that an arrest warrant had been issued against us.

That day in the Midyat courthouse, I was arrested on charges of involvement in democratic actions and events organized by a political party, such as naming the municipal women's center "Çiçek Women's Center,"* and stating that the construction of the Ilısu Dam would destroy local Kurdish history and culture, and publishing the slogan "Liberation with autonomy" in the town bulletin. It was absurd to consider these crimes. Nonetheless they took me to Midyat Prison and put me in a dingy 20-foot-square cell, because, they said, they had no ward for political prisoners.

Leyla Salman and I were held there for 15 days and then transferred to other prisons. They put us both in a transport vehicle and drove us nearly 20 hours. We arrived at Erzurum at around 2 a.m., to drop off Leyla at Erzurum Prison. I spent the night there and the next day they drove me for another 18 hours to Sincan Closed Women's Prison in Ankara. They could have flown me from Midyat to Sincan in an hour and a half, but instead they subjected me to a 38-hour journey in a prison transport vehicle as a kind of torture in its own right. Also, the very fact that they took me to Sincan, when there were other prisons nearby, even in Mardin itself, was an effect of the colonial logic of exile. I was, of course, enraged by my arrest, which revoked the will of the people who had elected me. Although I knew I was being held as a political hostage, the legacy of prison resistance gave me strength.

I was born in 1986 in Diyarbakır, the second of six children. Our house consisted of one main room, a kitchen, and a bathroom. My father was feudalistic and repressive, while my mother, despite her many troubles, was creative and resilient. She bore all kinds of hardships for the sake of her children but never once complained in our presence. Until third grade, I didn't speak much in school because I couldn't express myself easily in Turkish. When my

* Çiçek, which means "flower," was the code name of a PKK woman guerrilla.

mother realized I was retreating into my shell, she bolstered me and gave me courage. Thanks to her efforts, I was able to partially overcome my shyness.

I was educated in Diyarbakır. In middle and high school, I started to comprehend the difficulties of womanhood. There were rules that I always had to follow in school, on the street, and in family visits. The purpose of some of those rules was to assimilate us Kurds into Turkish culture. Other rules were imposed specifically on women, especially on the streets, which were male dominated. Although my family was Kurdish-patriotic, they still upheld patriarchal norms.

My high school years were contentious as I came up against these patriarchal norms. I especially clashed with my mother. When I was in my first year of high school, she told me, "Your dad doesn't want you to wear pants." I argued with her about it for months. Today, looking back, I can see that even though I had my worst conflicts with her, she was my biggest support. Mindful of my father's stern character and his potentially harsh punishments, she took it upon herself to be the one to enforce his rules. Now I understand that she did that to ease my life at home and she didn't deserve my resentment. Like many mothers, she turned herself into a shield for me. But as a teenager, I was oblivious to that.

In 2006, I enrolled as an undergraduate at Van University, to study sociology. Thanks to my department and my friends, my university years raised my consciousness about women's issues. I graduated in 2010, then moved to Mardin province to work at the Peljin Women's Center, in the town of Derik. At the women's center, we provided psychological and legal counseling services; organized trainings to raise gender awareness and combat violence against women; educated people on women's health; and undertook cultural activities. We held women's meetings in villages and neighborhoods to discuss issues and possible solutions. Working one on one with these women helped me understand myself better. At every opportunity—at condolence visits, in coffee shops, even in beauty salons—where women got together, we took apart the patriarchal mentality and sought to tap into the power of liberated women. It was the most meaningful, exciting, and invigorating time of my life. Every day brought new insights that the path to truth and justice runs through women's liberation.

However, every time we women organized an event, the Turkish authorities would launch an investigation, despite the ongoing peace dialogue. Every week they required us to go to the courthouse and give a statement. They were trying to intimidate us, but they failed—we continued our work as ardently as ever.

Unfortunately, the craze to arrest Kurdish politicians known as the "anti-KCK operation," started around this time. Among the politicians arrested was Derik's mayor Çağlar Demirel. Having a gender-conscious woman like her as our mayor had created very favorable conditions for us in organizing women's activities. Indeed, Mayor Çağlar always prioritized and supported women's projects. I'd like to emphasize that after she was arrested, we at the women's center had a very hard time. As I've said, it was very meaningful for me to work with the women of Derik, who were strong, hardworking, outgoing, talkative, self-confident, and diligent, and it was precious to earn their beautiful friendship and comradeship. I learned a lot from them. In this sense, it's no exaggeration to say that I consider myself one of the luckiest women in the world.

In 2014, as local elections approached, someone proposed that I run for our party's nomination to become co-mayor of Dargeçit. Having already worked in a town hall, I knew it wouldn't be easy to handle the responsibilities of that important position. After all, the municipality, the closest institution to the people, was pervaded by the patriarchal mentality. Although several municipalities had implemented various democratic practices in the previous decade, I admit that I felt apprehensive. I debated with myself for a long time but eventually decided it was a public duty that needed to be performed for the people, especially for women. *Show a little courage,* I told myself.

Dargeçit, a small and charming district in Mardin province, has a population of 29,000, including the surrounding villages. Among all the districts, it's the farthest from Mardin city, so it was relatively neglected. During the 1990s, it'd been hit hard by civilian massacres and forced village evacuations. Its natural beauty, on the other hand, is such that it reminds you of descriptions of heaven in holy books. I hope that one day, my women friends and I will have a chance to stroll through the beautiful villages of Miştê (Umutlu), Bekwan (Belen), Dîlan (Ulaş), Germero (Akbelen), and others.

When I decided to run for the nomination in this beautiful district, we were 33 candidates in total, 27 men and six women. At first, this imbalance felt odd to me, and I puzzled over it for a while. Over time, however, I began to understand it. A predominantly feudal social structure, especially in small areas, is a reality in Kurdistan. So being a young woman candidate in a small town along with 27 men wasn't easy. Frankly, it was one of the hardest things I ever did.

In the end I won the nomination, and when my candidacy was announced, most of the other candidates rallied to support me wholeheartedly. But a few couldn't accept it. Some of my former competitors went to the party headquarters in Mardin, their families in tow, to object to the result and even staged a sit-in protest. When I heard about it, I got very sad and suggested to the party that it might be better for them to withdraw my candidacy. They refused, but those few days of contention lay heavily on me.

About a week later, the party was preparing for an election rally in our district. When the day came, I traveled to the rally in an election bus with Ahmet Türk and Februniye Akyol, the party's co-mayor candidates for Mardin Metropolitan Municipality. I was fired up but also nervous. As we entered the district, a large crowd welcomed us and showered us with affection. What I felt when I saw that crowd are indescribable. Elderly mothers bubbled over with love and warmth, and the people's open-faced trust, fervor, and exhilaration cinched my commitment to taking on the responsibility.

Our campaign was dynamic. The co-mayoring system was still new, but the people endorsed and embraced it quickly. My fellow co-mayor candidate was a young man from Dargeçit. The candidacy of two young people as co-mayors created an energetic atmosphere and raised people's hopes. We won the election with 62 percent of the vote and got down to work.

Co-mayoring has been one of the most meaningful achievements for women's political representation in history. For me, fulfilling the responsibilities that came with that office required a great deal of hard work. I was planning to bring in participatory democracy and transparent governance and the principle of "equal representation, equal participation." Unfortunately, municipalities were still male-dominated. There were only two women employees in Dargeçit's 80-person staff, and women rarely visited the town hall. Only three of the town councilors were women.

We were just six women in all, but that didn't faze us, especially as the district's women embraced women's leadership. Still, it wasn't always easy to bring women's representation to every field. It required breaking the norms of an entrenched patriarchal mentality. We eventually raised the number of women staffers in the town hall. When they joined forces with the women in the party administration, our numbers reached a critical mass that drew ever more women in. We soon opened the Çiçek Women's Center, to the rejoicing of the district's women. Someone complained, half in jest, "They have turned this place into a women's municipality." Despite such remarks, most people in the district were more than happy with our innovations.

But let's face it, the process of making these changes was neither easy nor smooth. Co-mayoring allowed women to have equal representation and participation with men at all levels, but it took a while for it to sink in. The patriarchal mentality ran deep and persisted: seeing men as the ultimate decision makers, having them always at the forefront, allowing them to interfere in women's autonomous activities, relegating women to the back seat, and finding women's successes intolerable. It wasn't easy to unsettle the ruling power of patriarchy.

In fact, the most challenging issue for me was recruiting women personnel. Of course, while speaking of challenges, I must be honest: I made mistakes. I could have been more patient and constructive. I'm annoyed at myself for losing my cool sometimes. We women should have developed a relationship style that supported one another positively rather than tearing each other down. But we'd have needed a little more time and experience to make that a deliberate practice.

And I should have kept in mind that pitting women against one another is one of the most cunning tactics of patriarchy. One day a man in his mid-50s or 60s came to the town hall and met with us. He complained loudly and irritably about municipal services, but after listening to him for a while, I realized that his main object was to persuade me to hire one of his family members. I explained that the municipal administration lacked the resources to hire new workers just then. He got up and stalked off.

The next day a few elderly mothers descended on the town hall. I showed them into my office and hugged them one by one. They said they'd come to talk about the district's water shortage, and I explained what we did to address that problem. I told them that they were always welcome here to discuss whatever problems they had, and that the municipality belonged to women as well as men.

As we chatted, it occurred to me that the man who had come with the job request the day before had sent these mothers. And sure enough, when I stepped out into the hallway to see them off, the man was waiting there. Seeing that my demeanor was calm, warm, and smiling, he looked surprised. He'd obviously expected a less pleasant scene. Yes, he'd organized their visit, but I established a dialogue with them that brought the municipality and women together.

After that, women visited the town hall more frequently and spoke about the issues in their neighborhoods. Occasionally, I went back to their neighborhoods with them and inspected municipal projects. As days passed, women gradually came to view the town hall as their space.

If only my story could have ended there, with women coming together and providing municipal services in the best way possible. But my term as co-mayor coincided with a period of extraordinary developments. When Islamic State attacked Kobanê, people in Dargeçit protested, and three people lost their lives. A crowd joined the funeral procession and afterward marched solemnly toward the designated condolence site. As they approached, a Turkish army battalion opened fire on the crowd, killing one person and injuring five others. I'll never forget that day, seeing the wounded lying on the ground, mothers beating their knees and crying, children trembling with fear, and people running around in desperation. I was crying even as I helped the wounded and tried to calm people. You cannot imagine how difficult it is for me to write about those moments right now.

And now here I am within four walls. The authorities are trying to suppress the people's will by imprisoning us. But I believe that peace, freedom, the unity of peoples, and a dignified life will win out in the end.

22
Breaking Down the Doors

Selma Irmak

Translated by Semiha Arı and Hülya Osmanağaoğlu

Selma Irmak (b. 1971) was elected as an MP for Hakkâri in both June and November 2015 with 84 percent of the vote. She was arrested on November 4, 2016, and sentenced to ten years imprisonment. She was later released because she had served more time than her sentence required.

In 2015, the people of Hakkâri sent a woman to parliament for the first time. So many women had placed all their hopes in us. But at that time the Kurdish movement in Turkey was entering a catastrophic period, when a political hurricane would try to destroy all Kurdish hopes. On November 4, 2016, I was taken into custody at my home in the town of Kızıltepe at around 1:30 a.m. The police's attitude bordered on disrespect. Amid the tension, I said goodbye to my mother and siblings. I knew I wouldn't be home again for a long time.

As I stepped outside, I saw a terrifying scene. Special operations police and armored vehicles were posted around the house and at all the roads leading into and out of the neighborhood. All this force was deployed to detain an MP. They took me to Mardin Airport, where I was joined by Leyla Birlik and Gülser Yıldırım, whom they'd also just detained. They transported us to Diyarbakır by military helicopter.

Only after we arrived in Diyarbakır did we learn the extent of the arrest operation. That night 15 MPs, including Nursel Aydoğan, Abdullah Zeydan, and our co-chairs Figen Yüksekdağ and Selahattin Demirtaş, had all awakened to knocks on their doors. Some of the officers were polite, while others pounded forcefully and kicked down doors.

That night Nursel, Leyla, Abdullah, and I were flown to Şırnak, again by military helicopter. As we neared the city, my heart ached. For months, the entrances to our city had been barred. When I saw Şırnak from the air, tears filled my eyes. It looked like it'd been firebombed. The vibrant city I'd once known had fallen into a deep silence, sorrowful under the wreckage. So dignified, so sad.

We landed and Leyla and Nursel disembarked from the helicopter, surrounded by dozens of special operations forces. Meanwhile a dispute broke out between our friends and the gendarmerie, but I couldn't understand what it was all about over the helicopter's racket. After a while, I saw Leyla and Nursel being led away, hands cuffed behind their backs, and I understood the reason for the dispute. I couldn't restrain myself from saying, "Democracy doesn't come of a mindset that treats two women MPs like this."

The helicopter continued on to Hakkâri, carrying Abdullah and me. I looked out at the majestic mountains and thought of Ibn

Khaldun's remark, "Geography is destiny." But how difficult is a destiny determined by force!

As I struggled with these thoughts, the helicopter landed in a mountainous area in Hakkâri's gendarmerie zone. Abdullah and I were kept in a military booth for a while. Then Scorpion-type armored vehicles transported us to a downtown courthouse. They placed us in separate rooms. I wasn't allowed to meet with anyone, not even my lawyers, and I didn't see anyone. Hours later, Hakkâri's chief prosecutor began taking my statement. With an angry stare, he asked me absurd questions such as, "On whose instructions did you attend the March 8 protests?" "Who took you to the Newroz celebration?" I didn't respond, so I was brought before the judge.

There I saw my lawyers for the first time. I asked them why they hadn't come to see me. They said they'd been told that I didn't want them. "Really? The dirty liars!" In the courtroom, I told the judge that this arrest was part of a centralized political operation, not a judicial matter. I knew the verdict was already decided.

After a short break, Abdullah and I were informed that we were under arrest and would be transported to Kocaeli Prison. We were taken by helicopter to Van Airport, where we boarded a noncommercial plane. The plane landed not in Kandıra, where the prison is located, but in the town of Çorlu. The pilot explained that he'd been given a flight plan to Çorlu. Hearing that, our police escort got angry, because they didn't know where exactly we were to be taken either. We were held in Çorlu for a while, then were driven in separate vehicles to Silivri Prison. I saw that Nursel and Leyla were also there at Silivri Prison. After hours of processing, the authorities took us to separate rooms. I was so tired that I fell asleep in no time.

At Silivri, we were placed in solitary confinement in single rooms for three months. Just getting our basic needs met became a form of torture. Whenever we asked for a book, tea and a kettle, a television, or a newspaper, they told us, "We don't have any," "We ran out," or "We can't give it to you." I can't tell you how many times we heard these responses. Eventually the issue got resolved, but each and every one was like pulling teeth. And for over a month we got no mail—they didn't give us a single postcard or letter. When I asked about it, they said, "That means no one writes to you."

Yes, as the saying goes, human beings are born alone and die alone, but living alone, if it isn't a personal choice, is the greatest cruelty. The state isolates prisoners in order to break their will. When I was reunited with the friends three months later, we realized that every one of us had similarly thought with horror of prisoners who had to suffer life imprisonment in solitary confinement.

But for me, and I believe for my friends as well, this process was not only compelling but also empowering, even enlightening. One day while Nursel, Sebahat Tuncel, and I were talking about our time in solitary confinement, Nursel said, "Friends, do you know what I just realized? That you can cry alone, but you can't laugh alone." Sebahat completed her thought: "That's why laughing is a revolutionary act."

Our MPs Nursel, Leyla, and Meral Danış Beştaş were released on different dates. For a while longer, Sebahat and I were isolated in a two-person cell in Silivri. After some time, we applied for a transfer to Kocaeli Prison, where some of our women MPs and co-mayors were incarcerated. Two weeks later, on June 18, 2016, we were transferred to Kocaeli No. 1 F-type Prison. The court case that had been brought against me in Hakkâri First High Criminal Court was transferred to Diyarbakır Fifth High Criminal Court allegedly for "security reasons." The court concluded my case on November 3, 2017, rejecting my request to attend the hearing, hence without letting me present my closing statement. They sentenced me to ten years' imprisonment. My lawyers sent the case file to Antep District Court for appeal.

Every woman who takes part in the democratic struggle has a story, and all our experiences collectively make up the story of the monumental women's movement, the work it carries on with nonstop enthusiasm, and the achievements it has gained on behalf of all women. I like to think of women who set out on this journey with courage, wisdom, and willfulness as "little black fish." By challenging the limits that confine us to tiny lives, we set out for big seas. And we keep moving by growing in numbers.

I was born on January 9, 1971, in Eskin, a village outside Kızıltepe in the province of Mardin. I grew up in a big family with a grandma, a grandpa, an aunt, uncle, and aunt-in-law. I enjoyed being my parents' first child. The unrivaled head of our household was my grandma. My mother was kind of her assistant. The two women ran the household. My father and my uncle did whatever work they were assigned. I learned a lot from these strong women, who had a big impact on me. In 1978, for economic reasons, we moved to Konya, a city where the language, culture, and people weren't familiar to us. My mother had a hard time there, and so did we children.

I started learning Turkish in school when I was eight, but I had difficulty pronouncing certain words. *Leğen* (basin in Turkish) was the hardest word for me. It was so much easier to say *teşt* (basin in Kurdish). Also, I liked saying *kef* (foam in Kurdish) because I kept confusing *köpük* (foam in Turkish) with *köpek* (dog in Turkish). After elementary school, I continued on to secondary school thanks to my mother's support. Although she was illiterate, she had critical consciousness. She'd say, "My daughters will go to school so that they don't have to depend on men."

We lived in a western region, but we always talked about what was happening in Kurdistan: the numerous unsolved murders, the razing of Kurdish villages, and the forced displacement of Kurdish people. When the Kurdish poet Musa Anter was murdered in 1992, our family was overcome with grief. When we visited Mardin during summer months, we saw the implementation of the state of emergency, which affected us deeply. I finished high school and started university in this atmosphere. I enrolled at Selçuk University in early 1995. At that time the state launched a large detention operation in Konya. Police raided neighborhoods and student homes where Kurds lived and detained 70 people, including me. For 13 days, I was subjected to systematic torture while blindfolded. I was severely traumatized.

I was arrested and sent to Konya E-type Prison. There were 45 women inmates in two wards. Some were university students, others had been taken from their houses, and still others were guerrillas. Everyone had a different story, but our common denominator was that we were all subjected to the patriarchal injustices. There was an assault group in the prison called "A Team." Whenever we protested a violation of our rights, we'd incur the wrath of A Team. When they attacked, women defended themselves with slippers, and the prison filed a "slipper case" against them. Despite the harsh prison conditions, discussing our shared experiences helped us become more aware of our gender identity. So, Konya Prison was an important turning point for me.

I was released on October 23, 1996. At the time, HADEP was trying to form women's commissions. About six women and I formed a group to launch a local commission in Konya, to hold women's meetings. We couldn't find a meeting place in the provincial party building, so we got together in our homes. Finally, Leyla Güven, from the party's provincial administration, helped us secure a room in the party building for women's activities on certain days of the week. (Güven later served as the provincial chair of Adana, as mayor of Küçükdikili and Viranşehir, and as MP from Urfa.) Some of the women who came to our meetings had children. We let baby Zeynep (who is now a university graduate) sleep in a basket by the table, and we left the older kids with men friends at the youth branch—they minded them until our meeting ended. After a while, we announced our women's commission and started neighborhood organizing activities for women. Then I joined HADEP's Central Women's Commission. Establishing central and local women's commissions was the basis of women's organizing in the party. Today women's organizing continues based on the groundwork we laid.

Within the party, our men friends couldn't make sense of the women's commissions. Their attitude was "Why separate men and women? Our struggle is one. Organizing separately only divides the party's power." We women paid them no mind and continued our self-organizing. Based on our practical experiences, we also discussed our mistakes, especially when women echoed traditional gendered attitudes. It was like we had to reinvent ourselves. For instance, at our second 1997 women's conference in Ümraniye, Istanbul, we heavily criticized women's patriarchal mindset that perceived men who discounted women as powerful. Perhaps we were a bit harsh, but we condemned it as a mindset of "complicity." We emphasized that women should take strength from each other and act together. Indeed, we needed women's solidarity to be strong so that we could ensure that the party took women's organizational structure seriously.

In time, we also established a principle that women wouldn't argue with each other in the presence of men friends. Before any general meeting, women would get together, make a collective decision, and then defend that common decision in the meeting. Even if we had different opinions, we wouldn't express them in men's presence.

We party women needed that collective will then because we were initiating the discussion of the women's quota, and as we expected, all hell broke loose. The men, and even some of our women friends, viewed a women's quota as unnecessary. "A quota is an insult to women," they argued. "It diminishes women, and it presupposes that women are incompetent." In local and central women's commissions' discussions, the party women concluded that we needed the quota to ensure that women could participate in decision-making mechanisms. We fought hard, and succeeded, to insert the women's quota into the party bylaws.

In November 1998, I was imprisoned again because the three years and nine months of sentencing that I'd received on the basis of the Anti-Terror Law Article 169 got approved. I spent 13 months in Konya and Nevşehir prisons.

After my release, I worked at Mesopotamia Cultural Center (MKM) for about a year.* It was a very different milieu from the party—I met artist friends who had colorful personalities that changed my sense of form and substance. Form creates perception, whereas substance is truth. My perceptions and judgments based on form had prevented me from seeing truth. MKM greatly helped me realize the depths of humanity. It gave me the opportunity to see close-up how women were struggling just to survive. I realized that women had to fight against the patriarchal mindset not just in the political arena but in all areas of life, and that we had to treat women's struggle as a whole.

MKM had a women's unit that consisted of artists and executives. We'd get together sometimes, discuss women's problems, make decisions, and plan. At one such meeting, we decided that for a week we'd wear only traditional outfits and speak exclusively in

---

* MKM was established in Istanbul in 1991 to preserve and advance Kurdish culture.

Kurdish—at school, at the market, and in all other spaces. Our plan was to highlight women's demand "I want my language, culture, and identity." Thereafter this attitude became part of women's activities. Today almost every Kurdish woman has at least one set of *kiras* or *fîstan* in her closet.

In 2001, I returned to party work and joined DEHAP, participating in its Central Women's Branch. In my absence, women's activities in the party had gained momentum, and organizing had shifted from women's commissions to women's branches. The branch structure made women's self-organizing autonomous, as women's branches were organized separately from the party.

In the 2000s, DEHAP's local women's networks expanded greatly. Women's organizing spread to every province, district, and town. Thousands of women threw their hearts and souls into organizing these activities. Women gained a larger voice in the party's central structure as well. In 2001–2003, during activities at the women's branch, I observed that entering party work gave women a chance to socialize and gain awareness. Since we stayed at someone's home every day, we could actually witness the changing status of women within their families. When I worked in the Aegean coastal region, a woman who hosted me told me one day, "My husband doesn't treat me the way he used to. He doesn't cut my spending anymore either. He's afraid I'll report him to the women's movement!"

After spending a mellow spring in İzmir, in April I arrived in Van, where it was still the dead of winter—and got sick. The old woman with whom I was staying took care of me, preparing medicinal soups, *dewin*,* and herbal mixtures, and I recovered. My assignment was to organize women in Serhat district, and I'd soon find that its patriarchal structure was as hard, and women's reality was as wretched, as its climate was cold. Here it was almost impossible for women to be seen even inside their homes, let alone outside. It was as if the women cooked meals, set them on the doorstep, knocked on the door, and then disappeared.

An incident in Digor, a district of Kars, taught me a lesson about women's condition. I was in Digor hoping to recruit women for the

* A soup dish made with yogurt and bulgur.

party's district administration. I called a meeting and explained my objective. The answer was "*Heval*, no woman here is qualified to serve in the administration." I said to a young man friend, "During this term, your wife can be in the administration instead of you." "*Heval*, we have four children at home," he responded. "And who would look after the cattle? It's impossible."

"Okay then," I insisted, "up to now your wife has looked after the cattle. From now on you can do it." They growled their objections and refused my suggestion. But I wasn't about to give up. They'd won the first round, but the match had just started.

My next step was to call a meeting of women from the district. As I listened to those who attended, I was speechless. Almost every woman at the meeting said she'd lost a daughter, sister, or niece who, wearing ethnic attire, had been at the forefront of the march held in Digor on August 15, 1993, when soldiers opened fire on them.* I couldn't stop crying.

The saddest part was that this meeting was the first time the party ever brought them together or even checked on them to see how they were doing. For years, nobody had given a thought to these women or what they'd been through. Each story they told left me shocked, ashamed, and agonized. I've never forgotten, and never will, those mournful yet resilient women.

When the meeting ended, I told them about my goal, of having a woman in the party's district administration. A young woman with bright shining eyes said that she was a high school graduate and wanted to work at the party but first needed her husband and brother-in-law's permission. Later that evening, I visited their house. It was DEHAP's district chair's home—he was the brother-in-law she was talking about. He must have been democratic and progressive in his own way; after all, he was the party's district chair.

The dinner was prepared, and the table was set. The grandma, the district chair, and I took our places at the table. As we were about to start eating, I looked around. "Where are the other women?" I

* On that day a crowd of thousands, including children and elderly, marched toward Digor. Police opened fire without warning and killed 17 people, five of them children, wounding hundreds more. In 2006, the police were acquitted of this massacre on grounds that they'd fired in "justifiable self-defense."

asked. "Oh, they don't come to the table when their brother-in-law is here," the grandma said. "It'd be improper." I turned to our district chair and gaped at him as if to say *We expect actions, not just words*. After that, the women were brought in, and they sat down at the table with us. But this time the brother-in-law was absent. I looked at the women with inquiring eyes. "He doesn't sit at the table with us," they said. "When you insisted that we come and sit at the table, he left. It's okay, we'd feel embarrassed to eat with him anyway."

Besides the disappointment of that evening, despite all my efforts, I failed to recruit a woman for the party's district administration. In those days if you had told me that one day Digor would have a woman co-mayor and women councilors, I wouldn't have believed you. But it does now.

DEHAP's Central Women's Branch consisted of 35 to 40 women. Its elected members were women who had participated in local organizing, gained experience on the ground, and could work full time at women's activities. The Central Women's Branch chair was at the same time a member and vice chair of the party's Central Executive Committee. So we had the chance to influence the party's general politics. The chairs of local women's branches were also in the party administration in cities and districts. With this structure, women could have a voice and be part of decision making at all levels of the party. One of the main tasks of the Central Women's Branch members was to visit cities and assist with women's local organizing there. It wasn't easy to get women out of their homes and organize them. Even when a woman was willing, the men in her household had to be convinced.

Sometimes women, especially young women, who attended training workshops, meetings, and events and wanted to participate further needed our support. So, I would visit their families and talk to the men for hours, trying to persuade them to give permission. It was like performing some marriage ritual of "asking for the girl's hand."

In Malazgirt, a friend who wanted to work at the district women's branch needed this kind of support. One evening we went to her house. Over dinner, I spoke in general terms about the political situation. Her father listened attentively and approved me by joining in the conversation here and there. At one point I was talking about the importance of the Kurdish women's movement and said, "A society cannot be free unless the women are free." The father said that he wholeheartedly agreed. Then I got to the point: I explained to him that his daughter wanted to participate in party activities. Suddenly his face fell. Earlier he'd made the "mistake" of agreeing with me that women should be free. So now he couldn't step back. The woman friend was on the edge of her seat, awaiting her father's response. After thinking a while, he said "Of course she can take part in those activities. I'd be happy if she did."

To be honest, I was taken by surprise. I thought he'd allow only some conditional or temporary participation. But after we left, sure enough, her father told her off and laid down the law: "You're not participating in party activities." The next day, she told us what had happened. "We tried negotiating," she said, "but it failed, and now revolt is inevitable." She'd decided to participate in the women's branch regardless. We wished her luck and told her we'd stand by her no matter what. Despite the uproar at home, she did join the district women's branch.

It wasn't only the household men who hindered women from getting involved. Sometimes it was the mothers and grandmothers. During most of our home visits, the mother would greet and host us. The young women were always out of sight in the kitchen, busy preparing food for us. We had deep conversations about womanhood with the older women. Mostly they talked about being married off underage or for blood money, suffering domestic violence, and so on. While they were speaking, I could see deep sorrow etched on their faces. But they always ended with the same acceptance of "it's fate."

Of course, we wanted to get into those kitchens—they were our main organizing spaces. So we would do the dishes with the younger women. Those chats often formed the basis for taking steps toward freedom. The younger women couldn't wait to participate in life outside the kitchen.

Once women got out of their homes and came to the party, however, their problems weren't over. Now they had to struggle with the patriarchal mindset within the party and in politics generally, the mindset that looked down on women and refused to believe in their power. Another contrarian attitude perceived organized women as power-hungry, as rivals, and resorted to subterfuges to undercut them. That wasn't easy to deal with either. In our meetings, the most common complaint made by women friends was about men's behavior in the party administration.

The party's Central Women's Branch ultimately overcame lots of conventional patriarchal manners and carried a lot of weight at party headquarters, but that wasn't easy to replicate at the local level. At the women's branches conference, we discussed in detail the men's obstructive and exclusionary attitudes and grievances about our "shrewish" attitudes. We concluded that instead of complaining about the patriarchal mentality, the women's movement should demonstrate its preparedness for political struggle by asserting itself more forcefully.

The women's movement worked hard to support women's activism not only in the party but also in nonparty institutions. In 2003, since I spoke Kurdish well, I worked at the Istanbul Kurdish Institute.* I and the other woman on the institute's board suggested we include a positive discrimination principle for women in the bylaws. Almost all the men opposed the suggestion, claiming, "This institution produces scientific work, so we can't have positive discrimination." But the late İsmail Kılıçarslan, who called himself "feminist *mela*,"** supported us and explained at great length why a positive discrimination principle was necessary. İsmail Kılıçarslan, one of our distinguished *mela*, translated many important works from Arabic and Farsi into Kurdish and also wrote his own books. With his support and that of the Kurdish Institute's chair, Şefik Beyaz, positive discrimination was included in its bylaws.

In 2004, I returned to party work. For a year and a half, I was DEHAP's provincial chair in Konya. At the time, the only women provincial chairs were those of Yalova and Konya. Then in 2005, I

---

* The Istanbul Kurdish Institute was founded in 1992 to preserve and advance Kurdish literature, language, and culture.

** In Kurdish, a *mela* is a religious leader.

helped found DTH and DTP. For two years during that period, we suspended our women's activities. But when DTP came into being, I was elected to the Party Council, and women's activities resumed, even accelerated. Instead of women's branches, we decided to set up women's assemblies that would be more inclusive. And as a result of heated discussions during the founding period, the party decided to establish the co-chair system. Aysel Tuğluk and Ahmet Türk were elected DTP's first co-chairs.

In 2007, I took on the role of the party's central treasurer. It was the year of the general elections. The election expenses were daunting, but we managed to carry out a successful campaign. Because of the 10 percent electoral threshold, we decided to run independent candidates. In order to be candidates, our co-chairs Aysel Tuğluk and Ahmet Türk had to resign from the party. A Central Executive Committee meeting was held to designate acting co-chairs, and they chose me. I objected, but to no avail. Türkan Yüksel, our friend with the gentlest character and the warmest smile who also was the spokesperson of our women's assembly, told me, "Don't worry, you won't be on your own. I'll always be there with you." She won me over.

DTP ran our election campaign with independents. Twenty-two of our candidates were elected as MPs, enough to form a party group in the parliament. Our MPs, after getting their certificates of election, renewed their party membership. I felt so proud to present their dossiers to the parliamentary speaker's office as well as our application letter to form a party group in the parliament. After a while, I called an extraordinary congress and handed over the co-chair position to Emine Ayna.

For the 2009 local elections, I was nominated as a candidate for mayor of Derik, in Mardin province. Four days after the candidates' lists were announced, Turkey's Supreme Election Council unlawfully revoked my nomination. Derik ended up without a candidate because there wasn't enough time for DTP to nominate a new person. Everyone in Derik, young and old alike, revolted against this lawlessness. They took to the streets and stayed there, day and night—nobody went home. Women, carrying their children in their arms, stood in front of the town hall all day. Four days later the Election Council capitulated and let DTP nominate a new candidate.

Within a few hours, we prepared Çağlar Demirel's documents and delivered them to the district election board. Gültan Kışanak, who was then our Diyarbakır MP and parliamentary group vice chair, was on hand and said to the people waiting outside the building, "People of Derik! You won because you resisted!" Her words gave us goosebumps. Howls of joy pealed through the square. After that, the community poured its heart into the election campaign and DTP won the mayorship with almost 90 percent of the vote, as well as 14 of the district council's 15 memberships, and all four memberships of the provincial council.

Two weeks after the 2009 elections, at dawn, a simultaneous detention operation was initiated in 16 mostly Kurdish cities. The police had warrants for 192 people, including members of DTP's Party Council and Central Executive Committee, party provincial heads, members of the women's assemblies, activists from the Democratic Free Women's Movement (DÖKH), and mayors. In this first wave of the operation, police raided our homes and detained 50 of us. Later, with the second and third waves, they detained more every day. I was kept in the Counter-terrorism Office in Diyarbakır for four days. Then I was taken to the courthouse and arrested. The police gave away the motive for the operation when they said, "Congratulations, you worked hard in the elections. And so did we."

The detentions and arrests continued until 2012. In the main KCK case,* we were 92 defendants, 26 of us women. They'd managed to achieve the women's quota! At every session, every hearing, we put the patriarchal mentality on trial.

I was convicted and imprisoned for five years. Meanwhile significant changes happened in my life. In 2011, I was elected as MP from Şırnak—from prison. In fact, five people were nominated and elected as MPs from prison, two of us women. We spent about two and a half years of our MP terms in prison. I was released in January 2014. Faysal Sarıyıldız, the other Şırnak MP who had also

* Those arrested in the anti-KCK operation were tried in mass trials in Diyarbakır and Istanbul.

just been released, and I rushed to visit the town of Roboski. Seeing the graves of Roboski's beautiful children all lined up alongside each other, massacred, in the most shameful event of this country, tore our hearts out.*

In 2015, I was elected as MP from Hakkâri both in June and in November. HDP had great success electing women MPs. By increasing the number and percentage of women in the parliament, it achieved a place of honor in Turkey. We even formed a parliamentary Women's Group. We periodically held group meetings and invited women's organizations and activists. We shared the parliamentary rostrum with the women's organizations.

On May 20, 2016, the Turkish state unconstitutionally stripped us of our parliamentary immunity. The following November 4, I was detained. Once again, the Turkish state disregarded the people's will. All the MPs from Hakkâri, who had been elected with 84 percent of the vote—Abdullah Zeydan, Nihat Akdoğan, and I—were arrested. Nihat Akdoğan was released a few months later. I was sentenced to ten years, and Abdullah Zeydan to eight.

The patriarchal convention of not listening to the people's demands and treating democracy as a luxury continues to this day. But there's a difference. Today you can hear women's footsteps approaching. Women continue to challenge the patriarchal mentality, by resisting all attempts to silence and repress them. That's why the destructive power of violence always targets women. In war, truth is the first casualty, and women are shot.

We women are determined to expand the boundaries of our lives to wherever our passion for freedom takes us. We know that another world is possible, and we'll build that world.

My story is women's story. We began by breaking down the doors that were closed on us and we continue to break down doors, one after another, in our homes, streets, neighborhoods, and the whole society. Some of our stories are funny, and some are tragic. Some we should learn from; others should inspire us. Each of us has a different story of getting involved in the women's movement. We

---

* On December 28, 2011, near the Iraqi-Turkey border, the Turkish Air Force bombed a group of Kurdish civilians involved in smuggling gasoline and cigarettes, killing 34. The slaughter is known as the Roboski Massacre.

were like small creeks struggling against a million obstacles, but as our waters relentlessly kept flowing, we carved our streambeds. As our streams joined, we became a huge river. And now we're flowing into the magnificent sea of freedom. I'm honored to be part of the remarkable resistance story of women seeking freedom and truth.

Freedom for Aysel Tuğluk

In February 2022 a platform was established to call attention to the human rights violations of ill inmates in Turkish prisons, embodied by former HDP co-chair Aysel Tuğluk, who has been diagnosed with early-onset dementia. The Freedom for Aysel Tuğluk and Ill Prisoners Platform initiated a petition campaign, "A Call from 1000 Women for Freedom to Aysel Tuğluk" (copied here with permission). It affirms ill prisoners' right to life and demands that all ill prisoners, including Tuğluk, be released immediately, that their sentences be suspended, and that prison conditions in Turkey be improved. Overnight, the platform's campaign received thousands of signatures from women across Turkey. Since then, the platform has received ever-growing support from around the world. As of March 2022, 6,000 women from 54 countries signed the petition. If you'd like to add your signature, visit: https://ayseltuglukicin1000kadin.org/english/

A CALL FROM 1,000 WOMEN FOR FREEDOM TO AYSEL TUĞLUK

Aysel Tuğluk is a citizen of Turkey. She is among millions of women who were born to a difficult geography with layers of problems. She has chosen to use her time and energy to work with all people who were subjected to "othering" within power politics and relations, but especially Kurds and women, and struggle along with them against all forms of "othering." Instead of ignoring the problems of her land and pursuing a life of privilege, she has been a selfless and relentless advocate of rights, actively involved in both the women's and human rights movements. She is a proponent of democracy and engaged in Turkey's struggle for democratization and freedom. She is a lawyer and politician. She is an invaluable constituent of the women's struggle, which we carry out with a strong sense of camaraderie.

Aysel Tuğluk was put on trial for her speeches, which she delivered as a member of the parliament and by exercising her freedom of thought and expression, and she has been in prison for years. Although accredited local health institutions determined months ago that she could not survive in prison conditions, she remains in custody due to a report issued by the Istanbul Forensic Medicine Institute. While it is impossible for her to recover in prison conditions, her health is deteriorating rapidly and irreversibly.

Aysel is a sister, a comrade to all women in our country...

We can no longer stay silent when her life is blatantly put at risk. We can no longer remain mere spectators.

As 1,000 women from all walks of life and different branches of the women's movement, we invite everyone to become Aysel's voice. We don't want to be too late to save Aysel. We don't want to shed tears with remorse.

Turkey's prisons have several hundred more gravely ill prisoners. Just last month, seven inmates died in prison. The release of sick prisoners is a requisite of both national and international laws and conventions. Everyone has the right to live and receive care at home and among their loved ones. We claim people's right to life.

We demand freedom for Aysel Tuğluk, as well as for all ill prisoners, now, before it is too late to save them.

Translators and Coordinators

Anonymous Translator holds a PhD from Indiana University Bloomington and is currently working as an academic in Turkey.

Necla Açık is a Research Fellow at Middlesex University London and a member of the Kurdish Gender Studies Network.

Semiha Arı holds a PhD in Sociology from Anadolu University in Turkey and is a feminist activist and independent researcher based in Istanbul.

Demet Arpacık is a Postdoctoral Fellow at the Institute of Multilingualism, Fribourg, Switzerland.

Ronay Bakan is a PhD candidate in the Department of Political Science at Johns Hopkins University.

Susan Benson-Sökmen holds a PhD in History from the University of Toronto and is a lecturer at Ryerson University and University of Toronto.

Janet Biehl is the author of *Ecology or Catastrophe* (2015), translator of *Revolution in Rojava* (2016) and *Sara* (2018–19), and graphic novelist of *Their Blood Got Mixed* (2022).

Paula Darwish studied Turkish and Middle Eastern History at SOAS and Boğaziçi University. She is a professional translator and musician.

Dilar Dirik is a writer, postdoctoral researcher, and course convener at the Refugee Studies Centre at the University of Oxford.

Umut Erel is Professor of Sociology at the Open University, UK and author of *Migrant Women Transforming Citizenship* (2009).

Emek Ergun is a feminist translator and Associate Professor of Women's and Gender Studies and Global Studies at the University of North Carolina at Charlotte.

Ulrike Flader is a lecturer in the Department of Anthropology and Cultural Research at the University of Bremen, Germany.

Elif Genç is a PhD student in Politics at the New School for Social Research and an activist in the Kurdish women's movement.

Hazal Hürman is a PhD candidate in the Anthropology Department at Princeton University.

Dilek Hüseyinzadegan is a feminist political philosopher and Associate Professor at Emory University, Atlanta.

Ruken Isik holds a Ph.D. in the field of Gender and Women's Studies from the University of Maryland, Baltimore County, and is currently an Adjunct Professor at American University in Washington, DC.

İlkim Karakuş is a PhD Candidate in the Social Anthropology Department at Harvard University.

Gülay Kılıçaslan holds a PhD in Political Sociology from York University, Toronto.

Berivan Kutlay Sarıkaya holds a PhD in Adult Education and Community Development from the University of Toronto and is Lecturer at Trent University.

Hülya Osmanağaoğlu is the editor of original *The Purple Color of Kurdish Politics* and a feminist activist, translator, and editor.

Ebru Öztürk is an Assistant Professor of Sociology at Mid Sweden University, Sweden.

Suna Parlak is a feminist activist and independent domestic violence advocate and educator at the Asian Women's Resource Center, London.

Seda Saluk is Assistant Professor of Women's and Gender Studies at the University of Michigan, Ann Arbor.

Elif Sarıcan is a writer and an anthropologist trained at the London School of Economics.

Mediha Sorma is a PhD candidate at the Gender Women and Sexuality Studies Program at the University of Washington Seattle.

Kumru Toktamış is a transnational activist, human rights researcher, and Associate Professor of Political Sociology at Pratt Institute in Brooklyn.

Çağrı Yoltar holds a PhD in Cultural Anthropology from Duke University. She is currently a postdoctoral fellow at Koç University in Istanbul.

Index